David Clarke · Ingrid Preedy

Fundgrube
Englisch

 **Kostenloses Zusatzangebot
für die Käufer der Fundgrube:
Kopiervorlagen und Übungsbausteine im Internet**

Kopiervorlagen und Übungsbausteine dieser Fundgrube (Symbol:)
bieten wir Ihnen als kostenloses Zusatzangebot auch online an.

Sie können diese Übungsbausteine und Kopiervorlagen verändern und
Ihren Bedürfnissen anpassen, da diese im Word-Format angelegt sind.

Als Bonus stehen Ihnen online weitere ausgewählte Cornelsen-Materialien
für Ihre Unterrichtsvorbereitung kostenfrei zur Verfügung.

Wie finden Sie diese editierbaren Versionen der Übungsbausteine?
Rufen Sie einfach die Internetseite www.cornelsen.de/fundgruben auf
und geben Sie dort Ihren unten genannten Webcode ein. Sie werden
dann unmittelbar zu den Materialien weitergeleitet.

 http://www.cornelsen.de/fundgruben

Ihr Webcode für den Zugriff auf das Material: FGEN221879

David Clarke ist Brite. Nach langjähriger Tätigkeit als Englischlehrer ist er jetzt erfolgreicher Autor von Schulbüchern und anderen Materialien für den Englischunterricht sowie freier Verlagsredakteur.

Ingrid Preedy ist Schottin. Sie hat langjährige Erfahrungen als Englischlehrerin und Schulbuchautorin sowie als Verfasserin von Lernhilfen. Zudem ist sie in der Lehrerfortbildung tätig.

David Clarke/Ingrid Preedy

Fundgrube
Englisch

[Neue Ausgabe]

Die in diesem Werk angegebenen Internetadressen haben wir überprüft (Redaktionsschluss Januar 2006). Dennoch können wir nicht ausschließen, dass unter einer solchen Adresse inzwischen ein ganz anderer Inhalt angeboten wird.
Nicht in allen Fällen war es uns möglich, Rechteinhaber für Bilder und Texte ausfindig zu machen. Berechtigte Ansprüche werden selbstverständlich im Rahmen der üblichen Vereinbarungen abgegolten. Wir bitten um Verständnis.

 http://www.cornelsen.de

Bibliografische Information: Die Deutsche Bibliothek verzeichnet diese Publikation in der Deutschen Nationalbibliografie; detaillierte bibliografische Daten sind im Internet über http://dnb.ddb.de abrufbar.

Dieses Werk berücksichtigt die Regeln der reformierten Rechtschreibung und Zeichensetzung.

| 5. | 4. | 3. | 2. | 1. | Die letzten Ziffern bezeichnen |
| 10 | 09 | 08 | 07 | 06 | Zahl und Jahr der Auflage. |

© 2006 Cornelsen Verlag Scriptor GmbH & Co. KG, Berlin
Das Werk und seine Teile sind urheberrechtlich geschützt. Jede Nutzung in anderen als den gesetzlich zugelassenen Fällen bedarf deshalb der vorherigen schriftlichen Einwilligung des Verlags.
Hinweis zu § 52a UrhG: Weder das Werk noch seine Teile dürfen ohne eine solche Einwilligung eingescannt und in ein Netzwerk eingestellt werden. Dies gilt auch für Intranets von Schulen und sonstigen Bildungseinrichtungen.
Redaktion: Annegret Hauser, Berlin
Herstellung: Brigitte Bredow, Berlin
Illustration Innenteil: Dorina Teßmann, Berlin
Umschlagentwurf: Simone Büchner, Berlin, unter Verwendung einer Zeichnung von Klaus Puth, Mühlheim
Karten: Klaus Becker, Frankfurt a. M. (S. 115, 122–128); Rainer Fischer, Berlin (S. 92 und 94)
Satz: FROMM MediaDesign GmbH, Selters/Ts.
Druck und Bindearbeiten: Clausen & Bosse, Leck
Printed in Germany
ISBN-13: 978-3-589-22187-5
ISBN-10:   3-589-22187-9

 Gedruckt auf säurefreiem Papier,
umweltschonend hergestellt aus chlorfrei gebleichten Faserstoffen.

Inhalt

Vorwort	8
Kapitel 1: A joke a day	10
1 Simple Present	10
2 Simple Past	12
3 Present Perfect	13
4 Past Progressive	13
5 Future	14
6 Conditionals	14
7 Commands	15
8 Questions	15
9 American sports	17
10 Kids	17
For your amusement only	20
Kapitel 2: Games and activities	24
Kapitel 3: Activities at Christmas	46
Teil 1: Landeskundliche Informationen: Christmas in den angelsächsischen Ländern	47
Teil 2: Games and activities	53
Teil 3: 10 Christmas Tongue Twisters	54
Teil 4: Puzzles	54
Teil 5: Christmas songs	57
Teil 6: The Christmas Story	62
Teil 7: Dinner for one: a play	67
Teil 8: "Merry Christmas" in many languages	71
Kapitel 4: Englische Reime und Gedichte	73
For younger classes	73
For older classes	77
Kapitel 5: Antworten auf knifflige Fragen zur Landeskunde	92
1 What is the difference between the British Isles, Britain, Great Britain and the United Kingdom?	92
2 Are Northern Ireland and Ulster the same?	94
3 What are yellow lines? What do the different yellow lines mean?	94
4 Why do the British drive on the left?	95
5 Why do the British call *den deutschen Schäferhund* 'Alsation' and *die deutsche Dogge* 'Great Dane'?	97
6 Is it true that school attendance is not compulsory in Britain?	98
7 Do all British schools have a school uniform?	99
8 If you are a speaker of German, how do you pronounce Welsh place names?	100

9 What public holidays and 'special days' – other than
   Christmas and New Year – are there in Britain and Ireland? 101
10 How democratic is Britain? 107
11 Is it true that there is a clearer division of power in the UK? 110
12 What are the differences between Scotland and England? 110
13 Where was whisky invented? 113
14 What's the difference between the whisky made in Scotland
   and that made in other countries? 113
15 What is the difference between British gallons and US gallons? 114
16 How many times can Germany fit into the USA? 115
17 What is the difference between the Democrats and the
   Republicans in US politics? 115
18 What is the origin of the names 'Uncle Sam' for the USA
   and 'the Big Apple' for New York? 117
19 What is the 'American Creed'? 117
20 What is the text of the inscription on the Statue of Liberty? 118
21 Is it true that the Miss America contest says
   'gentlemen don't prefer blondes'? 118
22 What is the exact wording of the US presedential oath of office? 118
23 Is it true that America has only got two public holidays? 119
24 Are 'positive discrimination' and 'affirmative action'
   the same thing? 121
25 What are the regions of the USA? 121
26 What is a "ZIP code"? 129

Kapitel 6: Knifflige Fragen zur englischen Sprache 130
 1 When must/should I use a hyphen? 130
 2 How do I split …? Are there any rules of splitting? 134
 3 What are the 'comma rules' in English? 135
 4 Why is 'advertise' written with *-ise*, but 'recognize' with *-ize*? 137
 5 What are 'confusibles'? 137
 6 False friends 142
 7 What are the most commonly misspelt words in English? 143
 8 What is the English equivalent of *nichts anbrennen lassen*
   and similar idiomatic expressions? 144
 9 What are the differences between American English (AmE)
   and British English (BrE)? 156

Kapitel 7: Übungsbausteine 163
Lernjahr 1/2 164
   Grammatik 164 – Wortschatz 171 – Syntax (*word order*) 175
Lernjahr 3/4 178
   Grammatik 178 – Wortschatz 188 – Syntax (*word order*) 192

Lernjahr 5/6	194
Grammatik	194
Wortschatz	205
Syntax (*word oder*)	210
Oberstufe	212
Prüfungsfertigkeiten	212
Wortschatz	221
Kapitel 8: Lob und Kritik – Sprache des Klassenzimmers	238
1 Simple Instructions (*einfache Anweisungen*)	238
2 Exams and tests (*Prüfungen und Tests*)	242
3 Achievement: praising and criticising (*Leistung: wie man Lob und Kritik erteilt*)	245
4 Behaviour: Reprimanding somebody (*Benehmen: wie man jemanden zurechtweist*)	247
Kapitel 9: Deutschland auf Englisch	250
1 A tendency towards pessimism? (*Neigung zum Pessimismus?*)	250
2 Comparing political parties (*Politische Parteien im Vergleich*)	252
3 Germany's role in the extended EU (*Die Rolle Deutschlands in der erweiterten EU*)	253
4 Half-day schools (*Halbtagsschulen*)	254
5 Public holidays and religious feast days (*Feiertage und religiöse Festtage*)	256
6 Regional cuisine (*Regionalküche*)	257
Kapitel 10: Nützliche Informationen für den Englischunterricht	270
1 Same spelling, different pronunciation and meaning	270
2 Curious surname pronunciations	272
3 Cockney Rhyming Slang	273
4 How to spell with the International Aviation Alphabet	275
5 Acronyms to describe social groups	276
6 Acronyms that can be used in the chat room	277
7 Common Latin expressions and abbreviations found in English	278
8 How to read out email and website addresses in English	280
9 What's the equivalent of *Arzthelferin* in English?	281
10 Everybody knows 'Vienna' and 'Munich', but what other German place names have English equivalents?	285
11 What is the correct way of saying telephone numbers in English?	287
12 How do you express 'Null'/'null' and 'Bitte schön' in English?	288
13 What is the background of 'Ms', and when is it used?	289
14 Countries and nationalities	290
15 Mathematical terms in English	295
Übersicht: Lernjahre und Inhalte	296
Register	297

Vorwort

Die „Fundgrube Englisch" ist ein Sammelsurium von unterschiedlichen Themen, die alle irgendwo und irgendwie jedem zugänglich sind – allerdings nicht ohne lästige und zeitraubende Sucherei. Die übersichtliche Zusammenstellung so heterogener Materialien macht sicherlich die wichtige „lehrerentlastende Funktion" der Fundgrube aus. Dies ist besonders der Fall, da die Auswertung und Umstellung des Inhaltes für Schul- und Unterrichtszwecke ebenfalls schon weitgehend geleistet sind. Damit ist klar, dass die Fundgrube kein theoretisches Werk ist. Sie ist vielmehr eine praktische und – so hoffen wir – realitätstreue Hilfe für den Schulalltag.

Die „Fundgrube" ist für alle Englischlehrerinnen und -lehrer an Schulen im deutschsprachigen Raum bestimmt, ganz unabhängig von der Schulform und der Klassenstufe. Bei einem so breiten Spektrum ist es natürlich unvermeidbar, dass nicht alle Kapitel für alle Lehrkräfte gleichermaßen relevant sind. Die „Fundgrube" ist nicht ausschließlich für den Unterricht, sondern auch als Informationsquelle und Freizeitlektüre, eine Art *bedside book*, für Englischlehrerinnen und -lehrer gedacht.

Diese völlige Neubearbeitung der herkömmlichen „Fundgrube" wurde u. a. durch tiefgreifende Entwicklungen in der Informationsgesellschaft notwendig – vor allem durch die so genannte „Googlisation" des Internets. Daher haben wir bestimmte Kapitel bzw. Abschnitte gänzlich gestrichen und andere grundlegend revidiert. Das neue Kapitel 10 („Nützliche Informationen für den Englischunterricht") ist nur ein Beispiel für diese Bearbeitung. Hier finden Sie äußerst unterschiedliche Themen wie deutsche Berufsbezeichnungen auf Englisch, *rhyming slang* und wie man schwierige englische Nachnamen und Ortsnamen ausspricht.

Es folgt ein kurzer Überblick über einige der Inhalte und Möglichkeiten, die dieses Buch bietet.

Das Kapitel mit Witzen, die nach grammatischen Kriterien geordnet sind (Kapitel 1), gibt Ihnen die Möglichkeit, 1. Grammatik einzuführen, 2. Schüler an bestimmte grammatische Phänomene zu erinnern und 3. den Schülern zu zeigen, dass Grammatik Spaß machen kann! Der letzte Teil dieses Kapitels besteht aus 16 Witzen, die nur für die Lehrer bestimmt sind, deren Leben an der Schule nicht nur zum Lachen ist!

Wenn Sie jemals kurz vor Weihnachten verzweifelt nach dem Text von „Dinner for one" gesucht haben, werden Sie ihn hier finden, ebenso wie eine ungewöhnliche, humorvolle Version des Krippenspiels. Oft haben Sie Weihnachtslieder auf einer CD ohne die dazugehörigen Texte (ich jedenfalls scheine immer nur die Musik und nie die Texte zu haben!). Wir haben Ihnen hier die Texte einiger Lieder zusammengestellt. Sie reichen von „Frosty the snowman" als einem typischen amerikanischen Weihnachtslied bis zu „The 12 days of Christmas", einem traditionellen englischen Lied.

Auswendig zu lernen hilft Schülern, die Melodie und den Klang der englischen Sprache zu erfassen. Die Gedichte in diesem Buch bieten sich für den Gebrauch in einer EFL-Klasse an, und ich persönlich habe die ersten drei Gedichte dieses Buches erfolgreich mit jüngeren Schülern behandelt.

Der Auszug aus „Struwwelpeter" kann parallel zur deutschen Version verwendet werden. Möglicherweise kommen die Schüler selbst auf die Idee, das Gedicht in einer deutschen Fassung nachzuschlagen, die sie zu Hause oder in einer Bücherei finden. Auch Aspekte wie die Bedeutung der Interpunktion können mit Hilfe von Gedichten verdeutlicht werden, wie sich in dem kurzen, interessanten Gedicht „Private? No!" zeigt.

Für ältere Schüler haben wir Gedichte wie „Jabberwocky" von Lewis Caroll, dem Autor von „Alice im Wunderland", eingefügt, das zwar überhaupt keinen Sinn ergibt, aber mit dem Klang der Wörter in der englischen Sprache spielt und dadurch Schülern zeigen kann, dass es wichtig ist, die Wortreihenfolge zu begreifen, um die Bedeutung eines Satzes richtig zu verstehen. (Bevor Sie der Klasse die so genannte deutsche Übersetzung geben, lassen Sie die Schüler das Gedicht selbst interpretieren/übersetzen). Diese Beispiele sollen Ihnen einen Eindruck von den vielen Ideen und Informationen vermitteln, die in dieser „Schatzkiste" für die EFL-Klasse enthalten sind.

David Clarke, Ingrid Preedy

1 A joke a day

Jeder Lehrer hat manchmal Schwierigkeiten, die Stunde lebendig und originell zu beginnen. Wir wollen nicht immer mit Fragen nach dem Wetter, Datum, dem letzten Wochenende oder zu einem aktuellen Ereignis anfangen. Ein Witz zum Unterrichtsbeginn kann die Stimmung in der Klasse gut auflockern.

Wir haben den folgenden Witzekatalog hauptsächlich nach Grammatikthemen gegliedert. Ein Wort zur Erzähltechnik: Obwohl wir versucht haben, schwierige Wortspiele weitestgehend zu vermeiden (außer in den KNOCK, KNOCK-Witzen), kommen natürlich unbekannte Vokabeln vor. Solche Vokabeln sollten vorweg erklärt werden, nie während des Erzählens oder am Ende. Am besten schreibt man die betreffenden Vokabeln an die Tafel und gibt die deutsche Erklärung dazu. Übrigens, sollte es passieren, dass Sie einen Witz nicht verstehen, erzählen Sie ihn nicht. Ein Kollege berichtete, dass er einen Witz erzählt hatte. Seine Schüler hatten nicht gelacht, sondern gesagt, dass sie den Witz nicht verstünden. „Ich auch nicht", so der besagte Kollege.

1 Simple Present

1   A man drives to a gas station and asks the attendant to fill up his tank. The gas attendant sees two penguins sitting in the back seat of the car. He asks the driver, "Why have you got two penguins in the back seat?" The driver says "I found them. I asked myself what to do with them, but I haven't had an idea." The attendant thinks for a minute, then he says, "You should take them to the zoo." "Hey, that's a good idea," says the man in the car and drives away. The next day the man with the car is back at the same gas station. The attendant sees the penguins are still in the back seat of the car. "Hey, they're still here! I thought you were going to take them to the zoo." "Oh, I did," says the driver. "And we had a great time. Today I am taking them to the beach."

Simple Present

2 – I'm happy that I don't live in Germany.
   – Why?
   – I can't speak German.

3 – How many people work in this factory?
   – About half of them.

4 – How many months have 28 days?
   – All of them.

5 – Waiter, waiter, there's a fly in my butter.
   – Yes, it's a butterfly.

6 – Waiter, waiter, do you have frog's legs?
   – No, I always walk like this.

7 – Waiter, your finger is in my soup.
   – Don't worry, it isn't hot.

8 – Old man: My left leg hurts.
   – Doctor: That is because you are old.
   – Old man: But my right leg is OK and it is as old as my left leg.

9 – Waiter, this plate is wet.
   – That is not wet, sir. That is your soup.

10 – Waiter, there is no chicken in this salad.
   – Well, you don't get a dog in a dog biscuit.

11 – What is the weather like?
   – I don't know. I can't see because it is so cloudy.

12 – Do you like school, Billy?
   – I like going to school and I like going home.
   I don't like the bit in between.

13 LOST DOG
Black and white, three legs, one ear, can only see with one eye, only eight teeth, name is Lucky.

14 – My dog plays chess.
   – Your dog plays chess? He is very clever.
   – No, he isn't. I always win.

15 – Which has more legs, an elephant or no elephant?
   – No elephant. An elephant has four legs and no elephant has eight legs.

2 Simple Past

1 – What were you before you joined the army?
   – Happy.

2 – A ship with a lot of yoyos hit an iceberg.
   – It went up and down 46 times.

3 – This bread is lovely and warm.
   – I know. The cat sat on it all morning.

4 – There is a sausage behind your ear.
   – Oh, no. I ate my pencil.

5 A boy was on his bike.
"Look, mum, no hands. ... Look, mum, no feet. ... Look, mum, no teeth ...."

6 Little Johnny's kindergarten class was on a field trip to the local police station, where they saw pictures of the *Ten Most Wanted Men* tacked to a bulletin board.
One of the youngsters pointed to a picture and asked if it really was the photo of a wanted person.
"Yes," said the policeman. "The detectives want him very badly."
So Little Johnny asked, "Why didn't you keep him when you took his picture?"

7 It was a cold winter day when a man walked out on to a frozen lake, cut a hole in the ice, dropped in his fishing line and started to wait for a fish to bite.
He waited an hour and nothing happened.
Then a young boy walked out on to the ice, cut a hole in the ice not too far from the man and dropped in his fishing line. It only took about a minute and the boy pulled in a fish.
The man couldn't believe it but thought it was just luck. But the boy dropped in his line again and again within just a few minutes pulled in another fish. This went on and on until finally the man went to the boy and said, "Son, I've been here for over an hour without even a nibble. You have been here only a few minutes and have caught about half a dozen fish! How do you do it?"
The boy responded, "Roo raf roo reep ra rums rrarm."

"What was that?" the man asked.
Again the boy answered, "Roo raf roo reep ra rums rarrm."
"Look," said the old man, "I can't understand a word you are saying."
So, the boy spit something out of his mouth and said, "You have to keep the worms warm!"

8 Little Johnny was in the garden filling in a hole when his neighbour looked over the fence.
"What are you doing, Johnny?" he politely asked.
"Well, my goldfish died," replied Johnny with tears in his eyes, not looking at the man, "and I've just buried him."
The neighbour was concerned, "That's a very big hole for a goldfish, isn't it?"
Johnny patted down the last heap of earth then replied: "That's because he's inside your cat!"

3 Present Perfect

1 – Doctor, doctor, what can I do – my son has eaten my pen.
  – Use a pencil.

2 – I see you and your husband are taking German lessons.
  – Yes, we have adopted a little German baby and we want to understand him when he learns to talk.

3 – I have lost my dog.
  – Why don't you put a notice in the newspaper?
  – Don't be silly. My dog can't read.

4 – Jimmy, give the goldfish some fresh water.
  – But it hasn't finished the old water yet.

4 Past Progressive

1 One day a travelling salesman was driving down a country road at about 30 mph when he noticed that there was a three-legged chicken running beside his car.

He stepped on the gas until he was travelling 50 mph. The chicken was still keeping up. After about a mile of running the chicken ran up a farm lane and into a barn behind an old farmhouse.

The salesman had some time to kill so he turned around and drove up the farm lane. He knocked at the door and when the farmer answered he told him what he had just seen.

The farmer said that his son was a geneticist and he had developed this breed of chicken because he, his wife and his son each liked a chicken leg when they had chicken and this way they only had to kill one chicken.

"That's the most fantastic thing I've ever heard," said the salesman. "How do they taste?"

"I don't know," said the farmer. "We've never caught one."

2 Two men in a jungle come around a corner and meet a lion head-on pawing the ground.

One guy ever so carefully reaches into his rucksack and slowly takes out a set of Nike running shoes. The second man whispers: "What are you doing, you can't run faster than the lion." And the first man says: "No, but all I have to do is to run faster than you!"

5 Future

1. My husband is very religious. He won't work if there is a Sunday in the week.

2. – How long will the next bus be?
   – About eleven metres!

3. – When I'm older I'm going to have a farm two kilometres long and one centimetre wide.
   – What are you going to grow on it?
   – I'm going to grow spaghetti.

6 Conditionals

If Mr and Mrs Bigger had a baby, who would be the biggest of the three? The baby, because he's a little Bigger!

7 Commands

A priest at a village school, wanting to point out the proper behaviour for church, asked the young boys and girls about the rules that their parents might give before taking them to a nice restaurant.
"Don't play with your food," one boy said.
"Don't be loud," said another, and so on.
"And what rule do your parents give you before you go out to eat?" the priest asked of one little boy.
Without batting an eye, the child replied, "Order something cheap."

8 Questions

1 – Why did the scientist install a knocker on his door?
  – To win the Nobel Prize.

2 – Why did the balloon burst?
  – Because it saw a lolly pop!

3 – Why did the computer squeak?
  – Because someone stepped on its mouse.

4 – What kind of ship never sinks?
  – Friendship!

5 – Where's an astronaut's favourite place on the computer?
  – The spacebar!

6 – What goes up when the rain comes down?
  – An umbrella.

7 – What did the big chimney say to the small chimney?
  – You are too little to smoke.

8 – Why did the teacher jump into the lake?
  – Because she wanted to test the waters*!
    (**to test the waters* ~ [idiomatisch] die Lage peilen)

9 – What kind of lights did Noah use on the Ark?
  – Flood lights!

10 – Which is the longest word in the dictionary?
 – "Smiles", because there is a mile between each "s"!

11 – Why do golfers wear two pairs of pants?
 – In case they get a hole in one!

12 – Why did the sheep say "moo"?
 – It was learning a new language!

13 – What happens to cows during an earthquake?
 – They give milk shakes!

14 – Where do cows go on holiday?
 – Moo York.

15 – What has one head, one foot and four legs?
 – A bed.

16 – What gets bigger and bigger as you take more away from it?
 – A hole!

17 – What goes through towns, up and over hills, but doesn't move?
 – The road!

18 – How many books can you put in an empty bag?
 – One! After that it's not empty!

19 – What has four legs but can't walk?
 – A table!

20 – What has four eyes but no face?
 – Mississippi!

21 – Why do firemen wear red belts?
 – To stop their trousers falling down.

22 – Why does it rain?
 – To make the grass grow.
 – So why does it rain on the road?

23 – Which is nearer – the moon or America?
 – The moon. You can't see America.

24 – Why did you put that spider in my bed?
 – Because I couldn't find a frog.

25 – What is twelve and twelve?
   – Twenty-four.
   – Good.
   – What do you mean good? It is perfect.

26 – What is love, Dennis?
   – Well, sir. I like my mother and my father but I love chewing gum.

27 – And what is your baby brother's name?
   – I don't know. He can't talk yet.

9 American sports

A little boy was overheard talking to himself as he walked through the back garden, wearing his baseball cap and carrying a ball and bat. "I'm the greatest hitter in the world," he announced.
Then he tossed the ball into the air, swung at it, and missed.
"Strike One!" he yelled. Unworried, he picked up the ball and said again, "I'm the greatest hitter in the world!" He tossed the ball into the air.
When it came down he swung again and missed. "Strike Two!" he shouted.
The boy then stopped a moment to examine his bat and ball carefully. He spit on his hands and rubbed them together.
He straightened his cap and said once more, "I'm the greatest hitter in the world!" Again he tossed the ball up in the air and swung at it. He missed. "Strike Three!" "Wow!" he exclaimed. "I'm the greatest *pitcher* in the world!"

10 Kids

1 Teacher: Maria, go to the map and find North America.
   Maria: Here it is.
   Teacher: Correct. Now class, who discovered America?
   Class: Maria.

2 Teacher: Why are you late, Frank?
   Frank: Because of the sign.
   Teacher: What sign?
   Frank: The one that says, "School Ahead, Go Slow."

3 Teacher: John, why are you doing your math multiplication on the floor?
　John: You told me to do it without using tables.

4 Teacher: Glenn, how do you spell "crocodile?"
　Glenn: "K-R-O-K-O-D-I-A-L."
　Teacher: No, that's wrong.
　Glenn: Maybe it's wrong, but you asked me how I spell it.

5 Teacher: Donald, what is the chemical formula for water?
　Donald: H I I J K L M N O.
　Teacher: What are you talking about?
　Donald: Yesterday you said it's H to O.

6 Teacher: David, name one important thing we have today that we didn't have ten years ago.
　David: Me!

7 Teacher: Colin, why do you always get so dirty? I don't get dirty.
　Colin: Well, I'm a lot closer to the ground than you are.

8 Teacher: Meg, give me a sentence starting with "I."
　Meg: I is ...
　Teacher: No, Meg ... Always say "I am."
　Meg: All right ... "I am the ninth letter of the alphabet."

9 Teacher: George Washington not only chopped down his father's cherry tree, but also admitted it. Now, Linda, do you know why his father didn't punish him?
　Linda: Because George still had the axe in his hand.

10 Teacher: Now, Simon, tell me, do you say prayers before eating?
　Simon: No sir, I don't have to, my Mom is a good cook.

11 Teacher: Clyde, your composition on "My Dog" is exactly the same as your brother's. Did you copy his?
　Clyde: No, Teacher, it's the same dog.

12 Teacher: Harold, what do you call a person who keeps on talking when people are no longer interested?
　Harold: A teacher.

Kids

„Knock, knock-Witze" sind sehr kindisch, aber trotzdem lustig. Ihr Witz ist in einer Wortspielerei begründet. Sie brauchen immer einen Partner, der Gegenfragen stellt, wenn Sie solche Witze erzählen.

1. A: *Knock, knock*
   B: Who's there?
   B: Boo who?
   A: Boo!
   A: Don't cry, it's only a joke!

2. A: *Knock, knock*
   B: Who's there?
   B: Rita who?
   A: Rita.
   A: Rita (read a) book, you might learn something!

3. A: *Knock, knock*
   B: Who's there?
   B: Heaven who?
   A: Heaven.
   A: Heaven (haven't) you heard enough of these silly *knock-knock*-jokes?

4. A: *Knock, knock*
   B: Who's there?
   B: Lettuce who?
   A: Lettuce.
   A: Lettuce (let us) in, it's cold outside!

5. A: *Knock, knock*
   B: Who's there?
   B: Anita who?
   A: Anita.
   A: Anita (I need a) tissue … ah-choo! Too late!

6. A: *Knock, knock*
   B: Who's there?
   B: Honeycomb who?
   A: Honeycomb.
   A: Honeycomb (Honey, comb) your hair!

7. A: *Knock, knock*
   B: Who's there?
   B: Justin who?
   A: Justin.
   A: Justin (just in) time for dinner!

8. A: *Knock, knock*
   B: Who's there?
   B: Canoe who?
   A: Canoe.
   A: Canoe (can you) come out to play?

9. A: *Knock, knock*
   B: Who's there?
   B: Arthur who?
   A: Arthur.
   A: Arthur (are there) any more apples in the kitchen?

10 A: *Knock, knock*
    B: Who's there? A: Honey Bee.
    B: Honey Bee who? A: Honey bee (honey, be) a dear and get me a coffee.

11 A: *Knock, knock*
    B: Who's there? A: Gorilla.
    B: Gorilla who? A: Gorilla (grill) me a hamburger, I'm hungry!

12 A: *Knock, knock*
    B: Who's there? A: Tom.
    B: Tom who? A: Tom on (come on) you know who I am!

13 A: *Knock, knock*
    B: Who's there? A: Howard.
    B: Howard who? A: Howard (how would) I know?

14 A: *Knock, knock*
    B: Who's there? A: Roach.
    B: Roach who? A: Roach (wrote) you a letter, did you get it?

15 A: *Knock, knock*
    B: Who's there? A: Lettuce.
    B: Lettuce who? A: Lettuce (let us) out of here!

16 A: *Knock, knock*
    B: Who's there? A: A boy who can't reach the doorbell!

For your amusement only

1 This blonde decides one day that she is sick and tired of all these blonde jokes and how all blondes are perceived as stupid, so she decides to show her husband that blondes really are smart. While her husband is off at work, she decides that she is going to paint a couple of rooms in the house. The next day, right after her husband leaves for work, she gets down to the task at hand. Her husband arrives home at 5:30 and smells the distinctive smell of paint. He walks into the living room and finds his wife lying on the floor in a pool of sweat. He notices that she is wearing a parka and a leather jacket at the same time. He goes over and asks her if she is OK. She replies yes. He asks what she is doing. She replies that

she wanted to prove to him that not all blonde women are dumb and she wanted to do it by painting the house. Then he asks her why she has a parka over her leather jacket. She replies that she was reading the directions on the paint can and it said ...
"For best results, put on two coats."
(coats to keep you warm/coats of paint)

2   Two peanuts walk into a bar, and one was a salted.
    (assaulted/a salted peanut)

3   A sandwich walks into a bar. The bartender says, "Sorry we don't serve food in here."
    (Think about that one!)

4   A dyslexic man walks into a bra.
    (dyslexia rules K.O.!)

5   A man walks into a bar with a slab of asphalt under his arm and says: "A beer please, and one for the road."
    (a saying often heard before a person leaves a pub for the night)

6   Two cannibals are eating a clown. One says to the other: "Does this taste funny to you?"
    (Do I need to comment on this?)

7   "Doc, I can't stop singing 'The Green, Green Grass of Home'." "That sounds like Tom Jones Syndrome." "Is it common?"
    Doc says, "It's Not Unusual."
    (For this you need to know your Tom Jones.)

8   An invisible man marries an invisible woman. The kids were nothing to look at either.

9   A man takes his Rottweiler to the vet and says, "My dog's cross-eyed. Is there anything you can do for him?" "Well," says the vet, "let's have a look at him." So he picks the dog up and examines his eyes, then checks his teeth. Finally, he says, "I'm going to have to put him down." "What? Because he's cross-eyed?" "No, because he's really heavy."
    (To put an animal down is to kill it.)

10 What do you call a fish with no eyes? A fsh.
    (I like this one, it shows you we don't really need "eyes"!)

11 Polish joke: A Polish immigrant goes to the Wisconsin Department of Motor Vehicles to apply for a driver's license. He has to take an eye test. The optician shows him a card with the letters C Z W I X N O S T A C Z.
"Can you read this?", the optician asks.
"Read it?" the Polish man replies, "I know the guy."

12 Thought For The Day
"Good looks catch the eye but a good personality catches the heart. You're blessed with both!"
Don't be flattered, this message was sent to ME!! (And by *me*, I mean *me*.)

13 I've sure gotten old
I've had two by-pass surgeries, a hip replacement, and new knees. Fought prostate cancer and diabetes. I'm half blind, can't hear anything quieter than a jet engine, take 40 different medications which make me dizzy, winded and subject to blackouts. Have bouts of dementia. Have poor circulation; hardly feel my hands and feet anymore. Can't remember if I'm 85 or 92. Have lost all my friends. But, Thank God, I still have my driver's license!
(This sounds just like my mother!)

14 A new young monk arrives at the monastery. He is assigned to help the other monks in copying the old canons and laws of the church by hand. He notices, however, that all of the monks are copying from copies, not from the original manuscript. So, the new monk goes to the head abbot to question this, pointing out that if someone made even a small error in the first copy, it would never be picked up. In fact, that error would be continued in all of the subsequent copies. The head monk says, "We have been copying from the copies for centuries, but you make a good point, my son." So, he goes down into the dark caves underneath the monastery where the original manuscript is held in a locked vault that hasn't been opened for hundreds of years. Hours go by and nobody sees the old abbot. So, the young monk gets worried and goes downstairs to look for him. He sees him banging his head against the wall. His forehead is all bloody and bruised and he is crying uncontrollably. The young monk asks the old abbot, "What's wrong, father?" With a choking voice, the old abbot replies, "The stupid word was 'celebrate'."
(Subtle, eh?)

15 WARNING: The consumption of alcohol may make you think you are whispering when you are not.
WARNING: The consumption of alcohol is a major factor in dancing like an idiot.
WARNING: The consumption of alcohol may cause you to tell your friends over and over again that you love them.
WARNING: The consumption of alcohol may cause you to think you can sing.
WARNING: The consumption of alcohol may lead you to believe that ex-lovers are really dying for you to telephone them at four in the morning.
WARNING: The consumption of alcohol may make you think you can logically converse with members of the opposite sex without spitting.
WARNING: The consumption of alcohol may make you think you have mystical Kung Fu powers, resulting in you getting your ass kicked.
WARNING: The consumption of alcohol may cause you to roll over in the morning and see something really scary.
WARNING: The consumption of alcohol may create the illusion that you are tougher, smarter, faster and better looking than most people.
WARNING: The consumption of alcohol may lead you to believe you are invisible.
WARNING: The consumption of alcohol may lead you to think people are laughing *with* you.

16 A couple decide to go for a meal on their anniversary and after some deliberation decide on their local Chinese restaurant. They peruse the menu and finally agree to share the chef's special *Chicken Surprise*.
The waiter brings over the meal, served in a lidded cast iron pot. Just as the wife is about to start in on the meal, the lid of the pot rises a tiny amount and she briefly sees two beady little eyes looking around before the lid slams back down.
"My goodness, did you see that?" she asks her husband. He hasn't, so she asks him to look in the pot. He reaches for it and again the lid rises, and he sees two beady little eyes looking around before it firmly slams back down. Rather perturbed he calls the waiter over, explains what is happening and demands an explanation.
"Well sir", says the waiter, "What did you order?"
"We both chose the same", he replies, "the *Chicken Surprise*."
"Oh I do apologise, this is my fault," says the waiter. "I've brought you the Peking duck."

2 Games and Activities

Leider werden Sprachspiele, Wettbewerbe und ähnliche Aktivitäten oft bestenfalls als *time filler* betrachtet, die am Ende der Stunde oder des Halbjahres verwendet werden. Damit wird ein motivierendes methodisches Mittel unterschätzt. Vor allem im Bereich der Vokabelfestigung, der Aussprache, der Rechtschreibung und des Umgangs mit Zahlen können Sprachspiele zu einem echten Lernerfolg beitragen.

Wie bei allen Klassenzimmeraktivitäten ist es auch bei Spielen wichtig, den Grundsatz „wenig, aber häufig" zu beachten. Viel wirksamer als ein- oder zweimal im Jahr eine ganze Stunde mit Spielen auszufüllen ist es, Spiele als ein regelmäßiges Element in den Unterricht zu integrieren. Mit wenigen Ausnahmen benötigen die hier angebotenen Spiele nur wenig Zeit – zehn Minuten sollten als obere Grenze angesehen werden – und verursachen kaum Aufwand.

Mit dem Wort *games* meinen wir Spiele, die in der Lerngruppe weitgehend mündlich durchgeführt werden, zum Teil mit Hilfe der Tafel. Wir beschreiben zunächst den Spielverlauf und geben – wo nötig – Beispiele. Kommunikationsspiele im Sinne der situativ ausgerichteten Anwendung mündlicher Sprachmittel kommen weniger häufig vor. Dies hat folgende Gründe: Erstens sollen die Spiele alle Schüler, auch die lernschwächeren, ansprechen. Bei kommunikativen Situationsspielen bleibt gerade diese Schülergruppe häufig stumm und unbeteiligt. Zweitens sind solche freien Übungen in den Lehrwerken großzügig vertreten. Viele Kollegen und Kolleginnen unserer Bekanntschaft, insbesondere diejenigen, die lernschwächere Gruppen unterrichten, verzichten daher auf diese Übungen.

(Übrigens, wenn Sie hier nicht das finden, was Sie suchen, empfehlen wir Ihnen das Buch „Englisch in der Grundschule" von Friederike Klippel, Cornelsen Scriptor 2003. Lassen Sie sich von dem Wort „Grundschule" nicht abschrecken. Hier gibt es wunderbare Spielideen, die man sehr gut auch in weiterführenden Schulen anwenden kann.)

Articles, Adjectives

1 'A' and 'An'

Lerngruppe: Anfänger

Sprachliche Ziele: Regeln erkennen und anwenden, Vokabeln üben

Beschreibung: Teilen Sie die Klasse in zwei Mannschaften ein, die jeweils in einer Reihe vor Ihnen stehen. Schreiben Sie für jede Mannschaft ein großes *a* und großes *an* auf unterschiedliche Papierstreifen, die Sie auf den Tisch vor die jeweiligen Mannschaften legen. Es ist nett, wenn diese Wörter in amüsante Tierformen geschrieben werden. Das erste Kind jeder Mannschaft legt seine Hände auf seinen Kopf, um zu verhindern, dass es sie bereits in der Nähe der Papierstreifen hat. Zeigen Sie den Kindern ein Bild (*flashcard*). Beide Schüler berühren nun den Streifen *a* oder *an*, je nachdem, welcher Artikel für das Bild richtig ist. Wer den korrekten Papierstreifen zuerst berührt, erhält einen Punkt für seine Mannschaft, vorausgesetzt, er bzw. sie sagt den vollständigen Satz *It's a ...* oder *It's an ...* ohne Fehler. Wenn er bzw. sie einen Fehler macht, wird dem Kind der anderen Mannschaft die Chance gegeben, den korrekten Satz zu bilden. Sobald die Klasse die Idee verstanden hat, kann anstelle des Lehrers eins der Kinder die Karten halten.

▶ weckt das Bewusstsein für Konsonanten und Vokale

2 Adjective game (1)

Lerngruppe: ab 2. Lernjahr

Sprachliche Ziele: Vokabeln üben, Sprachstrukturen ergänzen

Beschreibung: Schreiben Sie drei Adjektive an die Tafel, z. B. *big*, *cold*, *beautiful*. Jetzt versuchen die Schüler jeweils zu zweit, so viele Dinge/Substantive wie möglich aufzuschreiben, auf die alle drei Adjektive zutreffen. So könnte auf die obigen Beispiele *snowman*, *mountain*, *icecream* oder *Alaska* passen.

▶ fördert Partnerarbeit und Wortschatzarbeit

3 Adjective game (2)

Lerngruppe: ab 2. Lernjahr

Sprachliche Ziele: Adjektive situativ erkennen

Beschreibung: Wählen Sie einige bekannte Werbeanzeigen in großem Druck und mit nicht zu viel Schrift. Nummerieren Sie sie. Schwärzen Sie zwei Adjektive von jeder Anzeige und bilden Sie eine Liste der getilgten Wörter. Übersetzen Sie diese ins Englische. Vor der Unterrichtsstunde heften Sie die Werbeanzeigen an die Wände des Klassenzimmers. Diktieren Sie den Schülern die Adjektive und erklären Sie ihnen, dass dies die englischen Äquivalente der deutschen Wörter sind, die aus den Anzeigen entfernt wurden. Das Ziel ist es, die Adjektive den richtigen Anzeigen zuzuordnen.

▶ Transfer von bekannter deutscher Werbung ins Englische; Bewusstmachen der Bedeutung von Adjektiven

4 Alphabet run

Lerngruppe: Anfänger

Sprachliche Ziele: Rechtschreibung stärken

Beschreibung: Erstellen Sie zwei Sätze Alphabetkarten, wobei jeder Buchstabe circa eine halbe DIN-A4-Seite füllt. Teilen Sie die Klasse in zwei Gruppen. Verteilen Sie je einen Satz Karten unter den Schülern einer Gruppe. Einige der Schüler können dabei zwei Karten erhalten. Die Lehrerin oder der Lehrer sagt ein Wort. Jede Mannschaft muss das Wort durchbuchstabieren, indem die Schüler mit den notwendigen Buchstaben nach vorn laufen und ihre Karten in der korrekten Reihenfolge hochhalten. Die schnellste Mannschaft gewinnt.

▶ fördert das Gruppengefühl; trainiert richtiges und schnelles Schreiben

5 Mixed up words

Lerngruppe: alle

Sprachliche Ziele: Vokabeln üben, Rechtschreibung verbessern

Beschreibung: Schreiben Sie die Buchstaben einiger Vokabeln, die gerade durchgenommen wurden, auf kleine Karten und mischen Sie diese. Die Schüler müssen die Wörter aus den Buchstaben richtig entziffern. Dies kann als Mannschaftsspiel, als Partnerspiel oder mit der ganzen Klasse gespielt werden. Die Mannschaft, die das Wort richtig erkennt (d.h. es auf Englisch sagt) und seine Bedeutung auf Deutsch angibt, erhält einen Punkt. Die Mannschaft mit den meisten Punkten gewinnt. Sie können zur Bedingung machen, dass die Schüler die Wörter richtig buchstabieren, bevor sie einen Punkt bekommen.

▶ unterstützt das Vokabellernen

6 Answers galore

Lerngruppe: ab 2. Lernjahr

Sprachliche Ziele: grammatische Strukturen üben

Beschreibung: Die Schüler versuchen, so viele unterschiedliche Antworten auf eine Frage zu geben wie möglich. Der Lehrer fragt z. B. *How many fingers do you have?* Der erste Schüler sagt vermutlich *I have ten fingers.* Der folgende Schüler kann sagen *I have more than nine fingers.*; der Nächste *I don't have sixteen fingers.*; der Nächste *I am an alien, so I have sixty fingers.* ... Die Schüler versuchen, die gerade durchgenommene Grammatik anzuwenden. Dieses Spiel bietet sich an, um z. B. *some/any* zu üben und zu wiederholen.

▶ Auch lernschwache Schüler können einen Satz bilden, nachdem sie das Prinzip verstanden haben.

7 On my back

Lerngruppe: ab 2. Lernjahr
Sprachliche Ziele: genaues Lesen eines Textes
Beschreibung: Nach dem Lesen eines Textes wählt jeder Schüler ungefähr fünf neue, schwierige und/oder ungewöhnliche Wörter aus diesem aus. In Partnerarbeit schreiben die Schüler die einzelnen Wörter (mit ihren Fingern oder einem umgedrehten Bleistift) auf den Rücken ihrer Partner. Der Partner versucht das Wort zu erraten. Variante: Der ratende Partner muss das Wort in einem Satz verwenden. Bei geschlossenen Büchern funktioniert es auch als Gedächtnisspiel. Bei offenen Büchern haben Sie eine *Scanning*-Übung.

▶ Der Tastsinn wird hierbei angesprochen.

8 Back again!

Lerngruppe: Anfänger
Sprachliche Ziele: akkurates Schreiben
Beschreibung: Teilen Sie die Klasse in vier bis fünf Gruppen ein, die jeweils in einer Reihe stehen. Die letzte Person in jeder Reihe kommt nach vorn und sieht sich eine Vokabelkarte an. Wenn alle Schüler zu ihren Gruppen zurückgegangen sind, sagt der Lehrer „Start!" und das Spiel fängt an. Die Schüler am Ende jeder Gruppe schreiben das Wort (mit ihren Fingern oder einem umgedrehten Bleistift) auf den Rücken der Person vor ihnen. Wenn diese Schüler glauben, das Wort zu verstehen, schreiben sie es ihrerseits auf den Rücken der Person vor ihnen. Die letzte Person (d. h. die am Anfang der Reihe) schreibt das Wort an die Tafel und geht dann zum Lehrerschreibtisch, um die nächste Karte zu lesen. Sobald sie sich die Vokabel eingeprägt hat, geht die Person ans Ende ihrer Reihe und alles fängt von vorn an.
Es gewinnt die Mannschaft, die die meisten Wörter korrekt an die Tafel geschrieben hat.

▶ Übungen des richtigen und klaren Schreibens; der Team- und der Wettbewerbsgeist werden gefordert.

9 Baseball

Lerngruppe: alle

Sprachliche Ziele: Fragen verstehen und richtig beantworten; Textverständnis überprüfen

Beschreibung: Die Klasse wird in zwei Mannschaften geteilt. Vier Stühle werden in der Form eines Rhombus oder einer Raute aufgestellt. Sie stellen dem ersten Mannschaftsmitglied eine vorbereitete Frage, die in einem kompletten Satz beantwortet werden muss. Dies kann z. B. eine Frage zum Textverständnis sein. Wurde die korrekte Antwort gegeben, darf der Spieler bzw. die Spielerin auf den ersten Stuhl umziehen. Wenn die Antwort falsch ist, ist der Spieler *out*. Wenn drei Spieler der Mannschaft *out* sind, ist die andere Mannschaft dran.

▶ Training der Konzentration und des richtigen Zuhörens

10 Baseball word game

Lerngruppe: ab 2. Lernjahr

Sprachliche Ziele: Fragen verstehen und richtig beantworten; Textverständnis fördern

Beschreibung: Teilen Sie die Klasse in zwei Mannschaften. Zeichnen Sie ein Baseballfeld (bestehend aus 4–6 Stationen) und eine Punktetabelle an die Tafel. Die Schüler einer Mannschaft sind der Reihe nach dran und wählen, wie schwierig eine Frage sein soll: Je nach Schwierigkeitsgrad („einfach", „doppelt", „dreifach" oder *homerun*) können die Schüler bei richtiger Beantwortung der Frage die entsprechende Anzahl von Stationen vorrücken. Spieler, die am *homebase*, also am Ende des Feldes ankommen, gewinnen einen Punkt für ihre Mannschaft. Wenn ein Spieler falsch antwortet, ist sie bzw. er *out*. Sobald eine Mannschaft drei *outs* hat, ist die andere Mannschaft am Zug.

▶ Training der Konzentration und des richtigen Zuhörens

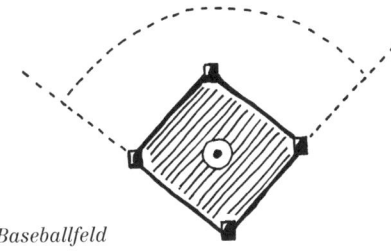

Baseballfeld

11 Word bingo

Lerngruppe: Anfänger

Sprachliche Ziele: Wörter im Satz wiedererkennen

Beschreibung: Das Spielbrett kann jede mögliche Größe (3 x 3, 4 x 4 etc.) haben. Die Schüler zeichnen sich ein solches Spielbrett auf und füllen die Felder mit Wörtern aus einer vorgegebenen Liste (die Liste muss mehr Wörter, als das Spielfeld Felder hat, enthalten). Lesen Sie jetzt Sätze, die Wörter aus der Liste enthalten, laut vor. Wenn die Schüler ein Wort hören, welches sie in ihr Spielbrett geschrieben haben, können sie das entsprechende Wort umkreisen. Ziel ist es, sämtliche Wörter in einer Reihe oder in zwei Reihen (oder wie immer Sie das Ziel definieren wollen – Sie können z. B. eine Form vorgeben wie ein „T" oder ein „X") umkreist zu haben. Übrigens, entdecken Sie, dass ein Schüler seine Wörter nicht richtig geschrieben hat, scheidet er aus.

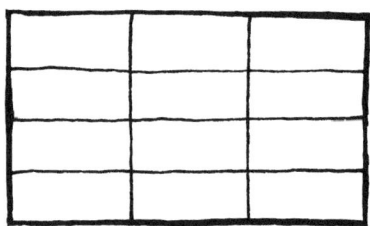

So kann das Spielbrett z. B. aussehen.

▶ richtiges Schreiben und genaues Zuhören

12 Blindman's buff

Lerngruppe: Anfänger

Sprachliche Ziele: Anweisungen geben und befolgen; Wege beschreiben

Beschreibung: Einem der Kinder werden die Augen verbunden. Während es auf Englisch bis zehn zählt, können die anderen Kinder sich im Raum bewegen. Das Kind, welches die Augen verbunden hat, fragt jetzt z. B. *Eva, where are you?*. Das angesprochene Kind muss Anweisungen geben, indem es z. B. sagt, *Go straight on/Turn left/Turn right/Stop*. Das „blinde" Kind darf nichts berühren, sonst ist das Anweisungen gebende Kind *out*. Wird das „blinde" Kind vernünftig durch das Klassenzimmer gelotst, werden anschließend dem „gefundenen" Kind die Augen verbunden.

▶ gut zuhören; Anweisungen geben; zweckgebunden kommunizieren

13 Chinese whispers

Lerngruppe: Anfänger

Sprachliche Ziele: Aussprache üben

Beschreibung: Sie oder ein Mitschüler flüstern einem Schüler etwas zu. Das Gesagte/Gehörte wird nun durch die Klasse weitergegeben. Die letzte Person sagt, was er bzw. sie gehört hat.

▶ großer Spaßfaktor, erst recht, wenn ein Nonsens-Wort das Ergebnis ist

14 Pantomime

Lerngruppe: ab 2. Lernjahr

Sprachliche Ziele: grammatische Strukturen üben

Beschreibung: Dieses Spiel funktioniert z. B. gut mit Verben. Die Schüler wählen eine Verbkarte aus und führen es pantomimisch vor. Die anderen Schüler versuchen zu erraten, um welches Verb es sich handelt. Das Spiel kann in zwei Mannschaften gespielt werden. Ältere Schüler bitten Sie um eine volle Satzantwort, z. B. *He is running.* oder *He has run.* anstatt *run*. Auch Fragen können hier geübt werden: *What am I doing?* oder *What have I done?* Dieses Spiel funktioniert auch mit Nomen und Adjektiven (*What am I eating?/What am I using?/What is this?*).
Eine andere Variante ist, ein Mitglied jeder Mannschaft raten zu lassen, was der Rest der Mannschaft pantomimisch darstellt. Verteilen Sie Punkte, wenn Sie das Spiel als Mannschaftsspiel durchführen. Wenn nach einer Minute die Mannschaft, die am Zug ist, noch nicht richtig geraten hat, darf die gegnerische Mannschaft es versuchen. Diese erhält den Punkt, wenn sie das Wort richtig rät. Oder Sie spielen nach „Tabu"-Regeln, wobei die Mannschaft innerhalb 90 Sekunden so viele Karten wie möglich erraten muss.

▶ Bekannte Vokabeln werden in großem Umfang wiederholt.

15 Miming in the middle

Lerngruppe: Anfänger

Sprachliche Ziele: Wortfeldarbeit

Beschreibung: Die Kinder sitzen in Stuhlkreis. Ein Kind steht in der Mitte und stellt pantomimisch einen Beruf, ein Tier etc. dar. Das Kind darf nichts darstellen, was bereits dargestellt worden ist oder wofür die Klasse die Bezeichnung (noch) nicht kennt! Die anderen Kinder versuchen zu erraten, was dargestellt wird und fragen also *Are you...?* Jedes Kind fängt mit fünf Punkten Guthaben an. Rät ein Kind falsch, verliert es einen Punkt. Wenn es richtig rät, erhalten sowohl das ratende Kind als auch das Kind, das in der Mitte steht, einen Punkt und wechseln die Plätze. Wird insgesamt dreimal falsch geraten, fragt die gesamte Klasse *What are you?* und das Kind in der Mitte antwortet *I'm a ....* Niemand erhält einen Punkt. Jetzt kommt ein anderes Kind in die Mitte. Gewonnen hat das Kind bzw. haben die Kinder mit den meisten Punkten.

▶ trainiert die Konzentration

16 Gap text activity

Lerngruppe: ab 2. Lernjahr

Sprachliche Ziele: Aussprache/Lesen üben; richtig schreiben; Fragen stellen

Beschreibung: Erstellen Sie zwei Kopien eines Textes, wobei Sie unterschiedliche Wörter auslassen (Lückentext). In Partnerarbeit lesen die Schüler abwechselnd ihren Text laut vor, so dass ihr Partner die fehlenden Wörter ausfüllen kann. Alternativ können die Schüler einander Fragen über die fehlenden Wörter stellen, nachdem zuerst jeder seinen Text für sich durchgelesen hat. Ein Schüler könnte z. B. fragen *What is the mother's name?*

▶ hoher Schüler-Sprechanteil

17 People's things

Lerngruppe: ab 1. Lernjahr

Sprachliche Ziele: Possessivpronomen anwenden; Genitiv üben

Beschreibung: Sammeln Sie von jedem Schüler einen Gegenstand ein und verstauen Sie sie alle in einem Beutel. Jetzt nimmt ein Schüler die Sachen einzeln nacheinander aus dem Beutel heraus. Er bzw. sie muss versuchen herauszufinden, wem die jeweilige Sache gehört, indem er bzw. sie ein Kind fragt, *Is this your...?* oder *Is this Martin's ...?* Er oder sie hat drei Chancen, um für jeden Gegenstand den richtigen Besitzer zu finden, darf aber für jeden Gegenstand jeweils immer nur dasselbe Kind fragen. Weiß das Kind die Antwort nicht, so muss es seinerseits ein weiteres Kind (z. B. „Martin") fragen, um sie zu finden. Nach drei erfolglosen Versuchen fragt das Kind, *Whose ... is this?* und der richtige Besitzer meldet sich.

▶ auch geeignet als Pfandspiel in Verbindung mit einer Vokabelabfrage (Kennt ein Kind die richtige Vokabel nicht, muss er bzw. sie einen Gegenstand als Pfand abgeben.)

18 Concentration, concentration

Lerngruppe: ab 2. Lernjahr

Sprachliche Ziele: Vokabeln üben; Kategorisierung

Beschreibung: Sagen Sie *Concentration, concentration now begins!* Nennen Sie eine Kategorie, z. B. Früchte/Sport/Kleidung. Alle Schüler müssen innerhalb einer bestimmten Zeit einen Gegenstand nennen, der zu dieser Kategorie gehört (normalerweise während Sie viermal klatschen).
Mögliche Kategorien sind: *food*; *drink*; *fruit*; *vegetables*; *vehicles*; *sport*; *clothes*; *family members*; *things with four legs*; *things made of wood*; *things on a farm*; *school things*; *things in your school bag*; *things in the classroom*; *things you can see in the street*; *buildings*; *colours*; *animals*; *pets*; *wild animals* etc.

▶ Verbwiederholungen müssen erlaubt sein, sonst kennen die Schüler nicht genügend Vokabeln.

19 Memory

Lerngruppe: ab 1. Lernjahr

Sprachliche Ziele: Vokabeln üben; Anweisungen geben und verstehen

Beschreibung: Bereiten Sie Karten mit englischen Wörtern sowie Karten mit der jeweiligen deutschen Übersetzung dieser Wörter vor. Heften Sie diese Karten so an die Tafel, dass die Schrift verdeckt ist. Zwei Schüler müssen abwechselnd jeweils zwei Karten umdrehen, bis sie ein Paar finden. Die Mannschaft oder der Schüler mit den meisten Karten gewinnt. Für Lernanfänger lassen Sie entweder die englischen oder die deutschen Karten sichtbar, so dass nur je eine Karte eines Paares verdeckt ist.

Bei fortgeschrittenen Lernjahren müssen die Schüler sagen, welche Karten sie umgedreht haben möchten, z. B. *Go up three cards and two left*. Diese Vorgabe wird nun von einem anderen Schüler ausgeführt.

Sie können den Schülern zu ihren gefundenen Karten Fragen stellen, z. B. *What colour is it normally?/Do you like it?/What do you need it for?* Wenn die Schüler eine falsche Antwort geben, erhalten sie die Karten nicht.

▶ Wettbewerbscharakter; Kinder mögen Memory-Spiele

20 People memory

Lerngruppe: Anfänger

Sprachliche Ziele: Fragen üben; Tätigkeiten wiederholen

Beschreibung: Sie benötigen zwei Sätze Karten, auf denen z. B. Tätigkeiten, die durch Personen, Roboter oder beliebige andere Figuren (Tiere, Schneemänner, o. Ä.) ausgeführt werden, abgebildet sind. Schicken Sie zwei Schüler hinaus in den Flur. Verteilen Sie die Karten unter den Schülern. Die beiden Schüler kommen wieder herein, und der erste Schüler stellt zwei beliebigen Schülern die Frage *What is your robot doing?* oder *What can your person do?* oder *What did your person do yesterday?* etc. Wenn die Tätigkeiten auf den Karten dieser beiden Schüler dieselben sind, erhält der Schüler diese Karten und fragt weiter. Wenn er bzw. sie durch das Fragen kein Paar findet, ist der zweite Schüler an der Reihe. Gewinner ist der Schüler, der die meisten Pärchen gefunden hat.

▶ eine der erfolgreichsten Methoden, grammatikalische Strukturen sinnvoll zu üben

21 Number game

Lerngruppe: Anfänger

Sprachliche Ziele: Zahlen üben, Zahlen verstehen

Beschreibung: Sie brauchen einen Würfel, der so groß wie möglich ist. Wiederholen Sie mit der Klasse die Zahlen 1 bis 20. Es wird jetzt gewürfelt. Nennen Sie zu der Zahl, die auf dem Würfel erscheint, eine zweite Zahl. Die Schüler müssen die beiden Zahlen addieren und das Ergebnis nennen. Sie können dieses Spiel in zwei Mannschaften durchführen, wobei immer zwei Kinder gegeneinander spielen. Diejenige Mannschaft erhält einen Punkt, deren Spieler die schnelleren (und richtigen) Antworten geben. Hilfe von anderen Schülern der Mannschaft wird mit Punktabzug bestraft!

Sie können höhere Zahlen üben, indem jeder der zwei Schüler einen Würfel bekommt und Sie zusätzlich eine dritte Zahl nennen.

▶ Mathematik auf Englisch – spricht auch weniger sprachbegabte Schüler an

22 Monster dictation

Lerngruppe: Anfänger

Sprachliche Ziele: Körperteile üben, verstehen und benennen

Beschreibung: Sie beschreiben ein Monster, welches die Schüler nach Ihren Anweisungen malen, z. B. *My monster has three heads. It has one long green arm and a short blue arm. It has a pointy nose ...* etc. Am Ende vergleichen Sie alle Monster. Die Schüler können als Hausaufgabe ihr eigenes Monster zeichnen und später kann eines der Kinder selbst ein Monsterdiktat durchführen.

▶ Eignet sich für ein Ratespiel: Wenn Sie alle Monster einsammeln, die die Kinder zu Hause gezeichnet haben und an die Tafel heften, können die Schüler raten, welches Bild von wem gemalt wurde: *Is your monster blue? Has your monster got three arms?* usw.

23 By heart

Lerngruppe: ab 1. Lernjahr

Sprachliche Ziele: flüssig sprechen

Beschreibung: Schreiben Sie einen Dialog (oder ein Gedicht) an die Tafel. Lesen Sie dieses Zeile für Zeile mit den Schülern durch. Schwierige Wörter oder Satzmelodien werden so oft wie nötig wiederholt. Jetzt wischen Sie einen Teil aus. Das können Sie entweder Wort für Wort oder einfach quer über die Tafel tun (was einfacher für die Schüler ist, da Wortstücke noch zu erkennen sind). Der Dialog wird nun wiederholt, wobei die Schüler auch die fehlenden Teile aus dem Gedächtnis ergänzen. Bald ist die Tafel sauber und die Schüler können den Dialog auswendig.

▶ Klappt auch wunderbar mit Liedern!

24 Read the sentence

Lerngruppe: Anfänger

Sprachliche Ziele: flüssig sprechen; sich Wörter merken

Beschreibung: Schreiben Sie einen Satz an die Tafel. Lesen Sie den Satz vor und bitten Sie die Schüler, ihn zu wiederholen. Bitten Sie alle Schüler aufzustehen. Wischen Sie ein Wort des Satzes weg. Jetzt versucht ein Schüler einer Tischgruppe den Satz vollständig zu lesen, einschließlich des fehlenden Wortes (Präpositionen und Adjektive eignen sich hierfür). Wenn der Schüler es richtig sagt, darf seine Gruppe sich hinsetzen. Wenn er es falsch sagt, bleibt die Gruppe stehen und ein Schüler der nachfolgenden Gruppe darf sich an dem Satz versuchen. Wichtig ist hier nicht nur das Ergänzen des fehlenden Wortes, sondern auch die Aussprache des gesamten Satzes.

▶ fördert die Aufmerksamkeit

25 Description of words

Lerngruppe: ab 1. Lernjahr

Sprachliche Ziele: Begriffe an ihren Eigenschaften erkennen

Beschreibung: Zeigen Sie den Schülern einige Bildkarten von Wörtern/Begriffen, die sie kennen. Bitten Sie sie, sich die Karten zu merken. Dann mischen Sie die Karten und fangen an, die obere Karte zu beschreiben, ohne sie den Schülern zu zeigen. Sie kommentieren: Wenn die obere Karte z. B. *apple* ist, könnten Sie sagen *It's red. You can eat it.* Die Schüler können das Wort jetzt sicherlich erraten, wenn die zur Wahl stehenden Bilder z. B. *apple, sun, jet, frog, milk* sind. Ihre Hinweise müssen jedoch spezifischer sein, wenn die Bilder z. B. *apple, banana, strawberry, orange, tomato, cherry* sind. Wer als Erste oder Erster das Bild errät, bekommt die Karte. Es gewinnt am Ende der Schüler (oder die Gruppe) mit den meisten Karten.

▶ Kann mit einer Hausaufgabe verbunden werden, wenn Sie die Schüler bitten, beschreibende Sätze über Gegenstände auf kleine Karten zu schreiben, die Sie dann einsammeln und im nächsten Spiel verwenden.

26 Family tree

Lerngruppe: ab 1. Lernjahr

Sprachliche Ziele: Wörter für Familienmitglieder lernen und wiederholen; Wiederholung von Possessivpronomen und Genitiv-*s*

Beschreibung: Zeichnen Sie Ihren eigenen Stammbaum und erklären Sie ihn den Schülern. (Tipp: Mit Fotos wirkt es besser.) Üben Sie die Aussprache der neu eingeführten Wörter. Es kommen einige *th* vor. Dafür können Sie folgenden Rap benutzen:

Me, my baby brother, *My neighbour next to me*
my sister, father, mother *my house is number three*

Die Schüler zeichnen nun ihren eigenen Stammbaum und erklären ihn in Partnerarbeit ihrem jeweiligen Partner. Danach muss ein Schüler der Klasse den Stammbaum seines Partners präsentieren.

Sie können das Vokabelspektrum erweitern, indem Sie solche Wörter einführen wie: *grandson, great-grandson; grandfather; great-grandfather; stepfather; cousin; aunt; uncle.*

▶ hoher Schüler-Sprechanteil

27 Countries and people

Lerngruppe: ab 1. Lernjahr

Sprachliche Ziele: Landeskundliche Informationen wiedergeben; grammatikalisch richtige Sätze bilden

Beschreibung: Zeichnen Sie ein Rasterfeld an die Tafel. Setzen sie die Namen einiger Länder in die oberste Zeile und bestimmte Verben in die letzte Spalte, so wie unten im Beispiel dargestellt. Füllen Sie dann die Mitte mit passenden Stichwörtern aus, mit denen die Schüler vollständige Sätze bilden müssen (z. B.: *In Canada we play hockey*). Diese können auch für die Bildung des Passivs verwendet werden, also z. B. *Hockey is played in Canada*. Die Schüler schreiben nun ihrerseits ein Rasterfeld, in das die Namen anderer Länder, allerdings dieselben Verben wie an der Tafel, eingetragen werden. Die Schüler müssen nun versuchen, die leeren Mittelfelder ihrer Tabellen auszufüllen. Dazu können sie passende Sätze schreiben.

England	Germany	Italy	USA	
English	German	Italian	English	speak
cricket	football	football	baseball	play
Ford	Volkswagen	Fiat	Chevrolet	make
sandwich	Bratwurst	spaghetti	hamburger	eat

▶ Kann mit exotischen Ländern wie z. B. Japan gespielt werden; der Phantasie sind dabei keine Grenzen gesetzt – Hauptsache, das Ergebnis sind grammatikalisch richtige Sätze!

28 Find the mistakes!

Lerngruppe: ab 2. Lernjahr

Sprachliche Ziele: Aussprache üben, Textverständnis fördern

Beschreibung: Die Schüler arbeiten zu zweit. Ein Schüler hat die Kopie eines Textes ohne Fehler und der andere Schüler eine mit inhaltlichen Fehlern. Der Schüler, dessen Text fehlerfrei ist, liest seine Version vor. Der andere Schüler hört zu und versucht die Fehler herauszufinden, die sich in seinem Text befinden. Er markiert sie auf seinem Blatt.

▶ hoher Schüler-Sprechanteil; die richtige Aussprache ist hier sehr wichtig, sonst versteht der Partner wenig

29 Group hunt

Lerngruppe: ab 1. Lernjahr

Sprachliche Ziele: Fragen bilden

Beschreibung: Sie fertigen Karten an, auf die Sie jeweils drei Wörter schreiben, die als Informationen über eine Person dienen. Dabei sind eine bestimmte Zahl von Karten komplett identisch, so dass im Ergebnis vier bis fünf verschiedene Gruppen entstehen, wenn sich die Schüler mit den gleichen Karten zusammenfinden. Allerdings wiederholen sich einige der Wörter einer Kartengruppe auch auf den anderen Karten (wie unten im Beispiel dargestellt). Jeder Schüler erhält nun eine Karte. Die Schüler müssen einander Fragen stellen, um herauszufinden, wer zur gleichen Gruppe gehört, also komplett identische Karten hat. Dabei müssen mit z. B. folgenden Verben Fragen gebildet werden: *be/like/play*.

Wenn auf der Karte steht *pizza, Turkey, volleyball*, dann muss der Schüler fragen *Are you Turkish?* oder *Do you like pizza?* oder *Do you play volleyball?* Die Schüler, die alle drei Fragen mit „ja" beantworten, gehören der gleichen Gruppe an. Wenn sich alle Mitglieder einer Gruppe gefunden haben, dürfen sie sich hinsetzen.

▶ sehr hoher Schüler-Sprechanteil, da alle Schüler gleichzeitig sprechen; Lehrer wird entlastet

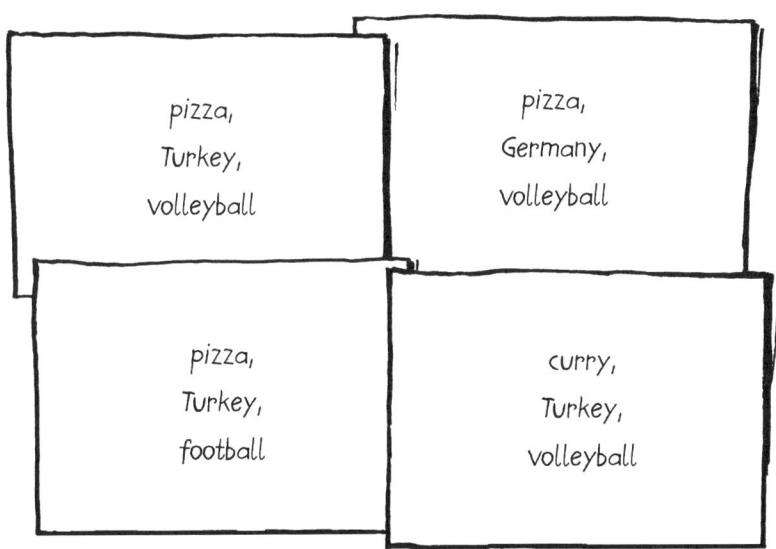

30 Pairs

Lerngruppe: ab 1. Lernjahr

Sprachliche Ziele: Vokabeln üben

Beschreibung: Eine etwas andere Methode, die Klasse in Paare für Partnerarbeit einzuteilen! Teilen Sie die Klasse in zwei Gruppen auf. Geben Sie einer Gruppe Karten mit englischen Wörtern und der anderen Gruppe Karten mit deren deutscher Bedeutung. Damit erhält jeder Schüler eine Karte. Wenn der Lehrer *start* ruft, versuchen die Schüler der einen Gruppe, ihren Partner in der anderen Gruppe zu finden. Um das Chaos überschaubar zu halten, kann eine Gruppe sitzen bleiben, während die andere Mannschaft herumläuft. Wenn jemand seinen Partner gefunden hat, setzen sich beide hinten hin.

▶ hoher Schüler-Sprechanteil

31 Fishy

Lerngruppe: ab 1. Lernjahr

Sprachliche Ziele: Vokabeln üben; Fragen verstehen und beantworten

Beschreibung: Zeichnen Sie eine Start- und eine Ziellinie auf den Fußboden. Teilen Sie die Klasse in zwei Gruppen auf. Jede Gruppe schneidet einen Papierfisch aus, und der erste Schüler jeder Gruppe legt ihn auf die Startlinie. Jedes Kind hat eine Zeitschrift (zur Not geht auch das Englischbuch). Sie stehen an der Ziellinie, halten eine Bildkarte nach der anderen hoch und stellen dazu Fragen, z. B. *What is it?*, *What colour is it?*, *What is she doing?* Das erste Kind jeder Gruppe, das den Fisch hat, versucht die Frage zuerst zu beantworten. Alternativ wird erst das Kind der einen Gruppe und dann das der anderen Gruppe drangenommen. Wenn ein Kind richtig antwortet, fächelt es mit seiner Zeitschrift über den Fußboden und bewegt auf diese Weise den Papierfisch seiner Gruppe (hoffentlich!) in Richtung Ziellinie. Jetzt geht dieses Kind zum Ende der Reihe und das nächste Kind der Gruppe steht hinter dem Fisch. Die Gruppe, dessen Fisch als Erster über die Linie geht, hat gewonnen.

▶ viel Bewegung, ausgeprägter Wettbewerbscharakter

32 Fruit salad

Lerngruppe: ab 1. Lernjahr

Sprachliche Ziele: Vokabeln üben; Grammatikstrukturen anwenden

Beschreibung: Bilden Sie einen großen Stuhlkreis. Teilen Sie Bildkarten aus, z. B. mit Obst. Die Vokabeln werden an die Tafel geschrieben (auch als Gedächtnisstütze, welche Karten im Spiel sind). Ein Kind erhält keine Karte. Es steht in der Mitte und sagt z. B. *I like apples*. Alle Schüler, die Apfelkarten haben, versuchen nun, die Plätze zu wechseln. Das Kind in der Mitte versucht dabei, einen Stuhl zu ergattern. Das Spiel kann mit verschiedenen Kategorien gespielt werden: *food (I like/I don't like …)*, *sport (I can play/do …)*, *languages (I can speak/I can't speak …)* usw.

▶ viel Bewegung; hoher Schüler-Sprechanteil

33 Words!

Lerngruppe: ab 1. Lernjahr

Sprachliche Ziele: Wörter in die richtige Reihenfolge bringen; Sätze bilden

Beschreibung: Teilen Sie die Klasse in Gruppen ein. Das erste Kind jeder Gruppe kommt nach vorn, wo Sie ihm ein Wort zeigen. Es geht zurück, und das zweite Kind kommt nach vorn. Das geschieht, bis allen Schülern ein Wort gezeigt worden ist. Jetzt versuchen alle Schüler einer Gruppe aus ihren Wörtern einen Satz zusammenzufügen.

▶ fördert das Zusammenarbeiten in Gruppen

34 Half sentences

Lerngruppe: ab 1. Lernjahr

Sprachliche Ziele: sinnvolle Sätze bilden; Sätze verstehen

Beschreibung: Den Schülern werden halbe Sätze gegeben. Sie müssen dann die Person mit der anderen Hälfte „ihres" Satzes finden. Der Anfang jedes Satzes ist nummeriert. Wenn alle ihre „Satzpartner" gefunden haben, wird die Geschichte oder der Dialog in Gänze von der ganzen Klasse vorgelesen. Eine Alternative wäre, dass die Schüler Antworten bekommen und die dazu passenden Fragen finden müssen.

▶ Die Übung erhöht die Sprechaktivität, da viele Schüler gleichzeitig sprechen.

35 Word hangman (1)

Lerngruppe: ab 2. Lernjahr

Sprachliche Ziele: ein Gefühl für die englische Satzform zu bekommen

Beschreibung: „Schreiben" Sie einen Satz an die Tafel, wobei Sie allerdings statt der Wörter jeweils einen Strich pro Wort malen. Sie können hierbei eine bestimmte zu übende grammatische Struktur verwenden. Die Kinder erraten nun die Wörter des Textes, welchen Sie bei richtigen Ansagen entsprechend ergänzen. Raten die Schüler ein Wort, welches nicht im Text vorkommt, vervollständigen Sie Strich um Strich ein Galgenmännchen.

Dieses Spiel ist gut für das Ende einer Stunde geeignet und sollte möglichst auf die in der Stunde durchgenommene Grammatik oder entsprechende Texte begrenzt werden.

The boy is going to school. =

_____ .

(Sie können schon ein Wort vorgeben, wenn Sie meinen, dass der Satz ohne Hilfestellung zu schwierig ist.)

Übrigens, diese Art von Lückensatz eignet sich für ein ganzes Lückendiktat. Lesen Sie einen Text zweimal vor. Die Schüler haben als Vorlage jetzt nur Lücken, die aus Strichen für die einzelnen Buchstaben jedes Wortes bestehen. Geben Sie ein bisschen Hilfe: *The longest word is* supermarket, oder/ und *The first word in sentence number four is* When; *The word after the question mark is* Then usw.

In Partnerarbeit werden die Lücken nun diskutiert und ausgefüllt.

▶ geeignet zum Üben gerade gelernter Grammatik, funktioniert z. B. gut mit der *present progressive*-Form

36 Word hangman (2)

Lerngruppe: ab 1. Lernjahr

Sprachliche Ziele: Vokabeln üben; Körperteile wiederholen

Beschreibung: Die Schüler spielen gegeneinander in Gruppen, die sich gegenseitig Vokabeln abfragen. Gibt eine Gruppe eine falsche Antwort, wird „ihr" Galgenmännchen um einen weiteren Strich vervollständigt. Die Gruppe, deren Galgenmännchen als erstes „fertig" ist, verliert. Alternativ haben

Sie das Galgenmännchen für jede Gruppe schon an die Tafel gemalt und wischen bei jedem Fehler der Gruppe einen Körperteil weg. Dabei kann die Gruppe dieses Körperteil jeweils bestimmen, z. B. *Rub out the left leg.*

▶ hoher Spaßfaktor

37 Hidden words

Lerngruppe: ab 1. Lernjahr

Sprachliche Ziele: Präpositionen sinnvoll anwenden

Beschreibung: Verstecken Sie Bildkarten im Raum (das Spiel kann auch draußen gespielt werden); stellen Sie dabei sicher, dass alle Karten sichtbar sind. Erklären Sie den Kindern, wie viele Karten versteckt worden sind. Die Kinder bewegen sich im Raum und schreiben Sätze über jede Karte und den Ort ihres Verstecks (z. B. *The horse is under the desk.*). Das Kind, das als Erstes alle Karten beschrieben hat, ist Sieger.

▶ Bewegung im Klassenraum oder draußen ist besonders gut für jüngere Klassen.

38 How many things can you think of?

Lerngruppe: ab 2. Lernjahr

Sprachliche Ziele: Vokabeln wiederholen

Beschreibung: Die Schüler versuchen, so viele Wörter zu schreiben wie möglich, die zu einer bestimmten Beschreibung passen, z. B. *How many things can you think of that are bigger than you?* Andere Ideen sind: *How many things can you think of that are round?*, *How many things can you think of that are long and thin?*, *How many things can you think of that make a noise?*, *How many things can you think of that work on electricity?*, *How many things can you think of that are made of wood/paper/glass?*, *How many things can you think of that you can sit on?*, *How many things can you think of that people enjoy looking at?*, *How many things can you think of that have four legs?* etc.

▶ gut, um Vokabeln zu üben

39 How to make toast

Lerngruppe: ab 2. Lernjahr

Sprachliche Ziele: Inhalte verstehen

Beschreibung: Schreiben Sie einfache Anweisungen für etwas wie *making toast* oder *doing the dishes* auf ein Blatt. Schneiden Sie die Sätze der Anweisungen auseinander. Jetzt müssen die Schüler versuchen, die Sätze wieder in die richtige Reihenfolge zu bringen. Vergessen Sie nicht, in die Sätze Wörter wie *first, next, then* und *finally* einzufügen.

▶ gute Vorübung für Erzähltexte

40 Draw a picture

Lerngruppe: ab 2. Lernjahr

Sprachliche Ziele: Anweisungen geben und verstehen

Beschreibung: Ein Schüler steht an der Tafel mit dem Rücken zur Klasse. Die anderen Schüler können ein Bild sehen (eine sehr einfache Skizze eignet sich gut). Die Gruppe gibt dem Schüler an der Tafel jetzt Anweisungen, was er bzw. sie zu zeichnen hat. Vergleichen Sie die ursprüngliche Skizze dann mit dem entstandenen Tafelbild.

▶ Es macht sehr viel Spaß, wenn der Schüler an der Tafel die Augen verbunden hat – die Schüler, die die Anweisungen geben, müssen genau überlegen, was sie sagen.

41 Listen for the sounds

Lerngruppe: Anfänger

Sprachliche Ziele: richtig zuhören

Beschreibung: Erteilen Sie den Schülern Anweisungen wie *Clap your hands when you hear a word that starts with S. Snap your fingers when you hear the [ʌ] -sound* (wie in *hug* [hʌg] – ersetzen Sie diesen durch jeden anderen beliebigen phonetischen Laut). *Stand up when you hear the end of sentence.* Dann lesen Sie einen Text vor. Die Schüler versuchen, Ihren Anweisungen zu folgen.

▶ Hier wird genaues Hinhören verlangt. Eine gute Übung z. B. zum Kontrastieren von [v] und [w].

42 Cloze text

Lerngruppe: ab 2. Lernjahr

Sprachliche Ziele: erkennen, welcher Satzteil fehlt und diesen ergänzen

Beschreibung: Dies ist ein *cloze text* (ein Ergänzungstext), in dem die Schüler Lücken in einer Geschichte ausfüllen müssen. Es gibt keine Regeln, wie die Geschichte zu schreiben ist, außer dass die grammatikalischen Strukturen korrekt sein müssen. Ein Beispiel für einen solchen Text wäre etwa:

This morning, I saw a _____. It was _____. It had many _____ and _____. It said _____. Then I said _____. Then it _____. Then I _____.

Geben Sie Zusatzpunkte für Kreativität.

▶ Ein etwas anderer Lückentext, in dem man zumindest keine inhaltlichen Fehler machen kann.

43 Number chain

Lerngruppe: Anfänger

Sprachliche Ziele: Zahlen üben

Beschreibung: Sie zählen die Schüler durch, wobei jeder Schüler „seine" Zahl zugeteilt bekommt. Alle Schüler stehen auf. Ein Kind beginnt, indem es zuerst seine Zahl und dann eine andere Zahl sagt, z. B. *Three ... Twenty-seven*. Die Zahl *Twenty-seven* bezieht sich auf einen anderen Schüler in der Klasse. Dieser Schüler muss jetzt reagieren, indem er nun seine Zahl sagt und dann eine weitere Zahl. Passt ein Schüler nicht auf und reagiert nicht, wenn seine Zahl genannt wird, verliert er eines seiner drei Leben. Hat ein Schüler alle Leben verloren, muss er sich hinsetzen. Nach einer vorbestimmten Zeit werden die Zahlen neu verteilt, sodass die Kinder sich auf eine neue Zahl konzentrieren müssen.

▶ trainiert die Wahrnehmung von Unterschieden zwischen ähnlich klingenden Zahlen, z. B. *thirteen* und *thirty*

3 Activities at Christmas

Dieses Kapitel enthält Vorschläge für unterschiedliche Aktivitäten, die man während der Weihnachtszeit einsetzen kann. Es ist gegliedert in folgende Teile:

1   Landeskundliche Informationen
Die landeskundlichen Informationen sind absichtlich in einfachem Englisch verfasst. Bezüglich des Wortschatzes sind sie den gängigen Lehrwerken weitestgehend angepasst. Unbekannte Wörter werden am Ende des Abschnittes zweisprachig erklärt. Mit älteren Lerngruppen kann der gesamte Teil als fortlaufender Text gelesen bzw. vorgelesen werden. Bei weniger erfahrenen Lerngruppen kann man den Text abschnittweise bzw. überhaupt nur einzelne Auszüge behandeln. Jeder Abschnitt ist ein in sich geschlossener Text.

2   Games and Activites
Hier bieten wir vier Spiele an, die man mit der ganzen Klasse bzw. Gruppe spielen kann. Sie verlangen kaum Vorbereitung.

3   Zehn Zungenbrecher
Diese Sätze haben einen weihnachtlichen Bezug, bieten aber auch die Möglichkeit, Aussprache in einer spielerischen Form zu üben.

4   Rätsel
Die drei Rätsel haben einen weihnachtlichen Bezug. Sie bieten sich für die Stillarbeit an und können die Schüler animieren, solche Rätsel selbst für ihre Mitschüler zu konzipieren.

5   Weihnachtslieder
Manchmal sucht man die Texte dieser bekannten Lieder – hier finden Sie sie!

6   Die Weihnachtsgeschichte
Hier wird die Weihnachtsgeschichte in einer nicht zu ernsten Art erzählt. Ältere Klassen bzw. Gruppen werden ihren Spaß an dieser Version haben.

7   *Dinner for one*, a play
Das Stück *Dinner for one* eignet sich auch für eine Aufführung bei einem Elternabend oder einem Schulfest. Varianten sind die Synchronaufführung in Deutsch und Englisch oder die Arbeit mit Untertiteln.

8   *Merry Christmas* – ein Wunsch in vielen Sprachen

Teil 1 – Landeskundliche Informationen: Christmas in den angelsächsischen Ländern

The British Christmas
There is not really such a thing as "the British Christmas". It should really be called "the German and American Christmas" because those are the places it really came from. In some parts of Britain, Christmas is much less popular than in England. In the old Celtic parts of the country (Northern Ireland, Scotland and Wales) Christmas is not so important. In these parts of Britain, New Year is the big festival of the year. In some more traditional Scottish families there is no real Christmas at all. Only families with young children do something at Christmas as well as at New Year.

1   Christmas Eve and the days before Christmas
Christmas cards
In the weeks before Christmas, people in Britain, America and other parts of the Anglo-Saxon world send each other millions of Christmas cards. They want to wish each other a merry Christmas and a happy New Year. Firms also send their customers Christmas cards. Most families get at least 20 or 30 cards; some families get over a hundred cards or more. People hang up the cards in ribbons in the windows and on the walls. Sometimes they hang them on special Christmas trees made of cardboard*. Christmas cards are much more popular in Britain than in Germany.

In many parts of Britain and the USA, Christmas Eve is a normal working day. More and more people, however, are allowed to go home two ore three hours earlier than usual. Some firms hold an office party on the afternoon of 24th December. On Christmas Eve the shops stay open until 6 o'clock, all the pubs and restaurants are open normally.

Once the shops stayed open late on Christmas Eve so that people could buy the presents they wanted to give to their families on Christmas Day and the food they wanted to eat. Today all that has changed. Now Christmas seems to start in October or even earlier.

(*cardboard* = Pappe)

Christmas decorations

The shops, streets and houses are full of Christmas decorations. In bigger towns there is often a big Christmas tree in the main square or in front of the town hall. People use a lot of holly* and ivy* to decorate their houses, as well as a Christmas tree. Often there is some mistletoe* hanging above the front door or in the entrance hall*. People also use coloured paper chains*, bells* and balloons to make their homes bright* and cheerful*.

(*holly* = Stechpalme; *ivy* = Efeu; *mistletoe* = Mistel; *entrance hall* = Diele; *chain* = hier: Girlande; *bell* = Glocke; *bright* = leuchtend; *cheerful* = fröhlich)

The Christmas tree

In Britain, the Christmas tree is only about 150 years old. Prince Albert of Saxe-Coburg and Gotha, the German husband of Queen Victoria, brought the idea to Britain and a lot of British people soon started to copy* it.

The biggest and most beautiful Christmas tree in Britain stands in front of the National Gallery in Trafalgar Square. It is huge*. The people of Norway still give the British people this wonderful tree to thank them for helping Norway against Hitler in the Second World War.

(*copy* = nachmachen; *huge* = riesig)

Why holly, ivy and mistletoe?

The holly, ivy and mistletoe are much older than the Christmas tree. They go back to Druid times, over two thousand years ago. In those days, they did not have anything to do with Jesus Christ or Christmas, of course. The Druids prayed* to the sun, the giver of warmth and light. The winter was a bad time for the Druids. The sun only came for a few hours a day. It was cold and dark. They thought the sun was angry with them. They prayed* to the sun god and asked him not to be angry with them any more. Then, towards the end of December, the days started to get longer again. The Druids decorated their houses with holly, ivy and mistletoe, three plants* that stayed green all through the winter, to thank the sun for coming back to them.

(*pray* = beten; *plant* = Pflanze)

Landeskundliche Informationen

Christmas stockings

Christmas Eve is still a very exciting time for younger children. Just before they go to sleep, they hang a Christmas stocking* at the end of their bed. When Father Christmas comes down the chimney* with his sack at 2 or 3 o'clock in the morning, he can put each child's present in the stocking.

Many parents still put some smaller presents and something to eat in their children's stocking. This is a good idea, because traditionally people do not get their bigger presents until after church on Christmas Day. Young children are happy with the smaller presents in their stocking until then. To put some food in the stockings is also quite a good idea. Cooking the Christmas dinner is a lot of work – no med for breakfast.

(*stocking* = Kniestrumpf; *chimney* = Kamin)

Carol singing

Another Christmas custom* is the singing of carols*. Groups of children go to their neighbours' houses and sing carols at the doors. They hope that their neighbours will be pleased with their singing and will give them some sweets, fruit or even money. In some parts of Germany, children go from house to house and sing songs, too. They do this on 6th January, though.

(**custom* = Brauch; *carol* = traditionelles Weihnachtslied)

2 Christmas Day

Going to church

Many people still like to go to church on Christmas Day, even if they do not go to church very often at other times of the year. The bigger churches hold a midnight service on 24th December and another one at 11 o'clock on Christmas Day. A lot of people like to go to the midnight service* because they have to stay up late to fill the children's stockings. Also, cooking the Christmas dinner makes it difficult to get away from home on Christmas morning.

(**midnight service* = Gottesdienst um Mitternacht)

Giving out the presents

People put bigger presents for the children and presents for grown-ups under the Christmas tree just like in Germany. Often, each member of the family gives out the presents he or she has bought or made personally. They do this at some time on Christmas morning.

Christmas dinner

After everyone has got their presents, the family sits down to Christmas Dinner. This is the biggest and most important meal of the year.
Here is a typical Christmas Dinner:

- roast* turkey* filled with chestnut stuffing* and/or mince*
- roast and/or boiled potatoes with vegetables (usually peas, beans, sprouts*)
- plum pudding (a very rich "hot cake" made of raisins*, sultanas* and spices) with cream* or brandy* sauce

The turkey came to Britain from America. Before the turkey came, people liked to eat roast beef* or roast lamb* at Christmas, and some families still do.

Some people like to cover the plum pudding with brandy or whisky and set it alight*. The pudding is made six or even eight weeks before Christmas. Everyone in the family stirs* the pudding mix and makes a secret* wish. But you must not wish for something for yourself. You must wish for something good for someone else. If you wish for something for yourself, you will never ever get it. In some families, people put a few silver coins into the plum pudding. If you find a coin in your bit of the pudding, it will bring you luck for the whole year.

(*roast* = gebraten; *turkey* = Truthahn; *chestnut stuffing* = Masse aus Esskastanien, Brot und Gewürzen; *mince* = Hackfleisch; *sprouts* = Rosenkohl; *raisins* = Rosinen; *sultanas* = Sultaninen; *cream* = Sahne; *brandy* = Weinbrand; *beef* = Rindfleisch; *lamb* = Lammfleisch; *set sth. alight* = etw. anzünden; *stir* = umrühren; *secret* = geheim)

The Queen's Speech

The most important thing after Christmas Dinner is the Queen's Speech*. This always comes on television and in radio at 3 o'clock in the afternoon on Christmas Day. People listen to the Queen's Speech all over the Commonwealth, in sunny Australia and New Zealand, in snowy Canada, in Africa, India and Asia. More people watch or listen to the Queen's Speech than any other programme. It is by far the most popular programme in the whole year. It is the one time of the year when the Queen can speak to her people as herself.

(*speech* = Rede)

Teatime on Christmas Day

At about five o'clock, people sit down for tea. For tea on Christmas Day there is a big Christmas cake and perhaps a Christmas log*. The cake is covered* with white icing* to look like snow and has little sugar trees and models of Santa Claus on it. The Christmas log is a roll of chocolate cake with chocolate cream icing on it. It looks like a log of wood.

(*log = (Holz-)Klotz; be covered = bedeckt sein; icing = Zuckerguss)

Christmas crackers

At teatime, everyone gets a Christmas cracker. When you pull the cracker with your neighbour it goes "bang!" and a small toy or model and a coloured paper hat fall out. Everyone puts on their paper hat and the candles are lit* on the Christmas tree.

(*light/lit/lit = anzünden)

3 Boxing Day

Boxing Day (the first day after Christmas Day that is not a Sunday, most often 26th December) has got nothing to do with the sport called boxing. In the middle ages* rich people gave their servants* and helpers presents of food and money, a "Christmas box", on 26th December. Later, shopkeepers and small business people* started to give their most important customers Christmas boxes (presents) on this day, too. It is a public holiday when people do not have to go to work.

Open house

Today, people no longer give presents on 26th December, but the idea of Boxing Day as a day for people outside your own family is still with us. Many people have "open house" on Boxing day. Friends and neighbours are welcome to call in for a drink and a snack between about 11 o'clock in the morning and 4 o'clock in the afternoon.

(*middle ages = Mittelalter; servant = Diener; business people = Geschäftsleute)

4 Between Christmas and New Year

The pantomime

Between Christmas and New Year many families still go to the pantomime. A pantomime is really a play without words, but the modern Christmas pantomime is a real show full of comedy, music and dancing. The pantomimes are based on* popular fairy stories* like *Cinderella*, *Sleeping Beauty* and *Aladdin and the Magic Lamp*. Traditionally, the main man's role* is played by a pretty girl. An older man, usually a famous comedy actor, takes one of the women's roles. Although once just for children, today pantomimes are also popular among grown-ups.

(*be based on* = basieren auf; *fairy story* = Märchen; *magic lamp* = Wunderlampe; *main man's role* = männliche Hauptrolle)

5 New Year

New Year is becoming more important than Christmas in many British families, especially* those without young children. Why is this so? One reason* is, perhaps, that New Year has always been more important in some parts of the country. Another is that many people are just getting bored and fed up* with Christmas. It used to start on Christmas Eve, now it starts as soon as the summer sales* are over in September. Christmas advertising* on television, in the newspapers and in the shops starts in late October and gets worse and worse as Christmas gets nearer. By the time Christmas actually* comes, people have had enough. New Year in Britain is just like *Silvester* in Germany. There are parties and fireworks*.

(*especially* = besonders; *reason* = Grund; *be fed up* = die Nase voll haben; *summer sales* = Sommerschlussverkauf; *advertising* = Werbung; *actually* = hier: tatsächlich; *fireworks* = Feuerwerk)

Teil 2 – Games and activities

1 Who am I, Santa?

Blindfold one pupil. The other pupils stand in a circle around the blindfolded pupil. Spin the pupil around and then stop him/her facing another pupil who says, "Ho ho ho. Who am I, Santa?" The blindfolded pupil must guess who that pupil is and call out his/her name.

2 Word Find

What you need: timer, paper, pens. Divide pupils into teams. Take a Christmas related word such as: Christmas, Christmas tree, Santa Claus etc. and find as many words as possible using the letters of that word. Give a time limit (e.g. two minutes). The team with the most words wins.
Example: Christmas → sit, is, his, miss, rat, tar, this, math, chair, rim …

3 Spelling Banner

Prepare two banners that say whatever you want them to say, i.e. *Merry Christmas*, *Seasons Greetings* etc. Also prepare a set of letters for the same words cut out and hidden around the room. Divide the class into two teams with two captains – the captains have the banners that their team cannot see. They now tell their team what letter they need. Their team have to look for the letter and bring the letters to their captain. The first team to cover the letters on their banner wins.

4 Christmas Story Exchange Game

Form a circle and give two pupils the same pictures of something relating to the Christmas story: star, manger, angels, shepherds, sheep, wise men etc. One child has no picture and stands in the middle of the circle. This child calls out the name of a picture. The children with these pictures try to exchange places before the "pictureless" child can get one of their places.

Teil 3 – Ten Christmas Tongue Twisters

a) Seven Santas sing silly songs.
b) Santa's sleigh slides on slippery snow.
c) Bobby brings bright bells to Brenda's bed.
d) Rudolph's reindeers run around red wrapped wreaths*.
e) Tiny Timmy trims the tall tree with tinsel.
f) Chilly chipper* children cheerfully chant.
g) Twelve terribly thundering trains travel together to Toyland.
h) Eleven elves eat eleven enormous eggs excitedly.
i) Santa slowly stuffs Stephan's striped stocking with silver spoons.
j) Ten tiny tin trains toot ten times.

(*wreath [riːθ] = Kranz; das [w] wird nicht ausgesprochen; chipper [informal] = fröhlich)

Teil 4 – Puzzles (Rätsel)

1 A letter to Santa

Can you read this letter? It is written in pictures and words.

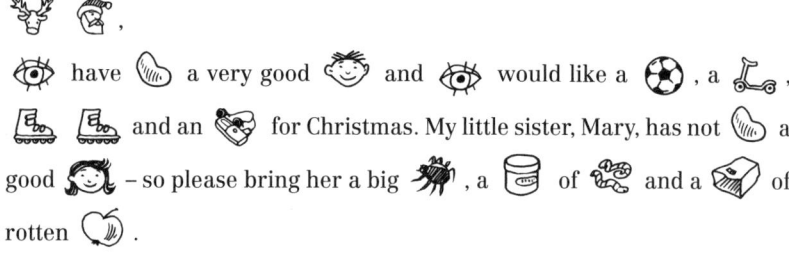

have a very good and would like a , a , and an for Christmas. My little sister, Mary, has not a good – so please bring her a big , a of and a of rotten .

I will leave a of and a of milk for you and in the living room under the .

Thank you,

Your friend Sam

Puzzles (Rätsel)

2 Find the words

There are 28 words hidden here. Can you find them all?
The words are:

1. CHRISTMAS PUDDING
2. FATHER CHRISTMAS
3. CHRISTMAS PARTY
4. WRAPPING PAPER
5. CHRISTMAS TREE
6. CHRISTMAS EVE
7. SANTA CLAUS
8. BETHLEHEM
9. CHOCOLATE
10. MINCE PIES
11. DECEMBER
12. HOLIDAYS
13. SLEDGING
14. REINDEER
15. CALENDAR
16. STOCKING
17. PRESENTS
18. CRACKERS
19. SNOWMAN
20. CANDLES
21. SKIING
22. ADVENT
23. TINSEL
24. CHURCH
25. CAROLS
26. JESUS
27. CARDS
28. STAR

M	T	T	R	E	I	N	D	E	E	R	A	D	V	E	N	T
K	X	S	T	O	C	K	I	N	G	C	A	N	D	L	E	S
T	C	Q	P	R	E	S	E	N	T	S	C	H	U	R	C	H
S	A	L	B	E	T	H	L	E	H	E	M	J	E	S	U	S
K	C	A	L	E	N	D	A	R	C	R	A	C	K	E	R	S
H	C	H	R	I	S	T	M	A	S	P	U	D	D	I	N	G
Z	U	S	C	H	R	I	S	T	M	A	S	P	A	R	T	Y
K	T	C	H	R	I	S	T	M	A	S	E	V	E	H	J	L
C	A	R	O	L	S	A	N	T	A	C	L	A	U	S	Y	D
T	I	N	S	E	L	Q	C	H	O	C	O	L	A	T	E	J
C	E	C	M	I	N	C	E	P	I	E	S	T	A	R	L	Y
O	M	D	E	C	E	M	B	E	R	S	N	O	W	M	A	N
Z	F	J	K	C	H	R	I	S	T	M	A	S	T	R	E	E
H	N	D	N	H	O	L	I	D	A	Y	S	C	A	R	D	S
Z	O	X	W	R	A	P	P	I	N	G	P	A	P	E	R	R
L	F	A	T	H	E	R	C	H	R	I	S	T	M	A	S	S
B	S	K	I	I	N	G	T	S	L	E	D	G	I	N	G	S

3 A ransom note!!!

Somebody has kidnapped Santa. Read the letter and help him.

reppandiK samtsirhC livE ehT :dengiS

!aH !aH !aH – samtsirhC on eb lliw ereht raey siht dna eloP htroN eht ot kcab mih dnes lliw I mih dnif ot yrt uoy fI. worromot thgindim ta dnuorgyalp loohcs eht ni eert eht rednu eniw fo selttob eerht dna seip ecnim evlewt, sgnidduP samtsirhC eerht evael uoy fi kcab atnaS evah nac uoY *start*

Answers:

1 A letter to Santa

Dear Santa,
I have been a very good boy and I would like a football, a scooter, inline skates and an MP3 player for Christmas. My little sister, Mary, has not been a good girl – so please bring her a big spider, a tin of worms and a bag of rotten apples.
I will leave a plate of biscuits and a glass of milk for you and Rudolph in the living room under the Christmas Tree.

Thank you,
Your friend Sam

2 Find the words (Duplikat ohne Füllbuchstaben)

			R	E	I	N	D	E	E	R	A	D	V	E	N	T
		S	T	O	C	K	I	N	G	C	A	N	D	L	E	S
			P	R	E	S	E	N	T	S	C	H	U	R	C	H
			B	E	T	H	L	E	H	E	M	J	E	S	U	S
	C	A	L	E	N	D	A	R	C	R	A	C	K	E	R	S
	C	H	R	I	S	T	M	A	S	P	U	D	D	I	N	G
			C	H	R	I	S	T	M	A	S	P	A	R	T	Y
		C	H	R	I	S	T	M	A	S	E	V	E			
C	A	R	O	L	S	A	N	T	A	C	L	A	U	S		
T	I	N	S	E	L		C	H	O	C	O	L	A	T	E	
			M	I	N	C	E	P	I	E	S	T	A	R		
		D	E	C	E	M	B	E	R	S	N	O	W	M	A	N
			C	H	R	I	S	T	M	A	S	T	R	E	E	
			H	O	L	I	D	A	Y	S	C	A	R	D	S	
		W	R	A	P	P	I	N	G	P	A	P	E	R		
	F	A	T	H	E	R	C	H	R	I	S	T	M	A	S	
	S	K	I	I	N	G		S	L	E	D	G	I	N	G	

Christmas songs 57

3 A ransom note!!!

You can have Santa back if you leave three Christmas Puddings, twelve mince pies and three bottles of wine under the tree in the school playground at midnight tomorrow. If you try to find him I will send him back to the North Pole and this year there will be no Christmas – Ha! Ha! Ha!
Signed: The Evil Christmas kidnapper

Teil 5 – Christmas songs

1 Rudolph the Red-Nosed Reindeer

Rudolph, the red-nosed reindeer had a very shiny nose.
And if you ever saw him, you would even say it glows.
All of the other reindeer used to laugh and call him names.
They never let poor Rudolph join in any reindeer games.
Then one foggy Christmas Eve Santa came to say:
"Rudolph with your nose so bright, won't you guide my sleigh tonight?"
Then all the reindeer loved him as they shouted out with glee:
"Rudolph the red-nosed reindeer, you'll go down in history."

© Johnny Marks (1949)

2 Frosty the Snowman

Frosty the snowman was a jolly happy soul,
With a corncob pipe and a button nose,
And two eyes made out of coal.
Frosty the snowman is a fairy tale, they say,
He was made of snow but the children know
How he came to life one day.
There must have been some magic
In that old silk hat they found.
For when they placed it on his head,
He began to dance around.
Frosty the snowman knew the sun was hot that day.
So he said, "Let's run and we'll have some fun
Now before I melt away."
Down to the village, with a broomstick in his hand,
Running here and there all around the square saying,
"Catch me if you can."
He led them down the streets
of town right to the traffic cop.
And he only paused a moment when he heard him holler* "Stop!"

© Nelson/Rollins (1950)

(*holler* = [AmE, ugs.] schreien, brüllen)

3 We Wish You a Merry Christmas

We wish you a Merry Christmas;
We wish you a Merry Christmas;
We wish you a Merry Christmas and a Happy New Year.
Good tidings to you wherever you are;
Good tidings for Christmas and a Happy New Year.

Oh, bring us a figgy pudding;
Oh, bring us a figgy pudding;
Oh, bring us a figgy pudding and a cup of good cheer.
Good tidings to you wherever you are;
Good tidings for Christmas and a Happy New Year.

We won't go until we've got some;
We won't go until we've got some;
We won't go until we've got some, so bring some out here.

4 The Twelve Days of Christmas

On the first day of Christmas, my true love gave to me
a Partridge in a Pear Tree.

On the second day of Christmas, my true love gave to me
Two Turtle Doves
and a Partridge in a Pear Tree.

On the third day of Christmas, my true love gave to me
Three French Hens, two ...
(*repetition of all gifts mentioned before*)

On the fourth day of Christmas, my true love gave to me
Four Calling Birds, three ...

On the fifth day of Christmas, my true love gave to me
Five Golden Rings, four ...

On the sixth day of Christmas, my true love gave to me
Six Geese A-laying, five ...

On the seventh day of Christmas, my true love gave to me
Seven Swans, A-swimming, six ...

On the eighth day of Christmas, my true love gave to me
Eight Maids A-milking, seven ...

On the ninth day of Christmas, my true love gave to me
Nine Ladies Dancing, eight ...

On the tenth of Christmas, my true love gave to me
Ten Lords A-leaping, nine ...

On the eleventh day of Christmas, my true love gave to me
Eleven Pipers Piping, ten ...

On the twelfth day of Christmas, my true love gave to me
Twelve Drummers Drumming, eleven ...

More information:

This song originates from 16th century England, which was stricken by religious wars and severe prohibition against catholic practice and tradition. Some historians believe *The Twelve Days of Christmas* contains hidden references to basic teachings of the Catholic Faith and served as a mnemonic device especially for children. By the way, the *Twelve Days* do not refer to the time before Christmas but they count from Christmas until the beginning of Epiphany: December 25th – January 5th.

The symbolic meaning of the gifts:

DAY	GIFTS FROM TRUE LOVE	Christian Interpretation
1st	A Partridge in a Pear Tree	Jesus Christ, the son of God
2nd	Two Turtle Doves	the Old and the New Testament
3rd	Three French Hens	Faith, Hope and Charity (1 Corinthians 13: 13)
4th	Four Calling Birds	the Four Gospels (Matthew, Mark, Luke, John)
5th	Five Golden Rings	the five Books of Moses (The Pentateuch: Genesis, Exodus, Leviticus, Numbers, and Deuteronomy.)
6th	Six geese A-laying	the Six days of Creation
7th	Seven Swans A-swimming	the Seven Gifts of the Holy Spirit (Prophesy, Ministry, Teaching, Exhortation, Giving, Leading, Compassion; Romans 12: 6–8)
8th	Eight Maids A-milking	the Eight Beatitudes (cf. Matthew 5: 3–10)
9th	Nine Ladies Dancing	the Nine Fruits of the Holy Spirit (Love, Joy, Peace, Patience, Kindness, Generosity, Faithfulness, Gentleness, Self-control; Galatians 5: 22)
10th	Ten Lords A-Leaping	the Ten Commandments
11th	Eleven Pipers Piping	the Eleven Faithful Apostles (i.e. all; apart from Judas Iscariot)
12th	Twelve Drummers Drumming	the Apostles' Creed (1) I believe in God, the Father almighty, creator of heaven and earth. 2) I believe in Jesus Christ, his only Son, our Lord. 3) He was conceived by the power of the Holy Spirit and born of the Virgin Mary. 4) He suffered under Pontius Pilate, was crucified, died, and was buried. He descended into the grave. 5) On the third day he rose again. He ascended into heaven, and is seated at the right hand of the Father. 6) He will come again to judge the living and the dead. 7) I believe in the Holy Spirit, 8) the holy Catholic Church, 9) the communion of saints, 10) the forgiveness of sins, 11) the resurrection of the body, 12) and life everlasting.

5 A Christmas poem

The remarkable cake

It's Christmas – the time when we gather to make
A truly remarkable once-a-year cake.
The recipe's written in letters of gold
By a family witch who is terribly old.

The rule of this cake is it has to be made
In a wheelbarrow (stirred with a shovel or spade)
At Christmas, the season of love and good will.
Other times of the year it might make you ill.

You must nail it together or stick it with glue,
Then hammer it flat with the heel of your shoe.
You must stretch it out thin, you must tie it in knots.
Then get out your paint box and paint it with spots.

What a taste! What a flavour! It's certain to please.
It's rather like ice cream with pickles and cheese.
In June it would taste like spaghetti and mud,
While its taste in September would curdle your blood.

Oh, what a cake! It looks simply delicious.
Now get out the carving knife, get out the dishes!
Be careful! Be careful! This cake might explode,
And blow up the kitchen and part of the road.

Oh dear! It's exploded! I thought that it might.
It's not very often we get it just right.
Let's comfort the baby, revive Uncle Dan,
And we'll start it all over as soon as we can.

For Christmas – that gypsy day – comes and goes
Far sooner than ever we dare to suppose.
Once more in December we'll gather to make
That truly remarkable once-a-year cake.

© Margaret Mahy

Teil 6 – The Christmas Story

1 Einleitung

Das Stück kann mit einer Doppelbesetzung 28 Schüler beschäftigen, wobei die Rolle des Sterns keinen Text hat, sondern mit Hilfe beschriebener Schilder kommuniziert. Die beiden Engel haben längere Texte, müssten also von Schülern übernommen werden, die problemlos etwas auswendig lernen können.

2 Bühnenaustattung

Die Szenen sind leicht mit wenigen Hilfsmitteln symbolisch darzustellen. Der Stern in Szene IV hält Schilder hoch, die groß genug sein müssen, dass alle sie sehen und lesen können. Man könnte hier einen zweiten Schüler beschäftigen, wobei der erste Schüler mit dem ersten Schild von links nach rechts über die Bühne geht und der zweite Schüler mit dem zweiten Schild von rechts nach links usw.

3 Text: The Christmas story

Characters: two angels, Mary, Joseph, Donkey (non-speaking), Innkeeper, three shepherds, three wise men, the star (sort of non-speaking), Herod
Props: gold, frankincense, myrrh, Baby Jesus, blankets, cards for the star, donkey's ears, Herod's crown etc.
Setting: Mary's home in Nazareth, Inn in Bethlehem, Hillside near Bethlehem, road between "The East" and Bethlehem, and wherever you find angels

Scene I
Mary's home in Nazareth, symbolised by a simple setting of a stool and a table
(Mary is sitting on a stool in the middle of the stage reading. First angel and Second angel are standing to the left of the stage.)

First angel: The story we are going to tell you took place many hundreds of years ago, but it has been told more often than any other story in the world. Because of this story, millions of people all over the world celebrate every year. This is the story of Christmas.

Second angel:	In a small town called Nazareth, a young girl sat alone in her room. Her name was Mary. Mary was going to be married to a carpenter called Joseph Bar Jacob. Mary was a very religious girl, and God was pleased with her.
First angel:	So he sent me to give her a message. (First angel jumps down onto the stage.)
First angel:	Boo!
Mary:	(Not very interested) Oh look. It's an angel.
First angel:	Don't be afraid, Mary, I've come to tell you good news.
Mary:	I'm not afraid.
First angel:	Oh. Well you're supposed to be.
Mary:	But I'm not.
First angel:	Well, anyway, I've been sent to tell you that God is pleased with you and he has chosen you to be the mother of a very special child. You must call him Jesus. I've got to go and save the universe now. (First angel goes back to the pulpit where Second angel is standing.)
Second angel:	'Save the universe now?'
First angel:	Well, I thought it sounded rather good, actually.
	(Joseph comes on. He goes and stands beside Mary. Mary stands up so they are standing together.)
Second angel:	Soon Joseph and Mary were married. At that time the ruler of the land, King Herod, said that every man in the country had to go to his home town to be counted, and he had to take his wife and family with him. Joseph's home town was Bethlehem.
	(Joseph brings on the "donkey" by his lead. The "donkey" should have a name tag or large ears so the audience know that he is a donkey.)
	So Mary and Joseph set off with their donkey. By this time Mary was soon going to have her baby.
	(The "donkey" gives a very pregnant Mary a piggyback.)
First angel:	The journey to Bethlehem was long and hard, especially for Mary. When they got to Bethlehem they could not find anywhere to stay, because so many people were there waiting to be counted and all the inns were full. Finally they came to the last inn in the town.

Scene II
Inn in Bethlehem, comprising of a door over which there is an inn sign
(The innkeeper comes on.)
Innkeeper:	No, sorry, we're full up.
Mary:	Haven't you got any rooms at all?
Innkeeper:	(Turning and walking away) Not unless you want to sleep in the cowshed.
Joseph:	Okay, we'll take that then. It's better than sleeping on the streets or under a bridge.
Innkeeper:	(Turning round) OK, fine. Come with me then. This way.
Second angel:	So the innkeeper led them to a small stable at the back of the inn, gave them some blankets and went back to his inn. Later that night, Mary gave birth to a baby son, and she called him Jesus.
	(Mary sits in the stable, holding baby Jesus. Joseph stands behind her. The "donkey" stands outside looking bored.)
First angel:	In the meantime, I had to go and tell some shepherds about the new baby. The shepherds were looking after their sheep in the fields just outside town.

Scene III
Hillside near Bethlehem, symbolised by a backdrop of hills
(The shepherds and the sheep come on. The "donkey" is still looking bored. First angel jumps back onto the stage.)
First angel:	Boo! (She pauses. The shepherds stare blankly at her.) Were you scared?
First shepherd:	(Sarcastically) Yep. Terrified.
First angel:	Oh good. Do not be afraid, for I bring you good news. Tonight, in Bethlehem, a baby has been born who will save the world. You will find him in a stable, under a bright star. (First angel goes back to the pulpit.)
Second shepherd:	Okay, let's go and find the new baby.
Third shepherd:	Hey, what are we going to do with all the sheep?
First shepherd:	I don't know. We'd better take them with us.
Second shepherd:	What – all four hundred and seventy two and a half of them?
Third shepherd:	And a half? Are you sure you counted them right?
Second shepherd:	I think so. But then, I was never very good at maths at school.

The Christmas story

Second angel: So the shepherds set off to Bethlehem, with their 472 and a half sheep. It didn't take them long to find the baby because there was a bright star above the stable, showing them the way.

Scene IV
On the road between "The East" and Bethlehem, a couple of road signs indicating that it is a road and between two important places
(The "star" comes on. The "donkey" looks even more bored. The shepherds go over to the stable and sit round it with their sheep.)

First angel: A long way away, in the east, some wise men saw the star too, and wondered what it was.
(The wise men enter. First wise man is wearing a Borussia Dortmund T-shirt. **Star** hold ups a sign "THIS WAY. YES; YOU TOO, YOU IN THE BORUSSIA DORTMUND T-SHIRT.")

First wise man: Hey, look. It's a star.
(**Star** holds up a sign: "FOLLOW ME.")

Third wise man: I think it wants us to follow it.
(**Star** holds up a sign: "WELL DONE.")

Second wise man: Well, we haven't got anything better to do. Come on then, let's go.
(**Star** holds up a sign: "GOOD IDEA." The wise men go up onto the stage and follow the star towards the stable.)

Third wise man: I'm tired.
(**Star** holds up a sign: "ALREADY?")

Third wise man: Can we stop and rest for a moment?
(**Star** holds up a sign: "NO!")

Second wise man: That's a good idea.
(**Star** holds up a sign: "NO IT ISN'T.")

First wise man: Here's a good place to stop.
(They sit down and look bored. **Star** holds up a sign: "GET UP!", then: "I HAVEN'T GOT ALL NIGHT YOU KNOW.", then: "HEY YOU", then: "WITH THE BORUSSIA DORTMUND T-SHIRT." First wise man looks up.)

First wise man: Hey, I think we should keep following that star.
(**Star** holds up a sign: "WHERE'D YOU GET THAT IDEA FROM?")

Third wise man: But I want to go to sleep.
(**Star** holds up a sign: "DO YOU THINK I CARE?")
Second wise man: No, we'd better get going. Come on.
(**Star** holds up a sign: "FINALLY!")
Second angel: So the wise men followed the star all the way to Bethlehem, where they found the baby Jesus and gave him presents of gold, frankincense* and myrrh. Then they returned home and told everyone they met about the baby who would be king of all Israel.
(Wise men go off.)

(*frankincense* = Weihrauch)

Scene V
In King Herod's palace, a chair draped with a golden cloth or so

First angel: Unfortunately King Herod heard about this, and he wasn't a happy king.
(King Herod comes on.)
Herod: I'm going to be the only king round here! I want all baby boys in the land to be killed! Killed!
Second angel: When Mary and Joseph heard what King Herod said, they ran away to Egypt, where they lived for two years. (Mary, Joseph and the "donkey" go off.) At last Herod died (Herod "dies" and is carried off.) and Mary and Joseph could safely come back to Nazareth with Jesus.
First angel: That's not the end of the story – it's only the beginning. But we angels aren't in the rest of it, so we thought you wouldn't find the rest of the story very interesting.
(All the members of the cast come on.)
Second angel: We hope you have a great Christmas and a wonderful New Year.
(Everyone sings "We wish you a Merry Christmas".)

Teil 7 – *Dinner for one*: a play

1 Einleitung

Das traditionelle Stück, das in Deutschland immer zu Silvester gespielt wird, hat nur zwei Rollen, kann aber in jeder Stufe gespielt werden. Da das Stück so verbreitet und die Handlung dadurch bekannt ist, wird es auch von jüngeren Klassen ohne Schwierigkeiten verstanden.

Miss Sophie feiert ihren 90. Geburtstag. Wie in jedem Jahr lädt sie dazu ihre vier engsten Freunde ein: Sir Toby, Admiral von Schneider, Mr Pommeroy und Mr Winterbottom. Die Geschichte hat nur einen Haken: Miss Sophie ist nicht mehr die Jüngste, und die Herren sind mittlerweile alle verstorben. Da sie aus verständlichen Gründen nicht persönlich anwesend sein können, muss Miss Sophies Butler James die Rolle aller vier Herren übernehmen. Er sieht sich genötigt, nicht nur seiner Arbeitgeberin das Essen, sondern auch den vier imaginären Herren die jeweils passenden Drinks (Sherry, Weißwein, Champagner und Portwein) zu servieren, in ihre Rollen zu schlüpfen, in diesen auf die Gastgeberin einen Trinkspruch auszubringen und jedes Glas zu leeren. Da er das für vier tut, wird er immer betrunkener, leert schließlich statt der Gläser Blumenvasen aus und treibt die albernsten Späße, wobei teilweise unklar bleibt, wie weit er die Trunkenheit der imaginierten Gäste nachspielt bzw. wie betrunken er selbst ist.

Vor jedem Gang und zunehmend lallend fragt Butler James: The same procedure as last year, Miss Sophie? Diese erwidert regelmäßig: The same procedure as *every* year, James, wobei die Betonung auf *every* liegt. Schließlich beendet Miss Sophie den Abend mit einem Augenaufschlag und einem einladenden I think I'll retire, was James nach dem obligatorischen The same procedure as last year? – The same procedure as every year mit einem Augenzwinkern und einem nonchalanten Well, I'll do my very best quittiert, um sich schließlich mit ihr in die oberen Räumlichkeiten zurückzuziehen.

In England selbst wurde *Dinner for One* nur bruchteilhaft ausgestrahlt und ist dort bis heute weitgehend unbekannt. In anderen Ländern, zum Beispiel der Schweiz, Österreich, Norwegen, Schweden, Südafrika, Dänemark, ist *Dinner for One* jedoch ähnlich wie in Deutschland ein alljährliches Kult-Ereignis.

2 Bühnenausstattung

The play takes place in a dining room. The table is laid for five people, each setting with four glasses, plates for soup, fish and chicken. The bearskin must, of course, be on the floor in front of the table, but imaginative classes could have a small pupil under a rug, playing the part and almost (!) tripping up James.

3 Text: Dinner for one

(© Lauri Wylie, 1953)

James: Good evening, Miss Sophie. Good evening.
Miss Sophie: Good evening, James.
James: You are looking very well this evening, Miss Sophie.
Miss Sophie: Well, I am feeling very much better, thank you, James.
James: Good, good …
Miss Sophie: Well I must say that everything looks very nice.
James: Thank you very much, Miss Sophie, thank you.
Miss Sophie: Is everybody here?
James: Indeed, they are, yes, yes … They all are here for your anniversary, Miss Sophie.
Miss Sophie: All five places are laid out?
James: All laid out as usual.
Miss Sophie: Sir Toby?
James: Sir Toby, yes, he's sitting here this year, Miss Sophie.
Miss Sophie: Admiral von Schneider? (gesprochen: [von])
James: Admiral von Schneider is sitting here, Miss Sophie.
Miss Sophie: Mr Pommeroy?
James: Mr Pommeroy, I put round here for you.
Miss Sophie: And my very dear friend, Mr Winterbottom?
James: On your right, as you requested, Miss Sophie.
Miss Sophie: Thank you, James. You may now serve the soup.
James: The soup, thank you very much, Miss Sophie, thank you. They are all waiting for you. Little drop of Mulligatawny soup* Miss Sophie …
Miss Sophie: I am particular fond of Mulligatawny soup, James.
James: Yes, I know you are.
Miss Sophie: I think we'll have sherry now, with the soup.
James: Sherry with the soup, yes … Oh, by the way, the same procedure as last year, Miss Sophie?

Dinner for one

Miss Sophie: Same procedure as every year, James.
James: (mimicking her) Same procedure as every year, James.
Miss Sophie: Is this a dry sherry, James?
James: Yes, a very dry sherry, Miss Sophie. A very dry. Straight out of the cellar, this morning, Miss Sophie.
Miss Sophie: Sir Toby!
James: Cheerio, Miss Sophie!
Miss Sophie: Admiral von Schneider!
James: Ad ... Must I say it this year, Miss Sophie!
Miss Sophie: Just to please me, James.
James: Just to please you, very good, yes, yes ... Skoll!
Miss Sophie: Mr Pommeroy!
James: Happy New Year, Sophie!
Miss Sophie: And dear Mr Winterbottom!
James: Well, here we are again, old lovely ...
Miss Sophie: You may now serve the fish.
James: Fish. Very good, Miss Sophie. Did you enjoy the soup?
Miss Sophie: Delicious, James.
James: Thank you, Miss Sophie, glad you enjoyed it. – Little bit of North Sea haddock, Miss Sophie?
Miss Sophie: I think we'll have white wine with the fish.
James: White wine with the fish. The same procedure as last year, Miss Sophie?
Miss Sophie: The same procedure as every year, James!
James: Yeah ...
Miss Sophie: Sir Toby!
James: Cheerio, Sophie, me gal ...
Miss Sophie: Admiral von Schneider!
James: Oh, must I, Miss Sophie?
Miss Sophie: James, please, please ...
James: Skoll!
Miss Sophie: Mr Pommeroy!
James: Happy New Year, Sophie gal.
Miss Sophie: Mr Winterbottom!
James: ... you look younger than ever! Younger than ever! He, he, he ...
Miss Sophie: Please, serve the chicken!
James: Ya ...
Miss Sophie: That looks a very fine bird?!
James: That's a lovely chu ... chuk ... chicken, that I'll tell you, a lovely ...

Miss Sophie:	I think we'll have champagne with the bird!
James:	Champagne, ya ... Sssame procedure as last year, Miss Sophie?
Miss Sophie:	Same procedure as every year, James!!! – Sir Toby!
James:	Sophie me gal ...
Miss Sophie:	Admiral von Schneider!
James:	Must I, Miss Sophie?
Miss Sophie:	James!
James:	Ssskoll!
Miss Sophie:	Mr Pommeroy!
James:	Happy New Year, Sophie gal ...
Miss Sophie:	Mr Winterbottom!
James:	It's one of the nicest little women ... hick ... one of the nicest little women, that's ever breathed, ever breathed ... I now declare this bazar open! – Would you like some fruit?
Miss Sophie:	I think we'll have port with the fruit!
James:	Oh, noo! Sssame procedure as last ...
Miss Sophie:	Yes, same procedure as every year, James!
James:	..........!!...
Miss Sophie:	Sir Toby!
James:	Sugar in the morning, sugar ...
Miss Sophie:	Admiral von Schneider!
James:	Ssskolll!
Miss Sophie:	Mr Pommeroy!
James:	I'm sorry, Madam, sorry.
Miss Sophie:	Mr Winterbottom
James:	... huuuh, That'll kill a cat!...uuuh!
Miss Sophie:	Well, James, It's been really a wonderful party!
James:	Well it's been most enjoyable.
Miss Sophie:	I think, I'll retire.
James:	You're going to bed?
Miss Sophie:	Yes.
James:	Sit down, I'll give you a hand up, Madam.
Miss Sophie:	As I was saying, I think, I'll retire.
James:	Ya ... Ya. – By the way, the same procedure as last year, Miss Sophie?
Miss Sophie:	The same procedure as every year, James!
James:	Well – I'll do my very best!

(*Mulligatawny* [ˌmʌlɪgə'tɔːni] *soup* = Currysuppe)

Teil 8 – "Merry Christmas" in many languages

Hier haben wir den bekannten Weihnachtsgruß in einer Vielzahl von Sprachen bereitgestellt. Vielleicht haben Sie Schüler einer der unten stehenden Muttersprachen und machen ihm bzw. ihr eine Freude.

Afrikaans – Geseende Kerfees en 'n gelukkige nuwe jaar
Danish – Glædelig Jul og godt nytår
Dutch – Vrolijk Kerstfeest en een Gelukkig Nieuwjaar!
English – Merry Christmas & Happy New Year
Esperanto – Gajan Kristnaskon & Bonan Novjaron
Finnish – Hyvää Joulua or Hauskaa Joulua
Flemish – Zalig Kerstfeest en Gelukkig nieuw jaar
French – Joyeux Noël et Bonne Année!
Greek – Kala Christougenna Kieftihismenos O Kenourios Chronos
Hebrew – Mo'adim Lesimkha. Shanah Tova
Hungarian – Kellemes Karacsonyiunnepeket & Boldog Új Évet
Irish – Nollaig Shona Dhuit
Italian – Buon Natale e Felice Anno Nuovo
Japanese – Shinnen omedeto. Kurisumasu Omedeto
Kurdish – Seva piroz sahibe u sersala te piroz be
Latin – Pax hominibus bonae voluntatis
Latvian – Prieci'gus Ziemsve'tkus un Laimi'gu Jauno Gadu!
Lithuanian – Linksmu Kaledu ir laimingu Nauju metu
Luxembourgeois – Schéi Krëschtdeeg an e Schéint Néi Joer
Macedonian – Streken Bozhik
Norwegian/Nynorsk – Eg ynskjer hermed Dykk alle ein God Jul og Godt Nyttår
Pennsylvania German – En frehlicher Grischtdaag unen hallich Nei Yaahr!
Polish – Wesolych Swiat i Szczesliwego Nowego Roku.
Portuguese – Boas Festas e um feliz Ano Novo
Romanian – Craciun fericit si un An Nou fericit!
Russian – Pozdravlyayu s prazdnikom Rozhdestva i s Novim Godom
Sardinian – Bonu nadale e prosperu annu nou
Scots Gaelic – Nollaig chridheil agus Bliadhna mhath ur!
Serbian – Sretam Bozic. Vesela Nova Godina
Sicilian – Bon Natali e Prosperu Annu Novu !
Slovakian – Vesele Vianoce a stastny novy rok

Slovene – Vesele bozicne praznike in srecno novo leto
Spanish – Feliz Navidad y Próspero Año Nuevo
Swedish – God Jul och Gott Nytt År
Turkish – Noeliniz Ve Yeni Yiliniz Kutlu Olsun
Ukrainian – Veseloho Vam Rizdva i Shchastlyvoho Novoho Roku!
Vietnamese – Chuc Mung Giang Sinh – Chuc Mung Tan Nien
Welsh – Nadolig LLawen a Blwyddyn Newydd Dda
Yiddish – Gute Vaynakhtn un a Gut Nay Yor

4 Englische Reime und Gedichte

Reime und Gedichte erfüllen viele Funktionen im Englisch-Unterricht. Das Auswendiglernen (*learning by heart*) unterstützt die Schüler

a) bei der Aussprache (mit Hilfe von Reimwörtern, die Orientierung bieten),
b) beim Vokabellernen (sie treffen auf bekannte Wörter in neuem Kontext und können Unbekanntes über den Sinn erschließen),
c) bei der Entwicklung eines Gefühls für den Rhythmus der Fremdsprache und
d) es bietet ihnen Spaß an der (Fremd-)Sprache.

For younger classes

1 As I was going to St. Ives

Ein Rätsel

As I was going to St. Ives I met a man
with seven wives,
Each wife had seven sacks, each sack
had seven cats,
Each cat had seven kits*
kits, cats, sacks and wives,
How many were going to St. Ives?

(**kits* = *kittens* = Kätzchen)

Answer: one: "As I was going to St. Ives"

2 Betty Botter

Ein Zungenbrecher-Gedicht

Betty Botter bought some butter,
"But," she said, "the butter's bitter;
If I put it in my batter*,
It will make my batter bitter;
But a bit of better butter,
That would make my batter better."
So she bought a bit of butter,
Better than her bitter butter,
And she put it in her batter,
And the batter was not bitter;
So 'twas better Betty Botter
Bought a bit of better butter.

(*batter* = Pfannkuchenteig)

3 Yellow butter

Noch ein Zungenbrecher-Gedicht

Yellow butter, purple jelly, red jam, black bread
Spread it thick. Say it quick

Yellow butter, purple jelly, red jam, black bread
Spread it thicker. Say it quicker

Yellow butter, purple jelly, red jam, black bread
Now repeat it while you eat it

(Spoken as if your mouth is full of bread and jam)
Yellow butter, purple jelly, red jam, black bread

Don't talk with your mouth full!

© Mary Ann Hoberman

4 From *Struwwelpeter*

Ein Gedicht mit einer Moral

Augustus was a chubby lad;
Fat ruddy cheeks Augustus had;
And everybody saw with joy
The plump and hearty healthy boy.
He ate and drank as he was told,
And never let his soup get cold.
But one day, one cold winter's day,
He threw away the spoon and screamed:
"O take the nasty soup away!
I won't have any soup today:
I will not, will not eat my soup!
I will not eat it, no!"

Next day! Now look, the picture shows
How lank and lean Augustus grows!
Yet, though he feels so weak and ill,
The naughty fellow cries out still:
"Not any soup for me, I say!
O take the nasty soup away!
I will not, will not eat my soup!
I will not eat it, no!"

The third day comes. O what a sin!
To make himself so pale and thin.
Yet, when the soup is put on table,
He screams, as loud as he is able:
"Not any soup for me, I say!
O take the nasty soup away!
I won't have any soup today!"

Look at him, now the fourth day's come!
He scarce* outweighs a sugar-plum;
He's like a little bit of thread;
And on the fifth day he was dead.

(*scarce* = *hardly* = kaum)

5 Homework

(*Ein Gefühl, das ich auch als Lehrerin gut kenne!*)

Homework sits on top of Sunday, squashing Sunday flat.
Homework has the smell of Monday, homework's very fat.
Heavy books and piles of paper, answers I don't know.
Sunday evening's almost finished, now I'm going to go
Do my homework in the kitchen. Maybe just a snack,
Then I'll sit right down and start as soon as I run back
For some chocolate sandwich cookies. Then I'll really do
All that homework in a minute. First I'll see what new
Show they've got on television in the living room.
Everybody's laughing there, but misery and gloom
And a full refrigerator are where I am at.
I'll just have another sandwich. Homework's very fat.

© Russel Hoban

6 Hugger Mugger

(*Ein Gedicht, dem alle jungen Leute sicherlich zustimmen werden*)

I'd sooner be
Jumped and thumped and dumped
I'd sooner be
Slugged and mugged ... than hugged ...
And clobbered with a slobbering
Kiss by my Auntie Jean.

You know what I mean:
Whenever she comes to stay,
You know you're bound
To get one.
A quick short peck* would be OK
But this is a whacking great,
Smacking great
Wet one!

© Kit Wright

(*peck* = Küsschen)

7 Private? No!

(Muss ich hierzu etwas sagen? Es ist selbsterklärend)

Punctuation can make a difference.
Private
No swimming
Allowed

Does not mean the same as
Private? No. Swimming allowed.

© Williard R. Espy

8 If only I had plenty of money

(nützlich für die Conditional Form)

If only I had plenty of money,
I'd buy you some flowers, and I'd buy you some honey,
I'd buy you a boat, and I'd buy you a sail,
I'd buy you a cat with a long bushy tail,
I'd buy you a brooch* and a bangle* as well,
I'd buy you a church, I'd buy you a bell,
I'd buy you the earth, I'd buy you the moon –
Oh, money, dear money, please come very soon.

(**brooch* = Brosche; *bangle* = Armreif)

For older classes

9 A poem full of nonsense and non-existant words

Die Schüler können ihren Spaß haben, indem sie versuchen sich mögliche Bedeutungen der Wörter auszudenken. Selbst die Aussprache mancher Wörter kann den Schülern überlassen werden. Die Melodie dieses Gedichtes ist nur einer seiner vielen Reize.

Jabberwocky

'Twas brillig, and the slithy toves
Did gyre and gimble in the wabe;
All mimsy were the borogoves,
And the mome raths outgrabe.

"Beware the Jabberwock, my son!
The jaws that bite,
the claws that catch!
Beware the Jubjub bird, and shun
The frumious Bandersnatch!"

He took his vorpal sword in hand:
Long time the manxome foe he sought
So rested he by the Tumtum tree.
And stood awhile in thought.

And as in uffish thought he stood,
The Jabberwock,
with eyes of flame,
Came wiffling through the tulgey wood,
And burbled as it came!

One, two! One, two!
And through and through
The vorpal blade went snicker-snack!
He left it dead, and with its head
He went galumphing back.

"And hast thou slain the Jabberwock?
Come to my arms,
my beamish boy!
Frabjous day! Callooh! Callay!"
He chortled in his joy.

'Twas brillig, and the slithy toves
Did gyre and gimble in the wabe;
All mimsy were the borogoves,
And the mome raths outgrabe.

(Lewis Carroll)

Der Jammerwoch

Es brillig war. Die schlichty Toven
Wirrten und wimmelten in Waben;
Und aller-mümsige Burggoven
Die mohmen Räth' ausgraben.

„Bewahre doch vor Jammerwoch!
Die Zähne knirschen,
Krallen kratzen!
Bewahr' vor Jubjub-Vogel, vor
Frumiösen Banderschnatzchen!"

Er griff sein vorpals Schwertchen zu,
Er suchte lang das manchsam' Ding;

Dann, stehend unterm Tumtum-Baum,
Er an-zu-denken-fing.

Als stand er tief in Andacht auf,
Des Jammerwochen's
Augenfeuer
Durch tulgen Wald mit
Wiffek kam
Ein burbelnd Ungeheuer!

Eins, Zwei! Eins, Zwei!
Und durch und durch
Sein vorpals Schwert
zerschnifer-schnück,
Da blieb es tot! Er, Kopf in Hand,
Geläumfig zog zurück.

„Und schlugst Du ja den Jammerwoch?
Umarme mich,
mien Böhm'sches Kind
O Freuden-Tag! O Halloo-Schlag!"
Er schortelt frohgesinnt.

Es brillig war. Die schlichte Toven
Wirrten und wimmelten in Waben;
Und aller-mümsige Burggoven
Die mohmen Räth' ausgraben.

(a sort-of German translation by Robert Scott)

10 The Owl and the Pussy Cat

Edward Lear (1812–1888) ist bekannt für seine Limericks, von denen einige weiter unten abgedruckt sind. Dieses Gedicht ist eines der bekanntesten englischen Kinderreime. Es besticht durch seine fließende Melodik.

The Owl and the Pussy Cat went to sea
In a beautiful pea-green boat,
They took some honey, and plenty of money
Wrapped up in a five-pound note.
The Owl looked up to the stars above,
And sang to a small guitar,
"O lovely Pussy, O Pussy, my love,
What a beautiful Pussy you are,
You are, You are!
What a beautiful Pussy you are!"

Pussy said to the Owl, "You elegant fowl!
How charmingly sweet you sing!
O let us be married! Too long we have tarried*:
But what shall we do for a ring?"
They sailed away, for a year and a day,
To the land where the Bong-tree grows
And there in a wood a Piggy-wig stood
With a ring at the end of his nose,
His nose, His nose,
With a ring at the end of his nose
"Dear Pig, are you willing to sell for one shilling
Your ring?" Said the Piggy, "I will."
So they took it away, and were married next day
By the Turkey who lives on the hill.
They dined on mince, and slices of quince*,
Which they ate with a runcible* spoon;
And hand in hand, on the edge of the sand,
They danced by the light of the moon,
The moon, The moon,
They danced by the light of the moon.

(Edward Lear)

(*tarry* = [lit.] zögern; *quince* = Quitten; *runcible spoon* = Löffel mit Gabelzinken)

11 Shall I compare thee to a summer's day (Sonnet 18)

Shall I compare thee to a summer's day?
Thou art more lovely and more temperate.
Rough winds do shake the darling buds of May,
And summer's lease hath all too short a date.
Sometime too hot the eye of heaven shines,
And often is his gold complexion dimmed;
And every fair from fair sometime declines,
By chance, or nature's changing course untrimmed.
But thy eternal summer shall not fade
Nor lose possession of that fair thou ow'st;
Nor shall death brag thou wand'rest in his shade,
When in eternal lines to time thou grow'st,
So long as men can breathe or eyes can see,
So long lives this, and this gives life to thee.

(William Shakespeare)

Or in other words:

Shall I compare you to a summer's day?
You are lovelier and more delightful.
Rough winds shake the much-loved buds of May,
And summer is far too short:
At times the sun is too hot,
Or often goes behind the clouds
And everything that is beautiful will lose its beauty,
By chance or by nature's planned out course;
But your youth shall not fade,
Nor lose the beauty that you possess;
Nor will death claim you for his own
Because in my eternal verse you will live forever.
So long as there are people on this earth
So long will this poem live on, giving you immortality.

Sonnet 18 is perhaps the best known and most well-loved of all 154 sonnets by Shakespeare. It is also one of the most straightforward in language and intent. The stability of love and its power to immortalize the poetry and the subject of that poetry is the theme. The poet starts the praise of his dear friend without ostentation, but he slowly builds the image of his friend into that of a perfect being. His friend is first compared to summer, but, then he is summer, and thus, he has metamorphosed into the standard by which true beauty can and should be judged. The poet's only answer to such profound joy and beauty is to ensure that his friend stays forever in human memory, saved from the ultimate oblivion that accompanies death. The sonnet reaffirms the poet's hope that as long as there is breath in mankind, his poetry too will live on.

12 In Flanders Fields

Dieses Gedicht von John McCrae ist noch heute eines der eindrucksvollsten Gedichte über den Krieg, die jemals in englischer Sprache geschrieben wurden. Es ist eine Erinnerung an die schreckliche Schlacht von Ypres im Frühling 1915. Zur Entstehungsgeschichte dieses Gedichts: Obwohl McCrae jahrelang als Arzt im Südafrikanischen Krieg diente, war es ihm unmöglich, sich an das Leiden, die Schreie und das Blut zu gewöhnen. Der Autor arbeitete 17 lange Tage als Chirurg in Ypres und behandelte verletzte Canadier, Briten, Inder, Franzosen und Deutsche.

McCrae schrieb später: „Siebzehn Tage im Hades! Wenn jemand am Ende des ersten Tages gesagt hätte, dass wir siebzehn Tage dort verbringen müssten, hätten wir unsere Hände gefaltet und erklärt, dass dies unmöglich sei."

Ein Tod berührte McCrae besonders. Ein junger Freund und Schüler von McCrae, Lieutenant Alexis Helmer aus Ottawa, wurde am 2. Mai 1915 durch eine Granate getötet.

McCrae begrub ihn persönlich am selben Tag auf einem kleinen Friedhof vor der Krankenstation, da kein Priester anwesend war, um die Beerdigungszeremonie durchzuführen.

Am nächsten Tag verfasste McCrae dieses Gedicht und brachte so seinen Schmerz zum Ausdruck. Er blickte dabei auf den wilden Mohn, der auf dem Friedhof wuchs.

In Flanders fields the poppies blow
Between the crosses, row on row,
That mark our place; and in the sky
The larks, still bravely singing, fly
Scarce heard amid the guns below.
We are the Dead. Short days ago

We lived, felt dawn, saw sunset glow,
Loved and were loved, and now we lie,
In Flanders fields.
Take up our quarrel with the foe:
To you from failing hands we throw
The torch; be yours to hold it high.
If ye break faith with us who die
We shall not sleep, though poppies grow
In Flanders fields.

(John McCrae)

13 The Soldier

If I should die, think only this of me:
That there's some corner of a foreign field
That is forever England. There shall be
In that rich earth a richer dust concealed;
A dust whom England bore, shaped, made aware,
Gave, once, her flowers to love, her ways to roam;
A body of England's, breathing English air,
Washed by the rivers, blest by suns of home.
And think, this heart, all evil shed away,
A pulse in the eternal mind, no less
Gives somewhere back the thoughts by England given;
Her sights and sounds; dreams happy as her day;
And laughter, learnt of friends; and gentleness,
In hearts at peace, under an English heaven.

(Rupert Brooke)

14 O Captain My Captain

O Captain my Captain! our fearful trip is done,
The ship has weathered every rack, the prize we sought is won,
The port is near, the bells I hear, the people all exulting,
While follow eyes the steady keel, the vessel grim and daring;
But O heart! heart! heart!
O the bleeding drops of red,

Where on the deck my Captain lies,
Fallen cold and dead.
O Captain! my Captain! rise up and hear the bells;
Rise up – for you the flag is flung for you the bugle trills,
For you bouquets and ribboned wreaths for you the shores a-crowding,
For you they call, the swaying mass, their eager faces turning;
Here Captain! dear father!
This arm beneath your head!
It is some dream that on the deck,
You've fallen cold and dead.
My Captain does not answer, his lips are pale and still;
My father does not feel my arm, he has no pulse nor will;
The ship is anchored safe and sound, its voyage closed and done;
From fearful trip the victor ship comes in with object won;
Exult O shores, and ring O bells!
But I, with mournful tread,
Walk the deck my Captain lies,
Fallen cold and dead.

(Walt Whitman)

15 When you are old

When you are old and grey and full of sleep,
And nodding by the fire, take down this book,
And slowly read, and dream of the soft look
Your eyes had once, and of their shadows deep;
How many loved your moments of glad grace,
And loved your beauty with love false or true,
But one man loved the pilgrim Soul in you,
And loved the sorrows of your changing face;
And bending down beside the glowing bars,
Murmur, a little sadly, how Love fled
And paced upon the mountains overhead
And hid his face amid a crowd of stars.

(William Butler Yeats)

16 I, too, sing America

I, too, sing America.
I am the darker brother.
They send me to eat in the kitchen
When company comes,
But I laugh,
And eat well,
And grow strong.

Tomorrow,
I'll be at the table
When company comes.
Nobody'll dare
Say to me,
"Eat in the kitchen,"
Then.

Besides,
They'll see how beautiful I am
And be ashamed –
I, too, am America.

(Langston Hughes)

This poem is full of symbolism when one recalls Americas policy of blacks not being allowed to eat with white people, a policy that was, by the way, also adopted by the White House.
Its main idea is alienation and loneliness through discrimination – the narrator eats in the kitchen. This is a simple construction of intolerance and bigotry, but as the poem ends, you will notice that the symbolism of revolution, be it metaphorical or reality based, empowers the isolated man to move, from which point the isolated becomes the isolator. The entire poem is a symbol of bigotry as a symbol of the flip-flopping of social power structures.
It is a very insightful and colorful poem that is clear and understandable and has a very deep meaning and it gives the reader an insight into the savage aspect of the American Dream, where equality etc. is supposed to be one of the main beliefs. However, the black slave is sent to the kitchen to eat. This goes against the religion of Christianity, which many Americans follow. Also, "They'll see how beautiful I am and be ashamed" suggests that the white people will be ashamed as they know it is contradictory to act in this way.

It is important to note that Hughes' pronouns are not collective as many people have assumed. "I am the darker brother" may be an allegorical reference to blacks in America but it is not "We are the darker brothers" and so it deserves a second look.

The circumstances that surround the poem play on individual circumstances, which is important because it doesn't feed into racist taxonomy. While many racists attempted to divide up racial groups (e. g. black, white) they strove to use language that would reflect this. Hughes, by using individualized pronouns such as "I" rejects this notion.

The use of individualized pronouns casts down racist taxonomists and makes people consider him on an individual (non-stereotypical) level.

17 Auld Lang Syne

Should auld acquaintance be forgot,
And never brought to mind?
Should auld acquaintance be forgot,
And auld lang syne?

For auld lang syne, my dear,
For auld lang syne,
We'll tak a cup o' kindness yet,
For auld lang syne.

And there's a hand, my trusty frien',
And gie's a hand o' thine!
And we'll tak a right guid-willie waught
For auld lang syne.

(Robert Burns)

The poem Auld Lang Syne *by Robert Burns has been immortalised by the tradition of singing the lyrics to* Auld Lang Syne *at Christmas and New Year parties.* Auld Lang Syne *is also sung on Burns Night, 25th January, to celebrate the life and works of Robert Burns.* Auld Lang Syne *was written in 1788 and the words 'Auld Lang Syne' literally translates from old Scottish dialect meaning 'Old Long Since' and is about love and friendship in times past. The words in the poem* Auld Lang Syne *referring to 'We'll take a Cup of Kindness yet' relate to a drink shared by men and women to symbolise friendship. Happy New Year!*

18 Limericks

Limericks are meant to be funny. They often contain hyperbole, onomatopoeia, idioms, puns and other figurative devices. The last line of a good limerick contains the *punch line* or "heart of the joke". As you work with limericks, remember to have pun, I mean *fun*! Say the following limericks out loud and clap to the rhythm.

A limerick is a five-line poem written with two couplets, the first consisting of two longer and the second of two shorter rhyming lines. It is completed by the last (= fifth) line which rhymes with the first couplet. The rhyme pattern is *a a b b a* with lines 1, 2 and 5 containing three beats and rhyming, and lines 3 and 4 having two beats and rhyming. Some people say that soldiers returning from France to the Irish town of Limerick in the 1700s invented the limerick.

1   A flea and a fly in a flue
    Were caught, so what could they do?
    said the fly, "Let us flee."
    "Let us fly," said the flea.
    So they flew through a flaw in the flue.

You will soon hear the distinctive beat pattern of all limericks. The rhythm is just as important in a limerick as the rhyme. Try completing this limerick.

2   There once was a pauper named Meg
    Who accidentally broke her _____.   (*leg*)
    She slipped on the _____.   (*ice*)
    Not once, but thrice
    Take no pity on her, I _____.   (*beg*)

Einige Limericks aus Edward Lears *Book of Nonsense* (1846)

3   There was an Old Man with a beard,
    Who said, 'It is just as I feared!
    Two Owls and a Hen,
    Four Larks and a Wren,
    Have all built
    their nests
    in my beard.'

4   There was an Old Person whose habits
    Induced him to feed upon rabbits;
    When he'd eaten eighteen,
    He turned perfectly green,
    Upon which he relinquished those habits.

5 There was an Old Man who supposed,
   That the street door was partially closed;
   But some very large rats,
   Ate his coats and his hats,
   While that futile old gentleman dozed.

6 There was a Young Lady of Norway,
   Who casually sat on a doorway;
   When the door squeezed her flat,
   She exclaimed, 'What of that?'
   This courageous Young Lady of Norway.

7 There was an Old Person of Hurst,
   Who drank when he had no thirst;
   When they said, 'You'll grow fatter,'
   He answered, 'What matter?'
   That globular Person of Hurst.

8 There was an Old Person of Chili,
   Whose conduct was painful and silly,
   He sat on the stairs,
   Eating apples and pears,
   That imprudent Old Person of Chili.

9 There was a Young Lady whose chin,
   Resembled the point of a pin;
   So she had it made sharp,
   And purchased a harp,
   And played several tunes with her chin.

10 There was a Young Lady whose bonnet,
   Came untied when the birds sat upon it;
   But she said: 'I don't care!'
   All the birds in the air
   Are welcome to sit on my bonnet.

11 There was an Old Man of Peru,
   Who never knew what he should do;
   So he tore off his hair,
   And behaved like a bear,
   That intrinsic Old Man of Peru.

12 There was an Old Man on a hill,
   Who seldom, if ever, stood still;
   He ran up and down,
   In his Grandmother's gown,
   Which adorned that Old Man on a hill.

13 There was an Old Man with a nose,
   Who said, 'If you choose to suppose,
   That my nose is too long,
   You are certainly wrong!'
   That remarkable Man with a nose.

14 There was an Old Person of Dover,
   Who rushed through a field of blue clover;
   But some very large bees,
   Stung his nose and his knees,
   So he very soon went back to Dover.

15 There was a Young Lady of Bute,
   Who played on a silver-gilt flute;
   She played several jigs,
   To her uncle's white pigs,
   That amusing Young Lady of Bute.

Einige anonyme Limericks

16 An exceedingly fat friend of mine,
   When asked at what hour he'd dine,
   Replied, "At eleven,
   At three, five, and seven,
   And eight and a quarter past nine."

17 There once was a fly on the wall
   I wonder why didn't it fall?
   Because its feet stuck?
   Or was it just luck?
   Or does gravity miss things so small?

18 A gourmet dining at Crewe
   Found a rather large mouse in his stew.
   Said the waiter, "Don't shout
   And wave it about,
   Or the rest will be wanting one, too."

19 There once was a slimmer named Steen
   Who grew so extremely lean
   And flat, and compressed,
   That his back touched his chest,
   So that sideways he couldn't be seen.

20 The incredible Wizard of Oz
   Retired from his business because
   Due to up-to-date science,
   To most of his clients,
   He wasn't the Wizard he was.

21 There was an old gent from Hyde
   Who ate rotten apples and died.
   The apples fermented
   Inside the lamented
   And made cider inside his inside.

25 An elderly man called Keith
   Mislaid his set of false teeth
   He put them on a chair,
   And forgot they were there,
   When he sat down they bit him beneath.

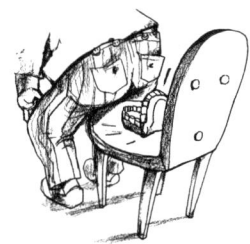

22 Said an ape as he swung by his tail,
   To his offspring both female and male,
   "From your offspring, my dears,
   In a couple of years,
   May evolve a professor at Yale."

26 There once was an old man of Esser,
   Whose knowledge grew lesser and lesser,
   It at last grew so small
   He knew nothing at all
   And now he's a college professor.

23 God's plan made a hopeful beginning,
   But Man spoilt his chances by sinning;
   We trust that the story
   Will end in great glory,
   But at present the other side's winning.

27 There was a young man of Japan
   Whose limericks never would scan.
   When they asked him, Why?
   He said, with a sigh,
   "It's because I always try to get as many words
   into the last line as I possibly can."

24 There was a young lady named Rose
   Who had a large wart on her nose.
   When she had it removed
   Her appearance improved,
   But her glasses slipped down to her toes.

19 Proverbs

Redensarten kann man nicht immer Wort für Wort übersetzen. Zum Teil kommt in Redensarten eine nationale Mentalität zum Ausdruck, die sich in anderen Sprachen so nicht findet. (z. B. *The cure is worse than the disease.* oder *Don't cry over spilt milk.*) Dennoch gibt es eine Vielzahl von Redensarten, die denselben oder zumindest einen ähnlichen Sinn ergeben. Hier eine Auswahl solcher Redensarten nebst ihrer deutschen Entsprechung.

Proverbs

1	Actions speak louder than words.	*Taten sagen mehr als Worte.*
2	All that glitters is not gold.	*Es ist nicht alles Gold, was glänzt.*
3	All for one and one for all.	*Alle für einen und einer für alle.*
4	All roads lead to Rome.	*Alle Wege führen nach Rom.*
5	All's well that ends well.	*Ende gut, alles gut.*
6	An apple never falls far from the tree.	*Der Apfel fällt nicht weit vom Stamm.*
7	April showers bring May flowers.	*Alles neu macht der Mai.*
8	Beauty is in the eye of the beholder.	*Schönheit liegt im Auge des Betrachters.*
9	Beggars can't be choosers.	*In der Not frisst der Teufel Fliegen.*
10	Better late than never.	*Besser spät als nie.*
11	Better safe than sorry.	*Vorsicht ist besser als Nachsicht.*
12	Birds of a feather flock together.	*Gleich und gleich gesellt sich gern.*
13	A bird in the hand is worth two in the bush.	*Lieber ein Spatz in der Hand als die Taube auf dem Dach.*
14	Carrying coals to Newcastle.	*Eulen nach Athen tragen.*
15	Do unto others as you would have them do unto you.	*Was du nicht willst, das man dir tu, das füge keinem anderen zu.*
16	A dog is a man's best friend.	*Der Hund ist des Mannes bester Freund.*
17	Don't count your chickens before they hatch.	*Kümmere dich nicht um ungelegte Eier.* *Lobe den Tag nicht vor dem Abend.*

18	Don't cross your bridges until you come to them.	*Kümmere dich nicht um ungelegte Eier.*
19	Don't look a gift horse in the mouth.	*Einem geschenkten Gaul schaut man nicht ins Maul.*
20	Don't put all your eggs in one basket.	*Setze nicht alles auf eine Karte.*

21 The early bird catches the worm.	*Der frühe Vogel fängt den Wurm.*
22 Early to bed and early to rise makes a man healthy, wealthy, and wise.	etwa: *Morgen Stund' hat Gold im Mund.*
23 Experience is the best teacher.	*Erfahrung ist der beste Lehrer.*
24 The grass is always greener on the other side of the fence.	*Auf Nachbars Feld steht das Korn besser.*
25 He who hesitates is lost.	*Wer zögert, verliert.*
26 He who laughs last laughs best.	*Wer zuletzt lacht, lacht am besten.*

27 Honesty is the best policy.	*Ehrlich währt am längsten.*
28 Laughter is the best medicine.	*Lachen ist die beste Medizin.*
29 Live and let live.	*Leben und leben lassen.*
30 Look before you leap.	*Erst denken, dann lenken.*
31 Make hay while the sun shines.	*Schmiede das Eisen, solange es heiß ist.*
32 A miss is as good as a mile.	*Knapp vorbei ist auch daneben.*
33 Money is the root of all evil.	*Geld ist die Wurzel allen Übels.*
34 The more the merrier.	*Je mehr desto besser.*
35 It never rains but it pours.	*Ein Unglück kommt selten allein.*
36 Never put off to tomorrow what you can do today.	*Was du heute kannst besorgen, das verschiebe nicht auf morgen.*
37 It's never too late to mend.	*Besser spät als nie.*
38 No pain, no gain.	*Ohne Schweiß kein Preis.*
39 Once bitten, twice shy.	*Ein gebranntes Kind scheut das Feuer.*
40 One rotten apple spoils the whole barrel.	*Ein fauler Apfel steckt hundert gesunde an.*
41 Out of sight, out of mind.	*Aus dem Auge, aus dem Sinn.*
42 Look after the pennies and the pounds will look after themselves.	*Wer den Pfennig nicht ehrt, ist des Talers nicht wert.*

43	People who live in glass houses shouldn't throw stones.	*Wer im Glashaus sitzt, soll nicht mit Steinen werfen.* 
44	One picture is worth a thousand words.	*Ein Bild sagt mehr als tausend Worte.*
45	Practice makes perfect.	*Übung macht den Meister.*
46	A rolling stone gathers no moss.	*Wer rastet, der rostet.*
47	Rome wasn't built in a day.	*Rom wurde nicht an einem Tag erbaut.* oder *Gut Ding braucht Weile.*
48	Silence is golden.	*Reden ist Silber, Schweigen ist Gold.*
49	Strike while the iron is hot.	*Schmiede das Eisen, solange es heiß ist.*
50	The pen (literally: the quill) is mightier than the sword.	*Die Feder ist mächtiger als das Schwert.*
51	Too many cooks spoil the broth. 	*Zu viele Köche verderben den Brei.* 
52	There is no accounting for tastes.	*Über Geschmack lässt sich nicht streiten.*
53	There's no place like home.	*Eigener Herd ist Goldes wert.* oder *Zu Hause ist's am schönsten.*
54	Time heals all wounds.	*Die Zeit heilt alle Wunden.*
55	When in Rome, do as the Romans do.	*Andere Länder, andere Sitten.*
56	When the cat's away the mice will play. 	*Ist die Katze aus dem Haus, tanzen die Mäuse auf dem Tisch.*
57	You have to break a few eggs to make an omelette.	*Wo gehobelt wird, fallen Späne.*
58	Necessity is the mother of invention.	*Not macht erfinderisch.*

5 Antworten auf knifflige Fragen zur Landeskunde

1 **What is the difference between the British Isles, Britain, Great Britain and the United Kingdom?**

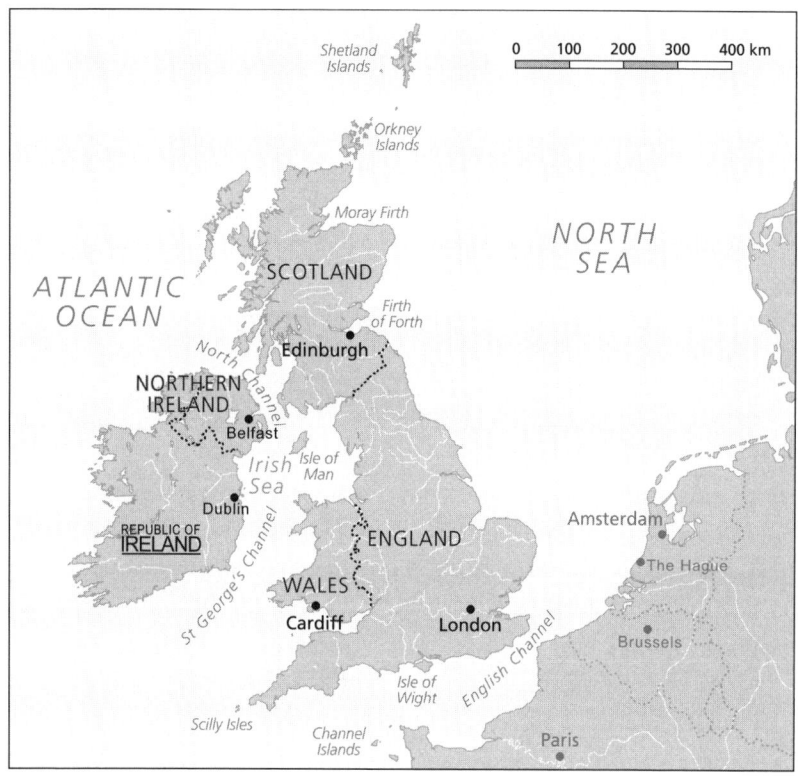

The Republic of Ireland, The United Kingdom of Great Britain and Northern Ireland

The facts

The British Isles is the geographical term for the two main British islands, Britain and Ireland, and the roughly 5,000 smaller islands around their coasts. The **Channel Islands** – in order of size: Jersey, Guernsey, Alderny and Sark – and their attendant smaller islands are geographically a part of France (*les Îles Normande*).

Nowadays **'Britain'** really exists only as a geographical name meaning the biggest island of the British Isles and as an historical name as in 'Roman Britain' and 'the Battle of Britain' (but see the note on usage below).

When James VI of Scotland became James I of England and Wales in 1603, a new name – **Great Britain** – was used for this 'personal union'. When the three countries were formally united by Act of Parliament in 1707, a completely new name was thought up, the **United Kingdom of Great Britain**. When Ireland was forcibly united with the rest of the British Isles in 1801, this name was simply expanded to the **United Kingdom of Great Britain and Ireland**. But that was not the end of the story. When the 26 counties of southern Ireland got their independence in 1921, the name was changed again, into the **United Kingdom of Great Britain and Northern Ireland**, and that is the full name of the country today.

The question of usage

Until the 1980s, most people used **Britain** for the whole country or 'England', 'Scotland', 'Wales' or 'Northern Ireland', as appropriate. In current usage, however, **the United Kingdom** or, more frequently and less formally, **the UK** has largely replaced 'Britain' as the name of the whole country.

What does all this mean?

The modern equivalent of *Großbritannien* in English is 'the United Kingdom' or 'the UK', not its exact translation 'Great Britain', which many people find a rather embarrassing archaism. And of course, never ever say 'England' unless you mean England and England alone.

2 Are Northern Ireland and Ulster the same?

Ulster: Northern Ireland plus three counties in the Republic of Ireland

No, Northern Ireland and Ulster are not interchangeable, although they are sometimes treated as if they were.

Northern Ireland consists of the six mainly Protestant counties of Londonderry, Antrim, Tyrone, Down, Armagh and Fermanagh which chose not to secede in 1921, when the rest of Ireland became independent. These six counties now make up the Province of Northern Ireland, which is part of the UK.

Ulster is a geographical term referring to the northern part of the island of Ireland. It is made up of the six counties of Northern Ireland (see above) and three counties in the Irish Republic, Donegal, Cavan and Monaghan. Hence people born in Northern Ireland can call themselves Ulstermen or Ulsterwomen, and they can say that they live in 'Ulster'. It is not, however, possible for them to refer to their country as 'Ulster'.

3 What are yellow lines? What do the different yellow lines mean?

It is often said by the British themselves that the UK is 'semi-detached' from Europe or that it forms a bridge between Europe and the USA. At a trivial level, nowhere does this mix become more telling than in the matter of road signs. For example, motorway signs on the continent of Europe are commonly white on a blue background. In the UK, they are yellow on a green background, as in the USA. It is similar when it comes to 'yellow lines' along the edges of roads, an American invention adopted by the British in preference to the continental European system of signs.

This is what the yellow lines, or the absence of them, mean:

No lines	You can park at all times.
Broken yellow line	You can park at the times shown on small signs.
Unbroken yellow line	No parking on weekdays, often until quite late.
Double unbroken yellow lines	No stopping at all except in an emergency.

4 Why do the British drive on the left?

There are **three** possible answers to this question:

(1) The British like to be different from everybody else, especially from other Europeans or 'the Continentals'.

It may well be right that the British like to be different, but their driving on the left isn't a good example of this trait. Until the late 18th century, driving on the left was the rule of the road throughout Europe, as the positioning of old milestones and signposts shows. Driving on the left is, therefore, at best evidence of British conservatism.

(2) In Roman times, the shield was carried with the left hand, and the sword or spear in the right. In the days of frequent ambushes, it was sensible for soldiers to march on the left so that the protected side of the body was nearest the likely direction of attack, and the right hand was free to fight off an attack with the sword or spear.

Not bad. Certainly better than (1).

(3) A horse is mounted from the left by putting the left foot in the stirrup and swinging the right leg over the animal's back. Especially near inns, toll-gates and other such places, mounting stones were often provided to help the short and fat to mount their horse. These mounting stones had to be located on the left hand side of the road, seen from the direction the rider was travelling. Hence 'driving on the left' is a natural development of 'riding on the left'.

Sounds more likely.

Until the rapid increase in car-ownership in the 1970s, there was some occasional discussion in the UK about changing over to driving on the right. The last time this seemed a real possibility was when Sweden abandoned driving on the left during the 1950s. Today, however, it looks as if things will certainly stay as they are. Why?

There are **five** reasons:

- The enormous cost of a change, for example repositioning road and traffic signs.

- The question of road safety during the change over, particularly as most cars would have the steering wheel 'on the wrong side' for several years.
- Unlike Sweden, a change is not essential as Britain is an island.
- Driving on the left means that the steering wheel is on the right and the gears are changed with the left hand. As most drivers are right-handed, this means that the 'preferred hand' stays on the steering wheel during gear changes, thus increasing road safety.
- Most countries drive on the left. (Yes, really!)

5 Why do the British call *den deutschen Schäferhund* 'Alsation' and *die deutsche Dogge* 'Great Dane'?

Just as the royal family's surname was 'Hanover' and that of the Mountbattens 'Battenberg' until the First World War, so were these two breeds of dog referred to by their German name, i.e. German Shepherd (Dog) and German Dogge. As a result of the highly emotional anti-German propaganda that accompanied the outbreak of war, the names were changed in Britain, though not in America. However, in modern usage the British are increasingly using the original, and accurate, names.

6 Is it true that school attendance is not compulsory in Britain?

Yes, this is quite true. The law simply says that parents of children resident in Britain must provide them with an appropriate education between the ages of 5 and 16. Whether or not this education takes place in a school or not is entirely up to the parents – and increasingly large numbers of parents are opting out of the school system in favour of home education.

Here is the FAQ page from the Home Education Advisory Service's website, which answers the most basic questions (www.heas.org.nk). It has been lightly modified to make it more readily comprehensible to a German reader.

Home Education – Frequently Asked Questions

Is home education legal?	**Yes, it is.** It is the parent's duty to ensure that the child receives a proper education as set out in the Education Act 1996, Section 7, the Education (Scotland) Act 1980, section 30 and the Education and Libraries (Northern Ireland) Order 1986, Article 45. Children of all ages can learn at home.
Do I have to get the permission of my local education authority (LEA) to educate my child at home?	**No, you don't.** If your child has never attended a state school, or if you move to an area served by another LEA, you are not even obliged to inform the LEA, although you may do so if you wish. If you are taking your child out of a state school in England or Wales, the head teacher must remove your child's name from the school register and inform the LEA. **Yes, you do** have to notify your local LEA of your intention to educate your child at home if you are withdrawing him or her from a state school in Scotland.
Are any grants available for home education?	**No, there are not.** Legally, you are in exactly the same position as parents who opt out of the state system to educate their children at private schools.
Do I have to follow the National Curriculum?	**No, you don't.** The Education Act 1996, Section 9, the Education (Scotland) Act 1980, Section 28 and the Education and Libraries (Northern Ireland) Order 1986, Article 44 state that children may be educated according to the wishes of their parents, not the state.
Will my child have to take tests at the Key Stages?	**No, he or she won't.** No formal testing is required by law. Your local LEA may check informally from time to time to ensure that your child is receiving the 'appropriate education' that the law requires.

Can a child with special educational needs be educated at home?	**Yes, he or she can.** Under Section 324 of the Education Act 1996 the LEA must make provision for a child's special educational needs **unless** the parent has made 'suitable arrangements' at home. Similar rules apply in Scotland and Northern Ireland.
Is home education costly?	**No, it isn't.** You don't need a lot of equipment to educate your child at home, and don't forget the internet.
Can GCSEs be taken at home?	**Yes, they can.** Some people enter as private candidates or arrange to study for their GCSEs at a local Further Education College. Others use correspondence or 'distance learning' courses.
Aren't the children deprived of a social life?	**No, there is no evidence of this.** In all areas home educators meet for social and educational activities, and their children also attend clubs, evening classes, sporting and leisure activities in the community just like anybody else.
Do I have to be a teacher?	**No, you don't.** Enthusiasm and commitment are needed, not formal teacher training. Many parents learn alongside their children so the whole family benefits from the experience.
Can you study science at home?	**Yes, you can.** Much of today's science is geared to real-life situations using equipment that is easily available at home. And don't forget the internet here, either.

7 Do all British schools have a school uniform?

No, they don't. It is now left to schools to decide whether to have a school uniform and, if they do decide to have one, which pupils should wear it.

Deregulation has not, however, led to schools giving up uniforms completely. Almost all primary schools and a big majority of secondary schools continue to have some sort of uniform or at least a very strict dress code that amounts to virtually the same.

A very typical 'uniform' is a white shirt with school tie, a dark blue, green or maroon pullover, and dark trousers for boys and a dark skirt for girls.

The most expensive and divisive items in the traditional school uniform – a blazer with the school crest woven into the breast pocket and a rather silly-looking cap – have been largely abandoned.

Nowadays, the most controversial aspect of school uniforms is the length of girls' skirts, which should reach to 'just above the knee', but are frequently much shorter. Related to this, there is some discussion about whether girls should be allowed to wear trousers or 'slacks' instead of skirts.

8 If you are a speaker of German, how do you pronounce Welsh place names?

Can you say these Welsh words and expressions so that they would be understood by a speaker of Welsh: Plyd Cymru (*Party of Wales*) – Yr Almaen (*Germany*) – nos dda (*good night*) – diolch yn fawr (*thanks*) – Croeso I Cymru (*Welcome to Wales*) – Wnaiff (*Britain*)?

As the answer is probably "No, I can't," here's some help.

Most consonants and vowels are pronounced as in English and/or German, but Welsh has some sounds not used in either language. You can, however, get fairly close to the correct pronunciation by using the following approximations:

Welsh	German	English
w	as **u** [uː] in *Kuchen*	
u	as **ie** [iː] in *Miete*	
ll	as **fl** [fl] in *Flur*	
dd		as **th** [ð] in *then*
th		as **th** [θ] in *think*
ff		as **gh** [f] in *cough*
f	as **w** [v] in *Wasser*	
y[1]	as **a** [ɑː] in *Vater*	
y[2]		as **y** [i] in *ferry*

[1] If before the last syllable of word
[2] If in the last syllable of word

9 What public holidays and 'special days' – other than Christmas and New Year – are there in Britain and Ireland?

The old distinction between religious and secular holidays has now fallen more or less out of use. People now say 'public holidays' (*Feiertag*) for both.

Public holidays

England and Wales
January 1st – Good Friday – the first Monday after Easter Sunday ('Easter Monday') – the first and last Mondays in May – the last Monday in August – Christmas Day – Boxing Day (December 26th)

Total free days per year: 8

Irish Republic
January 1st ('New Year's Day') – St Patrick's Day (March 17th) – Good Friday[1] – the first Monday after Easter Sunday ('Easter Monday') – the first Monday in June – the first Monday in August – the last Monday in October – Christmas Day – St Stephen's Day (December 26th)

Total free days per year: statutory 8, actual 9

Northern Ireland
January 1st – St Patrick's Day (March 17th) – Good Friday – the first Monday after Easter Sunday ('Easter Monday') – the first and last Mondays in May – the Battle of the Boyne (July 12th)[2] – the last Monday in August – Christmas Day – Boxing Day (December 26th)

Total free days per year:
statutory,
catholic areas 9;
protestant 10;
actual, both 10

---

1 Good Friday, a protestant festival, is not a statutory public holiday in the mainly catholic Irish Republic. It is, however, generally free for reasons of national cohesion.
2 Officially in protestant areas only, but in fact the whole country takes a day off, the protestants to celebrate, the catholics to mourn. (At the Battle of the Boyne, a river in Leinster, the protestant William of Orange defeated the catholic forces, hence ensuring the supremacy of calvinist protestantism in Northern Ireland.)

Scotland

January 1st – January 2nd – Good Friday – the first Monday after Easter Sunday ('Easter Monday') – the first and last Mondays in May – the first Monday in August – Christmas Day – Boxing Day (December 26th).

Total free days per year: 9

'Special days'

'Special days' are not necessarily public holidays, but they are days with some special meaning or significance.

St Valentine's Day (February 14th)

Myth: St Valentine's Day and the sending of Valentine cards originated in the USA and is a recent invention of the greetings card industry.

The historical background: Far from being a recent innovation, St Valentine's Day is one of the oldest 'special days' of all. St Valentine was an early Christian martyr who was put to death by the Romans in around 270 AD.

The practice of boys sending anonymous declarations of love to girls is of much older origin, however, and its only connection with St Valentine is that his saint's day, 14 February, more or less coincides with the Roman feast of Lupercalia. At Lupercalia, boys wrote the names of girls on small pieces of tile or soft wax and put them in an urn. Then the boys each drew a girl's name out of the urn to find their future partner.

Lupercalia came to Britain with the Romans. Towards the end of the 5th century, the church tried to forbid Lupercalia, but drawing names had by then become so popular that the ban was largely ignored.

The writing of Valentine verses in praise of a loved one – as opposed to simply writing her name on a bit of paper – was certainly well established by Shakespeare's day.

The first printed Valentine cards were produced in 1800 and the coming of the penny post and cheaper printing techniques made the sending of Valentine cards hugely popular throughout the 19th century. Today, Valentine cards are much more popular in Britain and America than in Germany. This may well have something to do with the greetings card industry that quickly saw the potential of this old custom. The sending of greeting cards is in any case more widespread in the Anglo-Saxon world.

The cards themselves are prettily decorated and carry verses expressing the sender's affection or are left blank so that the sender can write the message himself. They are still often sent anonymously, just for fun. Even so, most girls are very proud if they receive a large number of Valentine cards, though this is pretty tough on those who do not get any at all.

Here is a selection of typical Valentine's Day messages that your boys can write in their cards:

1 Tulips in the Garden
   Tulips in the Park
   The tulips I like best
   Are the two lips in the dark.

   (*Play on words:* tulips – two lips)

2 Snow on a Mountain
   The sun can't melt* it
   I love you but
   I can't help it.

   (**melt* = schmelzen)

3 Roses are Red
   Violets* are Blue
   God made me Beautiful
   But what happened to you?

   (**violet* = Veilchen)

4 Think of me on a River
   Think of me on a Lake
   Think of me on your Wedding Day*
   And send me a piece of your cake.

   (**wedding day* = Hochzeitstag)

5 Written with a Pen
   Sealed with a Kiss
   I love the girl
   Who opens this.

6 Butter is butter
   Jam is Jam
   I bet you can't guess
   Who I am.

7 Coffee is Coffee
   Mint* is Mint
   I live in (*Stadt, Straße oder anderer Anhaltspunkt*)
   That's a hint*.

   (**mint* = Pfefferminz; *hint* = Andeutung)

8 Darling be faithful*
   Darling be true*
   Tell me you love me
   As I love you.

   (**faithful* = true; *true* = hier: treu)

9 U R 2 GOOD
   2 B 4 GOT 10
   (You are too good
   To be forgotten.)

10 If you know my name
   One hundred kisses
   You may gain*.

   (**gain* = hier: erhalten)

11 East to East
   West to West
   But by far you
   Are the Best.

12 Roses are Red
    Violets* are Blue
    Sugar is Sweet
    And so are you.

    (*violet = Veilchen)

13 Think of M
    Think of E
    Put them together
    Think of ME.

14 Take a GLOVE
    Take away the G
    What is left
    I feel for thee*.

    (*thee you)

15 Remember that night
    We kissed in the hall*
    I missed your lips
    And kissed the wall.

    (*hall = hier: Diele)

A message, addressed to the postman ("Postie") delivering the card, is often written on the back of the envelope. These messages are also really intended for the girl, of course. Here is a selection of such envelope messages.

1 Postie, Postie
   Do not tarry*
   Take this to
   The one I'll marry*.

   (*tarry = verweilen;
   marry = heiraten)

2 Postie, Postie
   Do your stuff
   Take this to
   The one I love.

3 Postie, Postie
   Do not falter*
   This may lead me
   to the altar*.

   (*falter = zögern; "lead (a girl) to the altar" = zum Altar führen = heiraten)

4 Postie, Postie
   Don't be slow
   Be like Elvis
   Go – Man – Go.

5 Postie, Postie
   Don't be late
   This may lead me
   to a date.

6 Postie, Postie
   Be a dove*
   Take this to
   my own true love.

   (*dove = Taube)

7 Postie, Postie
   Do your duty*
   Take this to my
   Blue-eyed beauty.

   (*duty = Pflicht)

Holidays etc.

Sometimes the sender puts a coded message on the back of the envelope or in the card:

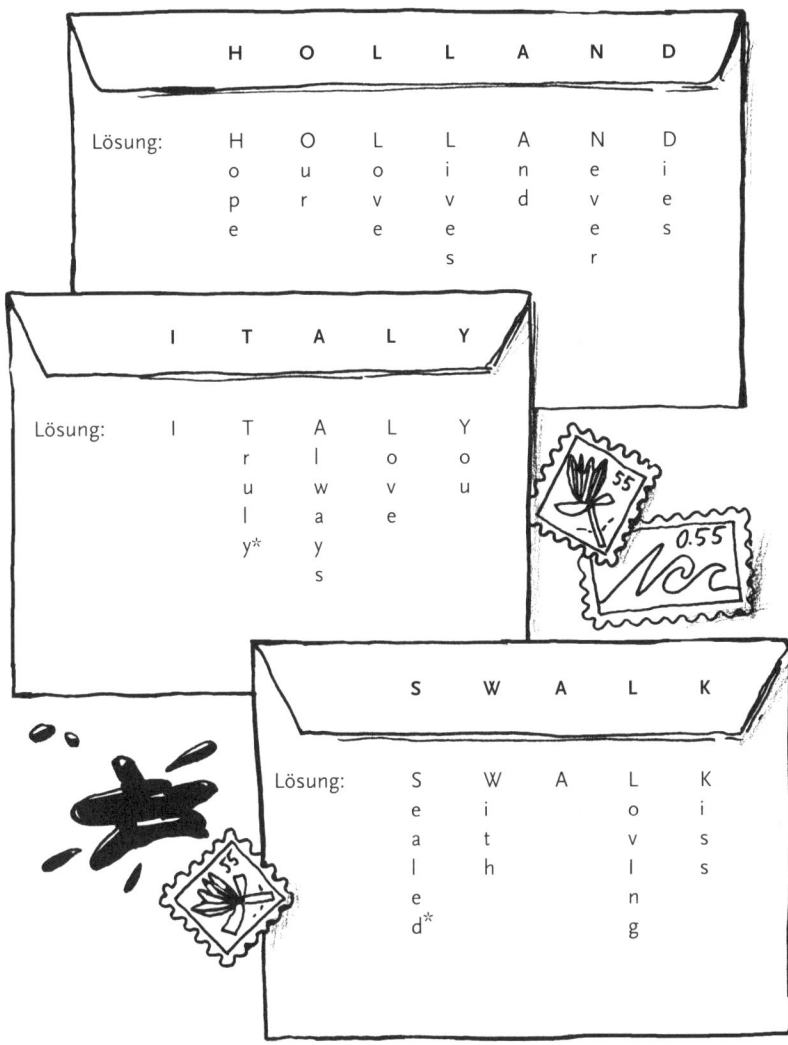

(* *truly* = wahrhaft,
* *sealed* = [Briefumschlag] zugeklebt)

Don't look under the table
Don't look under the lamp
If you want to know who sent this card
Just look under the stamp.

Hallowe'en (31st October, 1st November)

Hallowe'en (*AmE* Halloween) derives from "All Hallows", a form of "All Saints" (*Allerheiligen*). Like many Christian festivals, Hallowe'en is a christianised version of a very much older occasion, the Celtic Sambain festival. At Sambain, the Celts gave thanks for the summer just past, and tried to appease the spirits of nature at the onset of winter. Traditionally, it was a time when animals were brought in from open pastures and hillsides. Huge fires, symbolic of the sun, were built on hilltops to frighten away evil spirits. In addition, Hallowe'en was seen as an auspicious time to evoke the powers of light, i. e. the sun, against those of darkness, i. e. the long winter night. For this reason, it was considered a good time to get married, conceive or bear children, treat illnesses, die and so on.

Sambain was the only festival in which the Celts were willing to appease the forces of evil in an effort to reach good ends. This didn't please Christian missionaries too much, who quickly occupied the date with a festival of their own.

Today, at any rate in the Anglo-Saxon world, Hallowe'en has lost all its religious meaning and has become a purely secular occasion. The wearing of more or less ugly and frightening masks, generally made from hollowed out pumpkins (*Kürbis*), and the lighting of bonfires and candles do, however, refer back to the earlier Celtic festival.

Guy Fawkes' Day (5th November)

On 5th November 1605, the protestant King James VI of Scotland and I of England and Wales was due to open parliament in London. A group of catholic rebels planned to blow up the building with the king and his retainers in it. They stacked the cellar with barrels of gunpowder on the night of 4th November. News of the plot reached James, and when a search was made, Guy Fawkes, one of the rebels, was found hiding in the cellar. Under torture, Fawkes revealed the names of the other rebels and all were arrested and hanged.

A national holiday was declared to celebrate the failure of the plot and every year since then fires have been lit in gardens and parks all over Britain to mark the occasion. *Beefeaters* still search the cellars of the Houses of Parliament before members take their seats on the first day of a new session. They have done so, ceremonially, since 1605.

November 5th is not an official holiday today, but the evening of that day – *Bonfire Night* – is looked forward to weeks in advance by British children. They make dummies of Guy Fawkes out of straw and old clothes and happily carry these 'guys' through the streets, asking passers-by for 'a penny for the guy'. The 'guys' are placed on top of the fires and the children dance round them as fireworks soar out of the flames into the sky.

In some old towns, Lewes in Sussex is one, *Bonfire Night* is organized on a grand scale. Huge fires crown the hills surrounding the town, and hundreds of people march round the town from one fire to the next before the evening closes with a magnificent fireworks display.

Throughout British history many 'enemies' other than Guy Fawkes have been burned as dummies on November 5th. Napoleon Bonaparte became a 'guy' many times during his lifetime and in 1945 Adolf Hitler was burned as a dummy on fires all over Britain. In recent times, such dummies of Mrs Thatcher and President Reagan have also been burnt in some areas.

This is what children chant as the dummy goes up in flames:

Remember, remember
The fifth of November
Gunpowder*, treason* and plot*.

(**gunpowder* = Schießpulver; *treason* = Verrat; *plot* = Komplott)

10 How democratic is Britain?

In the past, Britain was often seen as the 'cradle of democracy' and its parliament as 'the mother of parliaments'. However, in recent years many people, not least politicians themselves, have become much more critical of Britain's political system. Here are some of the more obvious shortcomings or 'democratic deficits', as they are now often called:

The voting system
At present, there are 650 constituencies in the United Kingdom (523 in England, 38 in Wales, 72 in Scotland and 17 in Northern Ireland).

In an election, the candidate, that gets the most votes becomes the Member of Parliament (MP) for the constituency or 'seat'.

This simple majority or 'first past the post' (FPP) system is the only possibility when there are two political parties, which was the case before the Labour Party was founded in 1906. For the last hundred years, however, there have been three parties – i. e. the Conservatives, the Liberals and the Labour Party – in England and four in Scotland and Wales, where the Celtic nationalist parties receive a lot of support. In addition to these more traditional parties, newer parties such as the Greens also attract a significant number of votes in some constituencies.

This means that in modern elections anything between three and five serious contenders can take part, which immediately shows up the undemocratic nature of FPP. In some areas, it can even lead to the bizarre result that the opinions of a big majority of voters are not represented in parliament at all.

Here is an example of how easily this can happen. Let us take an average urban constituency of 100,000 voters in which there is a healthy turn-out of 70 % or 70,000 voters. At a close-run election, the three parties, A, B and C, receive the following number of votes:

Party A – 24,000 votes
Party B – 23,500 votes
Party C – 22,500 votes

According to the simple majority system, Party A has received the most votes and wins the seat. Parties B and C, with the combined support of 46,000 voters, go away empty-handed. If you take into account the 30,000 non-voters, the MP for this constituency has been elected by less than a quarter of the voters.

It is no wonder that more and more observers are calling for some kind of proportional representation (PR), such as that used in elections to the Scottish Parliament in Edinburgh.

Lack of a constitution

Unlike most modern democracies, Britain has no written constitution. However, books and articles on the British political system often refer to an 'unwritten' constitution. The problem is that nobody is certain exactly what this is. It is generally regarded as a collection of laws, judges' interpretations of these laws and various traditions about the way Britain is governed that have accumulated over the centuries.

But this collection is in itself so vague that it is practically meaningless. Some optimistic commentators try to make a virtue of this by claiming that an 'unwritten constitution' is more 'flexible', and therefore superior to a written constitution, which can quickly become 'obsolete'.

For all that, other political commentators point out that claiming the unwritten constitution is flexible is just another way of saying that the government can do whatever it wants. A British comedian once said that "Our unwritten constitution isn't worth the paper it isn't written on".

Dictatorship of parliament

Many people, and not only those from other countries, have little idea of just how powerful the British parliament is. Essentially, parliament in Britain means the House of Commons because the House of Lords is little more than a rather colourful chat show. It can delay laws which have been made by the House of Commons for a short period, but it can't stop or even change them. Because Britain has no written constitution there are no checks whatsoever on the power of the House of Commons – no constitutional court like the one in Karlsruhe, no federal states nor a president with independent powers. In short, there is nothing that the House of Commons can't do – and whatever it does is always automatically legal, though that has started to change with the emergence of the European Court of Justice whose judgements are binding in Britain as well.

Prime ministerial patronage

When the president of the USA appoints a supreme court judge, a minister or even a senior official such as the head of the Federal Reserve Bank, his or her choice has to be approved by the senate, usually after a thorough and sometimes punishing hearing.

None of the foregoing applies to British prime ministers, whose powers of patronage can hardly be exaggerated. Prime ministers have the final say when it comes to over 350 positions at the very top of British society, from bishops to the heads of universities. Prime ministers have no obligation to consult others, or even to inform them of the reasons for their choice. The positions are in their sole and personal gift. This may add immeasurably to prime ministerial power, but it can scarcely be called democratic.

11 Is it true that there is a clearer division of power in the UK?

Yes, it is. In the UK, there is a much clearer division between the people who make the laws (the legislature), those who administer the law (the judiciary) and those who execute the law (the executive) than is common in other European countries. Civil servants, police officers and judges (as well as criminals, archbishops, the insane and royalty) can't become a Member of Parliament. Compare this to Germany, where many members of the Bundestag are state employees and civil servants. Remember, too, that in the UK police officers, judges and teachers aren't civil servants.

12 What are the differences between Scotland and England?

England and Scotland have been united since the Act of Union of 1707, but Scotland has succeeded in keeping many of its old traditions and its separate identity alive. For this reason, there are some major differences between England and Scotland.

Language
Scottish-Gaelic is still spoken in the Highlands and on the Islands of Scotland, but only about 82,000 people have Gaelic as their mother-tongue, the rest speak English. But if you visit Scotland, you'll notice that the Scots speak English with a Scottish accent. (People in Scotland are Scottish or Scots, but never Scotch – only things and animals are Scotch: Scotch whisky, Scotch tape, Scotch terriers and so on.)

The Scottish accent varies a lot between the south of Scotland (the Lowlands) and the north of Scotland (the Highlands) and between big cities such as Edinburgh and Glasgow. Many English people think that the Scottish accent comes from Scotland's Gaelic history, but it's really an old dialect of English – the kind of English that was once spoken in Northern England.

About a thousand years ago 'England' included most of what is today the Lowlands of Scotland. William the Conqueror, the Duke of Normandy, defeated the Saxon Harald Godwinson at the Battle of Hastings in 1066 and became the new king of England. However, the North of England resisted the invaders and it took the Normans 80 years of hard fighting to reach Newcastle upon Tyne in Northumberland. The Normans tried to push their way further north but after several bloody defeats they gave up and 'England' ended at the River Tweed. The English lands north of the Tweed became part of Scotland more or less by default.

Government

The Scottish Parliament in Edinburgh was set up in 1998, making it the first Scottish parliament since Scotland united with England and Wales in 1707. The new parliament has wide-ranging powers to decide on purely Scottish affairs in such areas as agriculture, education, the environment, home affairs (including policing), health, transport and industrial development. In this, it is similar to federal states in Germany.

However, in external matters such as foreign policy, finance, relations with the EU and international trade, Scotland continues to be subject to the will of parliament at Westminster. For this reason, Scottish MPs still have seats at Westminster and the office of Secretary of State for Scotland continues to exist. Its incumbent is a member of the British government and has his or her headquarters in London.

This split between Scottish national affairs on the one hand and matters affecting Scotland as part of the UK on the other has reignited the old argument about the so-called 'Mid-Lothian question'. This focuses on the paradox that while Scottish MPs sitting in the House of Commons can vote on matters affecting England and Wales, English and Welsh MPs cannot vote on matters affecting only Scotland.

Opinions on the Scottish Parliament are divided. Some people see it as nothing much more than an expensive sham aimed at defusing Scottish nationalism. Such critics point to the fact that the Scottish parliament has only very limited tax-raising powers and is hence largely dependent on Westminster for funds. And everybody knows that "he who pays the piper, calls the tune". For all that, others are more charitable, seeing it as a first step towards virtual, if not formal independence.

Money

In England and Wales only the central bank, the Bank of England, can issue banknotes, but in Scotland several banks have the right to do so. This is why Scottish banknotes look different to English ones although the currency (the pound sterling) is the same. If you travel through Scotland, it's fun to see how many different kinds of banknotes you can collect. Scotland also has its own £1 coin. But be careful. Many shops in England and Wales won't accept Scottish money, although all British banks will.

Education

The Scots are rightly proud of the long tradition of education in Scotland. Scotland has had a national primary education for pupils from 5 to 10 years since 1560. A national system wasn't set up in England and Wales, and then unwillingly, until 1870.

As in England and Wales, almost all Scottish secondary schools for pupils from 11 to 16 are non-selective comprehensive high schools. However, all Scottish schools and universities have their own curriculum and are administered and financed by the Scottish parliament, not by the UK Ministry of Education in London.

In recent years there has been some tension between London and Edinburgh on several educational matters.

The first is about who controls the schools. Secondary schools in England and Wales can 'opt out' of being run by local educational authorities (LEAs) and can choose to be directly controlled and financed by the central Ministry of Education in London. This obviously reduces the power and influence of local government and increases that of central government. The Scottish parliament is currently refusing to allow its secondary schools to opt out in this way.

A second bone of contention is the question of a common national curriculum for the whole of the UK. The Scottish parliament tends to see London's ambitions to make one size fit all as nothing much more than an attempt to dilute the essential 'Scottishness' of Scottish schools and to reduce Scottish independence.

A third area of dispute involves the paying of university fees for first degrees. English and Welsh universities are allowed to charge their students these fees, whereas Scottish universities are not. London sees this as introducing unwelcome 'imbalance' in the tertiary education sector.

Law

Scotland has a different legal tradition to that of England and Wales. It is much closer to codified European law. In England and Wales, the verdict of a court must be either 'guilty' or 'not guilty', while Scottish courts have the third option of saying 'not proven'.

This is the verdict when a jury – in Scotland 15 people to avoid 'hung juries', in England 12 – think that there isn't enough evidence to say that a person is guilty beyond reasonable doubt, but the jurors are not convinced that the accused is not guilty beyond reasonable doubt, either.

Special days
The Scots have two 'special days', namely St Andrew's Day (November 30th) and Burns Night (January 25th). St Andrew is the patron saint of Scotland and St Andrew's Cross is the Scottish flag, a white diagonal cross on a dark blue ground, making it the white, X-shaped part of the Union Jack.
Robert Burns (1759–1796) is Scotland's greatest and most popular poet. On Burns Night, it is a tradition to eat a celebratory meal of haggis and read Robbie Burns' poems aloud.

13 Where was whisky invented?
Whisky has been distilled in both Scotland and Ireland for centuries. While there is good evidence to suggest that it was taken to Scotland from Ireland by Christian missionaries, it has never been proved that Highland farmers did not themselves discover how to distil spirits from their surplus barley.

14 What's the difference between the whisky made in Scotland and that made in other countries?

Scotch, Canadian and Japanese whisky
Whisky with a -*y*-ending is made in Scotland, Canada or Japan, with an -*ey*-ending in Ireland and the USA. This distinction applies to how, not where, the spirit is distilled.
Scotland produces two types of whisky: whisky made from grain (mostly maize) and whisky made from malted barley.
If a whisky is made only from malted barley and comes from one named distillery, it is called 'single malt'. Whisky made from grain has a more neutral flavour. It is also easier, and hence cheaper, to produce. Although single malt is becoming increasingly popular among whisky drinkers, in fact most of it is mixed or 'blended' with grain whisky to produce 'blended' whisky. There can be well over a hundred different malt whiskies and six or seven different grain whiskies in a blended whisky.

Blended whisky is the most popular type of whisky because it has a lighter flavour than most single malts and the blending process guarantees that it always tastes the same.

Before it can be sold, whisky must be 'matured' or 'aged'. The raw whisky – which is a clear spirit like vodka – is stored in oak barrels for at least three years. This gives the whisky its characteristic golden colour and improves the flavour, making it smoother.

The whisky which comes closest to genuine Scotch is made in Japan. Japanese whisky has a very good reputation among whisky drinkers, which isn't surprising as the first whisky-makers were trained in Scotland and the first Japanese distilleries were built by Scottish firms. The Japanese use exactly the same ingredients, and distillation and blending process, as in Scotland.

Irish and American whiskey

The whiskeys made in Ireland and the USA have a very different flavour to Scotch whisky. Irish whiskey is made by a different distillation process and mostly (or entirely) from maize. Sometimes a little rye is added to the maize to improve the flavour. Whiskey made in the USA is often called 'Bourbon' after Bourbon county in Kentucky where the maize used in the whiskey was (and still is) grown.

15 What is the difference between British gallons and US gallons?

A British gallon is a bit bigger than a US gallon. One British gallon is 1.2 US gallons or one US gallon is 0.83 British gallons, depending on how you look at it. The most frequently used measures of liquid capacity are:

	British	US	Metric
4 gills (gl)	1 pint (pt)	1.201 pints	0.568 litres (l)
2 pints	1 quart (qt)	1.201 quarts	1.136 litres
4 quarts	1 gallon (gal)	1.201 gallons	4.544 litres

16 How many times can Germany fit into the USA?

Flächenvergleich USA/Deutschland

The total area of the USA is 9,800,431 sq km, which makes it just over 27 times bigger than Germany (356,798 sq km). The biggest state is Alaska with an area of 1,700,138 sq km, which is about 4.8 times the size of Germany.

17 What is the difference between the Democrats and the Republicans in US politics?

Europeans tend to find the two American poltical parties, the Democrats and the Republicans, confusing because they often don't behave like parties in the European sense at all. There seem to be large areas of policy where there is little or nothing to choose between them and, indeed, this 'convergence' has become even more marked since the attack on the World Trade Center on 11th September 2001, perhaps in the interests of national cohesion.

The fact is that we are not talking so much about concrete policy differences as about 'tendencies' and, as important, historical allegiances. Until quite recently, the South voted Democrat simply because Abraham Lincoln was a Republican, for example.

For all that, there are some things that separate the Democrats and Republicans more clearly, even if we are still talking only of 'tendencies'.

The **Democrats** *tend* to be more willing to

- use public money to pay for social programmes to help those in need;
- invest in state-financed infrastructure projects in areas of high unemployment;
- legislate against discrimination and help the unfairly disadvantaged by means of affirmative action (see 24 below, p. 121);
- accept that the USA should play a leading international role in peacekeeping, environmental protection and foreign aid;
- place a higher value on federal, i. e. central, government in order to achieve their goals;
- place greater trust in international organisations such as the UN.

The **Republicans** *tend* to

- place great faith in free market forces as a 'natural regulator';
- call for a major shift of power from the centre to the states/local communities;
- be highly suspicious of, and often hostile to, 'liberal ideas' in such areas as abortion, drugs, (homo)sexuality, religion and the penal code;
- put 'America first' when defining foreign policy goals.

18 What is the origin of the names 'Uncle Sam' for the USA and 'the Big Apple' for New York?

Uncle Sam was Samuel Wilson, a merchant who became a government supply inspector in the war of 1812. Wilson was popular among his workpeople, who called him 'Uncle Sam'. When army supplies were delivered to warehouses, workers soon began to say "These goods are for Uncle Sam" meaning "These goods are for the US government".

The Big Apple was orginally used for any large American town (see *Dictionary of American Slang*, Crowell, New York, 1975), but in modern usage it applies only to New York.

'The Big Apple' is used in the sense of the apple being big enough for everybody to have a bite. In a narrow economic sense, this means that New York is large enough to provide everybody with a living. In a wider sense, it is so huge and diverse that it can satisfy every conceivable taste, inclination and desire.

19 What is the 'American Creed'?

In this sense, a creed is a solemn declaration of belief. The Commissioner of Education in New York, Henry S. Chapin, organised a competition in 1917 to find a form of words that embodied the ideals of America. The competition attracted over 3,000 entries. The winner was William Tyler Page with this text to be spoken in chorus like the Christian creed used in Anglican services:

"I believe in the United States of America as a government of the people, by the people, for the people; whose just powers are derived from the consent of the governed; a democracy in a republic; a sovereign Nation of many sovereign States; a perfect union, one and inseparable; established upon those principles of freedom, equality, justice and humanity for which American patriots sacrificed their lives and their fortunes. I therefore believe it is my duty to my country to love it, to support its Constitution, to obey its laws, to respect its flag, and to defend it against all enemies."

20 What is the text of the inscription on the Statue of Liberty?

The pedestal inscription on the Statue of Liberty in New York is from a poem by Emma Lazarus, 1883:

… Give me your tired, your poor; your huddled masses
yearning to breathe free. The wretched refuse of your
teeming shore. Send these, the homeless, tempest-tost,
to me: I lift my lamp beside the golden door.

21 Is it true that the Miss America contest says 'gentlemen don't prefer blondes'?

Yes, it is. The Miss America beauty contest has been held (with the odd break) annually since 1921, making it the world's oldest event of this kind. Here are the statistics of winners' hair colour (1921–2003):

blondes	24 %
brunettes	70 %
redheads	6 %

22 What is the exact wording of the US presidential oath of office?

At an inauguration, the new president places his or her left hand flat on an open bible and raises his or her right hand almost vertically above head level and says:

I do solemnly swear* that I will faithfully execute the office of President of the United States, and will, to the best of my ability, preserve, protect, and defend the Constitution of the United States.

(*'swear' can be replaced by 'affirm')

23 Is it true that America has only got two public holidays?

No, this is untrue. (You can't help wondering where these delusions about America come from. Another favourite myth dear to European hearts is that America hasn't got any 'real countryside', whatever that may mean.)
In fact, America has ten national public holidays and several state ones. The ten national holidays are:

New Year's Day	fixed date
Martin Luther King, Jr. Day	3rd Monday in January
'Presidents' Day	3rd Monday in February
Memorial Day	last Monday in May
Independence Day	fixed date: 4 July
Labor Day	1st Monday in September
Columbus Day	2nd Monday on October
Veterans Day	fixed date: 11 November
Thanksgiving Day	4th Thursday in November
Christmas Day	fixed date

Here are a few more remarks about American public holidays, in date order where possible:

As in the UK, most American public holidays fall on a Monday. This is to give people the benefit of a long or 'stretched' weekend. Other than the obvious exceptions of Christmas Day and New Year's Day, only Independence Day and Veterans Day have fixed dates. It is important to say here that when these 'fixed date holidays' fall on a Saturday or Sunday, then the following Monday is automatically a holiday. This is also the case in the UK and Ireland, but not of course in Germany.

The most recent public holiday is **Martin Luther King, Jr. Day**, which was declared a national holiday by President Reagan in 1983. This decision was harshly criticized by some conservatives, who argued that it was 'inappropriate' to honour King's memory in the form of a national holiday as he had divided the American people.

'Presidents' Day honours two presidents, George Washington and Abraham Lincoln, both of whom were born in February – Washington on the 22nd and Lincoln on the 12th.

Initially, **Memorial Day** honoured soldiers of the Union or Northern States – not, however, those of the rebel South – who died in the Civil War (1861–1865). Since then Memorial Day has been widened to honour all American soldiers who died while serving their country, whether in war or peace.

Independence Day is best seen as America's birthday. It is the anniversary of the signing of the Declaration of Independence by the 13 British colonies on 4th July 1776.

Columbus landed in what is today the Bahamas on 12th October 1492. **Columbus Day** falls on the second Monday in October, which is the nearest Monday to this date.

Veterans Day should not be confused with Memorial Day (see above). Veterans Day honours all those who served in the American armed forces, whether living or dead. (Memorial Day honours only the dead.)

Thanksgiving Day – often called simply 'Thanksgiving' – is the oldest American national celebration, going right back to colonial days.

The first settlement in what later became New England was established by 102 English settlers at New Plymouth, Massachusetts in December 1620. The settlers were heading for the British colony of Virginia but their ship, the *Mayflower*, was driven far to the north by storms.
During the first winter in America 48 of the colonists died of hunger and disease. Many more would have probably died if the local Wampanoag Indians had not helped them through those first terrible months. In the spring of 1621 the Indians helped the settlers further by showing them how to grow maize as well as how to hunt and trap. Luckily for the settlers, 1621 was a good year with a bumper harvest. For this reason, the settlers went into their second winter with plenty of food – hence Thanksgiving.

There are probably two reasons why many Europeans think that the USA has few public holidays:

1 While the Constitution guarantees Americans absolute religious freedom, the USA is constitutionally a secular state without any religious bias. Hence there are no 'religious holidays' as in Europe – even Christmas and Thanksgiving have long since become wholly secularised. This public avoidance of religious festivals such as Easter, Whitsun and so on may lead people to assume that Americans don't celebrate public holidays at all.

2   This misunderstanding may arise from confusing public holidays with annual vacations. American workers have much shorter holidays – 14 working days is the norm – than do their European colleagues, who get double that number of days off or even more. Ironically, though, the main reason why American employers are unwilling to give more generous annual vacations is the high number of public holidays.

24 Are 'positive discrimination' and 'affirmative action' the same thing?

No, they are not. Think of 'positive discrimination' as a bulldozer being used to level a playing-field. In other words, positive discrimination does not give an artificial advantage, but irons out social and economic disadvantages.

Staying with the sport metaphor but changing the sport, think of 'affirmative action' as a golf handicap. As the name implies, affirmative action not only irons out unfairnesses to level the playing-field, but gives deprived groups extra privileges on top.

Many people, particularly conservatives, find this problematical and affirmative action measures have led to a number of legal battles. Generally speaking, courts have come out against affirmative action. Judges accept the moral justification for affirmative action, but find that it offends against the fundamental constitutional requirement that everybody be treated equally.

25 What are the regions of the USA?

The USA comprises 50 federal states, but the states are too small, too numerous and either too similar or too diverse for many purposes. Bigger regional units are needed for things like, for example, economic and environmental planning, defence, tourism, weather forecasting and transport.

The country is commonly divided up in three ways depending on the criteria used. There are, however, other subdivisions or 'sub-regions', generally mountain ranges or historical factors, such as the original 13 colonies and the Confederate States in the Civil War.

The three most common national regional divisions are:

Geographic regions

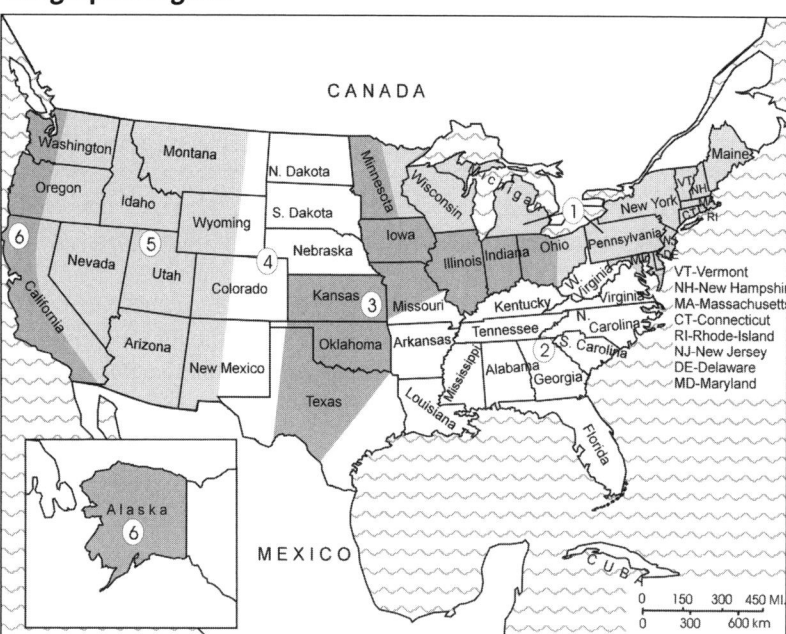

USA – geographische Regionen

① **Northeast:** Maine, New Hampshire, Massachusetts, Rhode Island, Connecticut, New Jersey, New York, Maryland, Michigan, eastern Minnesota, eastern Ohio, Pennsylvania
② **Southeast:** Delaware, Virginia, West Virginia, District of Columbia, Kentucky, southern Missouri, Arkansas, Tennessee, North Carolina, South Carolina, Georgia, Florida, Alabama, Mississippi, Louisiana, eastern Texas
③ **Central Basin:** Oklahoma, Kansas, central Texas, western Ohio, Indiana, Illinois, Iowa, central and western Minnesota, northern Missouri
④ **Great Plains:** North Dakota, South Dakota, Nebraska, eastern Colorado, western Texas, eastern New Mexico, eastern Wyoming, eastern Montana
⑤ **Mountains and Deserts:** western Montana, western Wyoming, western Colorado, western New Mexico, Idaho, Utah, Arizona, Nevada, eastern California, eastern Oregon, eastern Washington
⑥ **Coastal Valleys:** western California, western Oregon, western Washington, Alaska
⑦ **Pacific Region:** Hawaii *(ist nicht im Kartenausschnitt)*

Cultural and historic regions

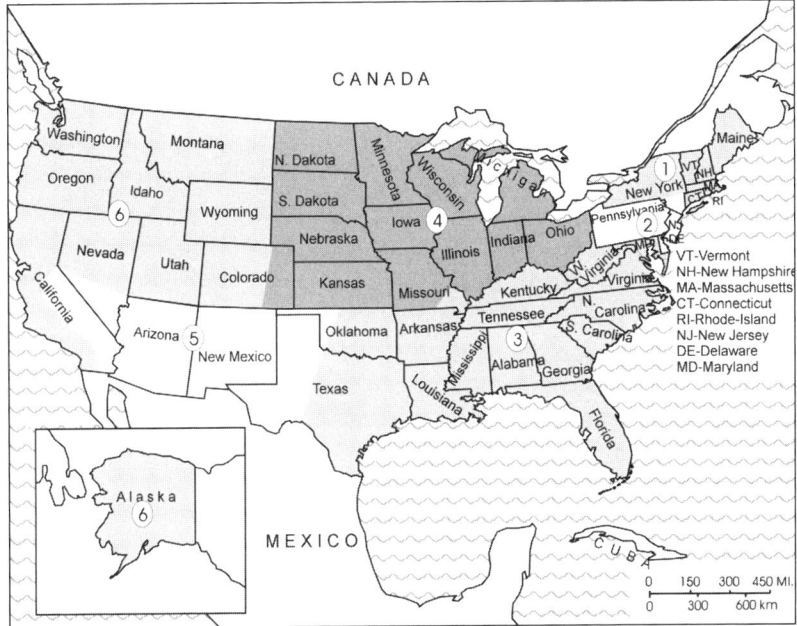

USA – historische Regionen

① **New England:** Maine, New Hampshire, Massachusetts, Rhode Island, Connecticut, northern New York State, Vermont
② **Middle Atlantic:** southern New York State, New Jersey, Pennsylvania, Delaware, Maryland
③ **The South:** Virginia, West Virginia, North Carolina, South Carolina, Georgia, Florida, Kentucky, Tennessee, Mississippi, Alabama, Louisiana, Arkansas, eastern Missouri, eastern Oklahoma, eastern and central Texas
④ **The Midwest:** North Dakota, Minnesota, Wisconsin, Michigan, Ohio, Indiana, Illinois, Iowa, Nebraska, western Missouri, Kansas, eastern Colorado
⑤ **The Southwest:** western Texas, western Oklahoma, New Mexico, Arizona, southern Nevada, southern interior of California
⑥ **The West:** western Colorado, Wyoming, Montana, Utah, northern California and the Pacific coastal strip of southern California, northern Nevada, Idaho, Oregon, Washington, Alaska, Hawaii

Tourist regions

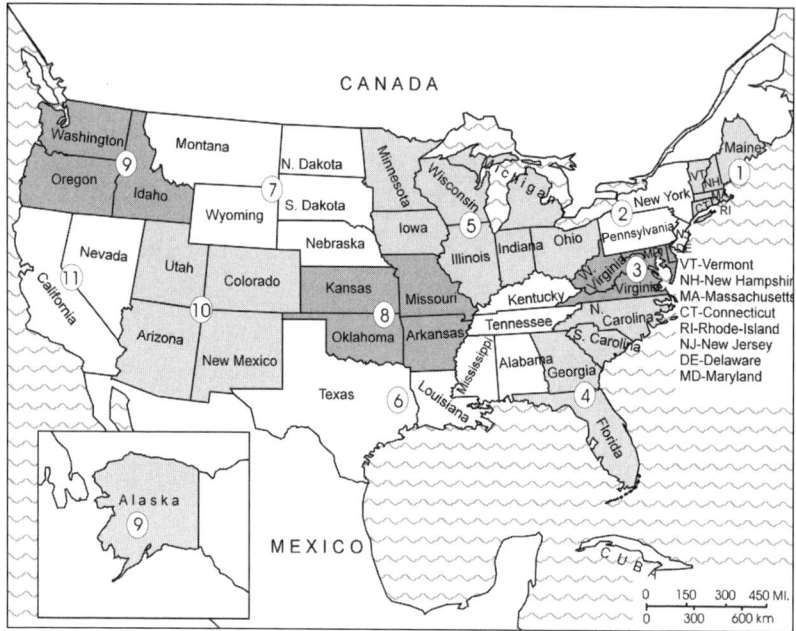

USA – touristische Regionen

① **New England:** Maine, New Hampshire, Vermont, Rhode Island, Massachusetts, Connecticut
② **Eastern Gateway:** New York, Pennsylvania, New Jersey
③ **Historic Washington Country:** Delaware, Maryland, District of Columbia (Washington), Virginia, West Virginia
④ **Southeast Sun Country:** North Carolina, South Carolina, Georgia, Florida
⑤ **The Great Lakes:** Michigan, Wisconsin, Minnesota, Iowa, Illinois, Indiana, Ohio
⑥ **The Southern Heartland:** Kentucky, Tennessee, Alabama, Mississippi, Louisiana, Texas
⑦ **The Old West:** Montana, North Dakota, South Dakota, Wyoming, Nebraska
⑧ **Heart of America:** Kansas, Missouri, Oklahoma, Arkansas
⑨ **Pacific Northwest and Alaska:** Washington, Oregon, Idaho, Alaska
⑩ **Great Southwest and Rocky Mountains:** Utah, Colorado, Arizona, New Mexico
⑪ **The Golden West:** California, Nevada
⑫ **The Pacific Islands:** Hawaii, dependant areas of Micronesia (island groups of Marianas and Guam), American Samoa *(nicht abgebildet)*

The most important regional sub-groupings

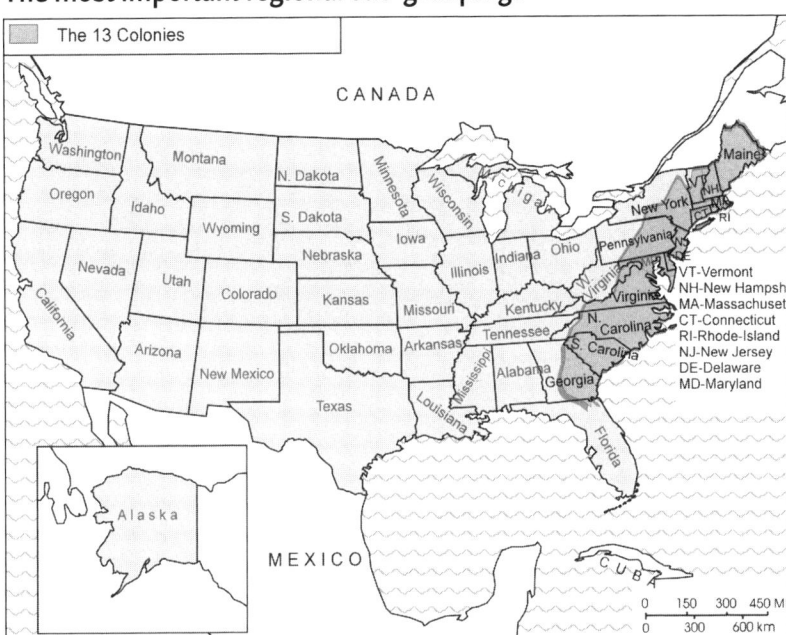

USA – Die 13 ursprünglichen britischen Kolonien

The 13 Colonies: Massachusetts, New Hampshire, New York State, Rhode Island, Connecticut, New Jersey, Delaware, Pennsylvania, Maryland, Virginia, North Carolina, South Carolina, Georgia

The **13 Colonies** fall into one of three groups, i.e. the four **New England Colonies** of Rhode Island (1636), Connecticut (1636), Massachusetts (1630) and New Hampshire (1638), the four **Middle Colonies** of Delaware (1638), Pennsylvania (1682), New York (1626) and New Jersey (1664), and finally the five **Southern Colonies** of Maryland (1633), Virginia (1607), North Carolina (1653), South Carolina (1663)and Georgia (1732).

The British assumed responsibility for military defence and purchased raw materials – mainly tobacco, cotton and furs – from the colonies. These became two major areas of conflict in the years leading up to the War of Independence (1775–1783). Firstly, the British expected the colonists to finance their own defence by taxation, although they were not represented in parliament in London. Secondly they determined the prices and the colonies were not allowed to sell their produce elsewhere.

USA – Die Konföderierten Staaten

The Confederate States: North Carolina, South Carolina, Georgia, Texas, Virginia, Arkansas, Tennessee, Mississippi, Florida, Alabama, Louisiana

Although eleven states finally seceded from the Union, they did not do so together as a united group and some, most influentially Virginia, only did so with very great reluctance.

The first state to secede was South Carolina immediately after Abraham Lincoln became president in November 1860 and for three months it was alone in doing so. South Carolina was followed by the six 'deep south' states of Georgia, Texas, Mississippi, Florida, Alabama and Louisiana, which officially declared their independence under the first Confederate president, Jefferson Davis, on 7th February 1861. The remaining four Confederate states – Virginia, North Carolina, Arkansas and Tennessee – hesitated until the Union attacked Fort Sumter in South Carolina on 12th April 1861.

The four southern states of Delaware, Maryland, Missouri and Kentucky, which border on the North, decided not to secede but to stay in the Union.

Regions of the USA

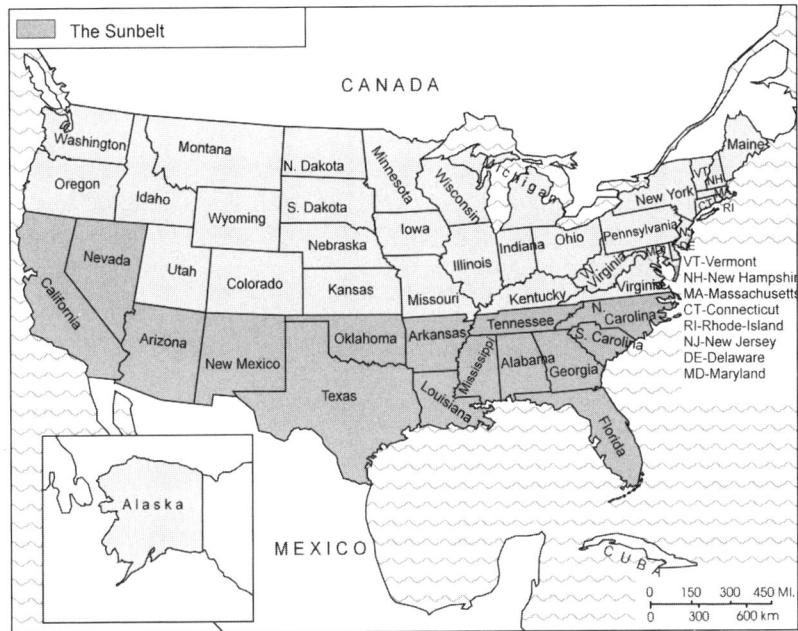

USA – Sunbelt states

The Sunbelt: North Carolina, South Carolina, Georgia, Florida, Tennessee, Alabama, Mississippi, Arkansas, Louisiana, Oklahoma, Texas, New Mexico, Arizona, Nevada, southern California

Since the 1950s, the USA has seen a major migration from the cold and snowy north to the warm and sunny south, i. e. to the 'sunbelt'. The coastal states of the Carolinas, Georgia and Florida have attracted huge numbers of retired people, while the dry and healthy southwestern states of New Mexico, Arizona, Nevada and southern California have attracted many new industries.

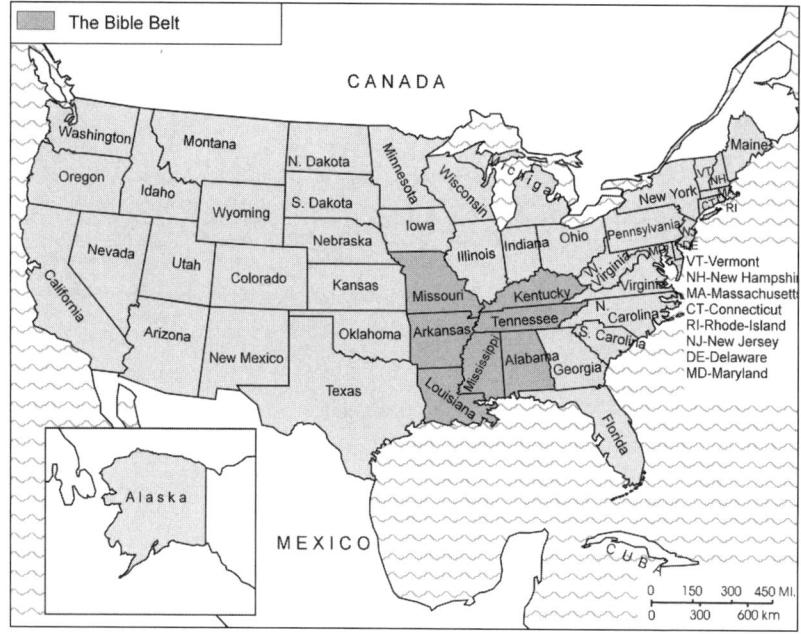

USA – Bible Belt States

The Bible Belt: This is an area of the interior of the southern USA which is socially and culturally highly conservative and tends to interpret the bible very literally. It is, in other words, characterised to a greater or lesser extent by religious fundamentalism. You need, however, to be extremely careful not to stereotype the states in the following list and, in particular, to distinguish between urban and rural areas.

The bible belt states are generally seen as those west of the Appalachian Mountains in the valley of the Mississippi River, i. e. Kentucky, Tennessee, Mississippi, Alabama, Louisiana, Arkansas and Missouri.

There are, however, fundamentalist protestant communities in many parts of the USA, including parts of New England and the Great Lakes area. The religious life in the Mormon (Church of the Latter Day Saints) state of Utah is also fundamentalist.

26 What is a "ZIP code"?

The verb 'zip' is sometimes used to mean 'move very fast', as in "the rumour zipped round the school in no time." This is a happy coincidence, but it has nothing to do with the expression ZIP code. Here ZIP stands for the more mundane 'Zone Improvement Plan'. ZIP codes are, then, the American equivalent of the German *Postleitzahlen* and the British postal codes.

ZIP codes are made up of two letters (for the state) and five numbers (for the town and neighbourhood) with one space between the letters and the numbers, for example **CA 89754**. The code is positioned on the same line as the postal town, but is separated from it by a comma and one space, e. g. **Buffalo, NY 14209**.

Please note
1. The spacing and positioning of the ZIP code is important because of electronic sorting machines.
2. It is compulsory to use the codes, and the United States Postal Services do not guarantee to deliver letters without the code or with wrongly written codes.

Here are the official abbreviations of state names:

Alabama	AL	Kansas	KS	Ohio	OH
Alaska	AK	Kentucky	KY	Oklahoma	OK
Arizona	AZ	Louisiana	LA	Oregon	OR
Arkansas	AR	Maine	ME	Pennsylvania	PA
California	CA	Maryland	MD	Rhode Island	RI
Colorado	CO	Massachusetts	MA	South Carolina	SC
Connecticut	CT	Michigan	MI	South Dakota	SD
Delaware	DE	Minnesota	MN	Tennessee	TN
District of Columbia	DC	Mississippi	MS	Texas	TX
Florida	FL	Montana	MT	Utah	UT
Georgia	GA	Nebraska	NE	Vermont	VT
Hawaii	HI	Nevada	NV	Virginia	VA
Idaho	ID	New Hampshire	NH	Washington	WA
Illinois	IL	New Jersey	NJ	West Virginia	WV
Indiana	IN	New Mexico	NM	Wisconsin	WI
Iowa	IA	New York	NY	Wyoming	WY
		North Dakota	ND		

6 Knifflige Fragen zur englischen Sprache

1 When must/should I use a hyphen?

A **hyphen** – the name is derived from a Greek word meaning 'together' – is used to aid understanding, as in 'extra-marital sex', meaning sex outside marriage, and 'extra marital sex', meaning more sex within marriage.

Although there is a very marked trend in modern usage to dispense with hyphens, particularly in compound nouns like **ice cream** and **living room**, there are still nine situations in which a hyphen is at least helpful when not essential. Here they are:

(1) A hyphen is always used to show that a word has been split at the end of one line and is completed on the next line. All good dictionaries show where words can be split. You should, however, never split a word in such a way that the reader has absolutely no idea of how it might go on.
The word **hopeful**, for example, should be split after **hope-** and not after **hop-** or **ho-**. The first split suggests the complete word might be 'hopping' and the second 'ho-tel'. (→ 2 How do I split ...?, S. 134)

(2) In spite of the current trend towards either writing compounds together as one word or as separate words without a hyphen, a relatively small number of compounds, mainly adjectives and verbs, continue to be hyphenated. Examples are **man-made** (adjective), **two-piece** (adjective), **video-tape** (verb), **window-shop** (verb). By the way, the compound noun 'video tape' does not make use of a hyphen.

(3) A fixed group of words which together make up a single unit of sense is always hyphenated when it is used attributively, i. e. as an adjective before a noun:

> ▶ the **out-of-date** catalogue but the catalogue is **out of date**
> the **out-of-work** actors but the actors are **out of work**
> the **ten-thousand-euro** prize but the prize was **ten thousand euros**

(4) A small group of compounds which are treated like single words also use hyphens as an aid to understanding. **Mother-in-law, great-grandparents, lieutenant-colonel, governor-general, wing-threequarter** (position in rugby football) are examples.

(5) As a pronunciation aid, a hyphen is often used when the last vowel of a prefix is the same as the first letter of the stem word: **co-operate, re-enter**. Here, one should think of the reader and be generous. Words like **re-alight** (get off again) and **co-alesce** (combine to form a whole) could also be written with a hyphen for this reason.

(6) A hyphen is often used between prefixes of Latin origin (*ante-*, *anti-*, *ex-*, *inter-*, *intra-*, *pre-*, *pro-*) and the stem: **ante-room, anti-British, ex-husband, pre-war, inter-city, pro-government**.

(7) Hyphens are always used in compounds made up of names:
The M4 is the **London-Cardiff motorway**.
There's a lot of interest in **Chelsea-Arsenal** matches.

(8) Hyphens must be used to avoid a breakdown in understanding, i. e. to make meaning clear. Compare these pairs of sentences:

> **Small-car drivers** have less trouble parking. (= the drivers drive small cars)
> **Small car-drivers** will find it difficult to park such a heavy car. (= the drivers themselves are small)
> **Sweet-shop** assistants don't get much pay. (= assistants who work in sweet shops)
> Sweet **shop-assistants** sell more. (= shop assistants who are sweet)

(9) Place names made up of three or more words almost always take hyphens: **Ashby-de-la-Zouche, Bourton-on-the-Water, Burnham-on-Crouch, Wells-next-the-Sea**.

But please note: 'Bury St Edmunds', 'Newcastle upon Tyne', 'Burton on Trent'.

A final word
Hyphening is often a kind of halfway house between writing the word of a compound separately and writing them together as a single word. Obviously, the more common a particular compound is, the more likely it is to be written as one word without hyphens, i. e. 'closed'. There is thus a large class of very common compounds which have already become practically single words and are now hardly recognised as compounds at all.

Here is an overview of problematical words that sometimes cause trouble. If this list conflicts with anything written above, trust the list.

One word without hyphen

anticlimax
antidote
antiseptic
backlog
bilingual
blueprint
businessman
businesswoman
bypass
ceasefire
coastguard
comeback
commonsense (as adjective)
foothold
goodwill
halfhearted
handout
handpicked
hijack
lacklustre
loophole
lopsided
lukewarm
multilingual
nationwide
offshore
oilfield
onshore
overpaid
overrated
override
overrule
overrun
peacekeepers
peacekeeping
profitmaking
salesforce
shortlist
statewide
stockmarket
strongman
subcommittee
subcontinent
subcontract
subhuman
takeover
threshold
turnout
underdog
underpaid
underrated
videocassette
videodisc
wartime
workforce
worldwide

Two words without hyphen

air base
air force
aircraft carrier
arm's length
drug dealing
errand boy
girl friend
health care

ballot box
birth rate
child care
chip maker
coal miner
common sense (as noun)
drug dealer

microchip maker
on to
steel maker
steel worker
under way
vice versa

Two words with hyphen

agri-business*
asylum-seeker**
build-up
catch-phrase
death-squad**
drawing-board**
end-game
faint-hearted
fund-raiser
fund-raising
heir-apparent**
hot-head
ice-cream**
infra-red
inter-governmental*
know-how
long-standing

mid-week, mid-May etc.
nation-state**
post-war
pre-war
re-sort (= sort again)
starting-point**
sticking-point**
stumbling-block**
talking-shop**
task-force**
think-tank**
time-bomb**
turning-point**
working-party

*   (also as one word)
** (also without hyphen)

Three words without hyphens

ad hoc agreement
capital gains tax
chiefs of staff

in as much
in so far
value added tax

Three words with hyphens

chock-a-block
commander-in-chief
no-man's-land

prisoners-of-war
second-in-command

2 How do I split ...?
Are there any rules of splitting?

Yes, there are, and they're not all that difficult. Here they are:

(1) In British English, you can split words of more than one spoken syllable between the syllables as long as this leaves more than one letter before the hyphen at the end of the first line, and – other than in the case of the ending -*ly* – more than two letters at the beginning of the run-on line.

Because of this rule, you cannot split short words of two syllables like **a·long**, **al·so**, **du·et**, **laugh·ed**, **play·er** and so on. You can, however, split words ending in -*ly* like **easi·ly**, **high·ly**, **week·ly** etc.

(2) Compound words written as a single word (**postman**, **football**) and hyphenated words (**son-in-law**, **well-paid**) should only be split between the individual words: **post·man**, **foot·ball**, **son-·in-·law**, **well-·paid**

The same rule applies to words containing prefixes and suffixes.

anti·social, inter·national, jump·ing, soci·able, un·tidy

(3) Notice that words containing **double letters** are split between those letters, not after the second of them:

let·ter, put·ting, swim·ming.

Please note: Only split when really unavoidable. In handwriting, splitting is only necessary in the case of very long words like 'internationalism', 'self-consciousness' and so on. Splitting is rather ugly and makes a text difficult to read. Most people would rather see bigger gaps within and at the end of lines, and less splitting. Try and avoid splitting at the end of two or more consecutive lines.

3 What are the 'comma rules' in English?

The obligatory use of commas

Commas must be used

(1) To separate the *if/when*-clause and the main clause in sentences beginning with *if* and *when*:

> ▶ If I see her, I'll give her your message.
> When Tom got home, he went to bed.

(2) After the introductory verb in reported speech:

> ▶ Helga said, "Let's go to the theatre next week."

(3) To show that a non-defining relative clause (*nichtnotwendiger Relativsatz*) is not necessary to an understanding of the main clause:

> ▶ Smallpox, which once killed thousands of people, has now disappeared from Europe.

(4) Between the items in a list except before *and**:

> ▶ Don't forget to buy some bread, butter, milk, sausages and beer.
>
> * In AmE a comma is often used before *and* in such lists.

(5) To separate words like *however*, *nonetheless*, etc. from the rest of the sentence:

> ▶ In my opinion, however, the government should do something about it.
> Nonetheless, there's no doubt the firm will do better next year.
> Jane had, luckily, not forgotten to turn off the cooker after all.

The obligatory non-use of commas

(1) The big mistake made by German-speaking users of English is putting commas into the sentence unnecessarily. This should be avoided as commas act as a brake in English so their unnecessary or unexpected use makes reading quite hard going.

Here are some examples of the most common 'German errors'. The first sentence in the pair illustrates the error, the second sentence the correct form.

▶ ~~None of the others noticed, that Bob was no longer with them.~~
None of the others noticed that Bob was no longer with them.

~~No one told me, what to do or, who to ask.~~
No one told me what to do or who to ask for help.

~~Dr Davids told me, to go straight to hospital.~~
Dr Davis told me to go straight to hospital.

~~I thought, I saw you in town today. Or was I mistaken?~~
I thought I saw you in town today. Or was I mistaken?

~~Tom went to hospital, because he hurt his leg.~~
Tom went to hospital because he hurt his leg.

~~Sally reached the station on time, but the train had already left.~~
Sally reached the station on time but the train had already left.

⚠ We **do not use** a comma in front of noun clauses beginning with *that*, *what*, *where* and so on. In reported speech, we do not use commas before verbs of saying, thinking, wondering etc. We do not use a comma before *because* or *but* in the sense of German *aber*.

▶ ~~The man, who came into the bank, was carrying a gun.~~
The man who came into the bank was carrying a gun.

~~The dog, that bit the little girl, belongs to my neighbour.~~
The dog that bit the little girl belongs to my neighbour.

⚠ We **do not use** commas to separate defining relative clauses (*notwendige Relativsätze*) from the rest of the sentence because they are essential to understanding. They are thus treated as an integral part of the subject they qualify.

4 Why is 'advertise' written with -ise, but 'recognize' with -ize?

There was a time when there were clear conventions about verbs ending in -ise and -ize when pronounced 'eyes' [aɪs].

In British English, apart from a small group of verbs – most common **advertise, advise, comprise, compromise, despise, devise, disguise, exercise, improvise, supervise, surprise, televise** – ending in -ise, all other such verbs were written in -ize (of Greek origin), for example **characterize, economize, formalize, industrialize, mechanize, organize, recognize, realize** and so on.

However, as any reader of the British press will know, in BrE – though in AmE less so – -ise seems to have largely replaced -ize.

This means that the current convention in BrE is:

Verbs ending in -ise (see list above) must be written in this way. Verbs ending in -ize can be written in -ise as well, and this is becoming increasingly common. As always, the big thing is to **be consistent**.

5 What are 'confusibles'?

Confusibles are generally pairs of words that are frequently mixed up or 'confused' not only by foreign learners, but by native speakers as well. Confusibles should not be, well, confused with 'false friends', which are words that look very similar to each other in two languages, but have different meanings.

Here is a list of common 'confusibles':

Verbs

abuse	Some parents **abuse** their children.	*missbrauchen*
misuse	If you **misuse** the machine, it'll break down.	*falsch bedienen*
affect	Smoking **affects** your health.	*beeinflussen*
effect	He **effected** his escape by stealing a car.	*bewirken*
arbitrate	We asked the court to **arbitrate** in the dispute.	*schlichten*
mediate	The UN is trying to **mediate** in Angola.	*vermitteln*

assume	I'm not sure, but I **assume** Tom will be there.	*ausgehen von*
presume	His car is still here, so I **presume** he's in his office.	*annehmen*

Although these two verbs can always be replaced by *suppose* without change of meaning, **presume** should only be used when there is good evidence to support a supposition. If no such evidence is present, then **assume** is more appropriate.

avoid	I **avoid** using the car whenever possible.	*vermeiden*
evade	Many people **evade** paying taxes.	*ausweichen*
become	Susan wants to **become** a nurse.	*werden*
get	Did you **get** many Valentine's cards?	*bekommen*
borrow	Can I **borrow** your bike this weekend?	*sich etwas leihen*
lend	I'm sorry. I never **lend** my bike to anybody.	*jmdm. etwas leihen*
convince	John tried to **convince** me of his political views.	*überzeugen*
persuade	Can't I **persuade** you to accept the job?	*überreden*
do	I must **do** my tax returns this evening.	*tun, erledigen*
make	Please don't **make** so much noise.	*machen, herstellen*
happen	The accident **happened** in heavy rain.	*passieren*
take place	The meeting **takes place** at 7 pm on Friday.	*stattfinden* (+ *Zeitangabe*)
imply	Are you **implying** that I'm not really ill?	*unterstellen, andeuten*
infer	From his behaviour we **inferred** he was drunk.	*(er)schließen*
lay	The teacher **laid** the books on the desk.	*legen*
lie	Get up. You can't **lie** in bed all day.	*liegen*
lie	Don't **lie** to me. I saw you do it myself.	*lügen*
look at	We have been **looking at** old buildings all week.	*anschauen*
watch	I **watch** a lot of tennis, but I don't play it myself.	*zuschauen*

The 'rule' is that we use **look** at for static objects and **watch** for activities. In modern colloquial usage, however, 'look at' is often also used for activities, as in 'We looked at the children playing in the park'. You cannot say 'She watched the Rembrandt for hours', however.

Confusibles

orient	Stonehenge is **oriented** on an east-west axis.	*orientieren*
orientate	Stonehenge is **orientated** on an east-west axis.	*orientieren*

Both these verbs are identical in meaning. **Orientate** is simply an alternative spelling, which only occurs in BrE.

prescribe	FIFA **prescribes** the rules of football.	*vorschreiben*
proscribe	The export of living animals should be **proscribed**.	*verbieten*
remark	Tom **remarked** that he'd seen me in town.	*beiläufig erwähnen*
notice	We **noticed** two men hiding behind a wall.	*wahrnehmen*
repel	The idea of eating dogs **repels** many people.	*abstoßen*
repulse	Chelsea easily **repulsed** Arsenals's attack.	*abwehren*
say	I'm sorry. What did you **say**?	*sagen*
tell	Can you **tell** me the way to the station, please? Mrs Adams **told** us a story.	*mitteilen* *erzählen*

Nouns

inquiry	The Iraq war is the subject of a UN **inquiry**.	*Untersuchung*
enquiry	We made an **enquiry** about their new paint.	*Anfrage*

In BrE, **inquiry** is mainly used to mean a formal investigation into an event or situation. **Enquiry**, on the other hand, is used for the simple act of asking for information. Please note, though, that in AmE inquiry / enquiry can be used practically interchangeably.

play	Hamlet is a **play** by Shakespeare.	*Theaterstück*
game	Football is the world's most popular **game**.	*Spiel*
recipe	She gave me a **recipe** for pancakes.	*Rezept*
receipt	Did you get a **receipt** for your purchases?	*Quittung*
prescription	You must have a **prescription** for this medicine.	*Arztrezept*
town	Holt is a small **town** in Norfolk.	*Stadt*
city/town	Salisbury is an interesting old **city/town**.	

We use **city** for a) towns with cathedrals and b) some important centres like Leeds and Newcastle that have been 'promoted' to cities by Act of Parliament. However, we can always use **town** without distinction. The German use of *City* to mean town centre, historic town (*Altstadt*) and even shopping centre is not possible in English.

Qualifiers

biannual	The report is **biannual**, in January and August.	*halbjährlich*
biennial	The fair is **biennial** – it's every other May.	*zweijährlich, alle zwei Jahre*
big	Lake Constance is a **big** lake in Germany.	*(physisch) groß*
great	J. S. Bach was a **great** composer.	*(geistig) groß*

Great meaning 'big in size' is used in place names, as in 'Great Britain', 'Greater London' etc., and sometimes when speaking of buildings, for example 'Great St Mary's', the university church in Cambridge.

continual	I dislike these **continual** interruptions.	*ständig*
continuous	They're forecasting **continuous** rain tomorrow.	*unaufhörlich, kontinuierlich*
definite	Can you give me a **definite** answer tomorrow?	*eindeutig*
definitive	That's my **definitive** opinion and it won't change.	*endgültig*
disinterested	Journalists should be **disinterested** reporters.	*unparteiisch*
uninterested	I'm totally **uninterested** in video games.	*uninteressiert, gleichgültig*
economic	The **economic** data suggests things are improving.	*Wirtschafts-*
economical	Small cars are more **economical** than big ones.	*sparsam*
heavy	Can't you help me to carry this **heavy** table?	*(physisch) schwer*
difficult	The test was much too **difficult** for my class.	*(geistig) schwer/ schwierig*
inapt	Telling jokes at funerals is completely **inapt**.	*unpassend*
inept	He's so **inept**. Nobody understood a word he said.	*unbeholfen*
industrial	Lille is an **industrial** town in northern France.	*industriell*
industrious	Bees and ants are incredibly **industrious** insects.	*fleißig, emsig*
little	They've bought a sweet **little** puppy.	*klein (niedlich)*
small	Dutch houses are far too **small** for us.	*(physisch) klein*
practical	Children learn best by doing **practical** things.	*praktisch*

practicable	It's a nice idea, but it's just not **practicable**.	*durchführbar, umsetzbar*
tasty	These sandwiches are very **tasty**. Have one.	*lecker*
tasteful	It's not **tasteful** to swear in company.	*geschmackvoll*
sociable	Jane loves parties. She's a very **sociable** girl.	*gesellig*
social	Racism is still a major **social** problem.	*Sozial-*
unsatisfied	You have everything, but you are still **unsatisfied**.	*unbefriedigt*
dissatisfied	I'm **dissatisfied** with my boring job.	*unzufrieden*

You are **unsatisfied** when you don't have enough of something you think you should have. You are **dissatisfied** when you have to put up with something that you don't want.

Miscellaneous confusibles

advice	I'm going to ask a lawyer for **advice**.	*Rat(schlag)*
advise	The doctor **advised** me to give up smoking.	*beraten*
finished	Have you **finished** your work?	*erledigt, beendet*
ready	Make sure you're **ready** to leave at 4.	*fertig (bereit etwas zu tun)*
licence	Give me your driving **licence**, please.	*Berechtigungsschein*
license	This café isn't **licensed** to sell alcohol.	*Erlaubnis haben*
loose	Two wheels of the truck were **loose**.	*locker*
lose	For heaven's sake don't **lose** the key.	*verlieren*
past	Just forget it, okay? Let the **past** be the **past**. I haven't been here for the **past** ten years. She walked **past** me on her way out.	*Vergangenheit vergangenen vorbei*
passed	The car **passed** us at a very high speed.	*vorbeifahren*

The word **past** occurs as a noun (*die Vergangenheit*), an adjective (*vergangene/r/s*) and as a preposition (*vorbei*). **Passed** is the simple past form and past participle of the verb **pass**.

principal	His **principal** argument was the high cost.	*Haupt-*
principle	I won't do it as a matter of **principle**.	*Prinzip*
stationary	Don't open the door until the train's **stationary**.	*stehend*
stationery	You can buy **stationery** at all bigger post offices.	*Schreibwaren*

6 False friends

Some words sound similar to German words but don't be too sure. Look at these examples!

German	English	English	German
aktuell	current	actual	tatsächlich
Artist	performer	artist	Künstler
Geldschein	bill (AmE), banknote (BrE)	bill (BrE), check (AmE)	Rechnung
blamieren	embarrass	blame	beschuldigen
Brief	letter	brief	kurz
Boot	boat	boot (BrE), trunk (AmE); boot (AmE) = Stiefel	Kofferrraum
Chef	boss	chef	Koch
Chips	crisps (BrE), chips (AmE)	chips (BrE), French fries (AmE)	Pommes frites
eventuell	maybe	eventually	schließlich
Gymnasium	high school	gymnasium	Turnhalle
konsequent	strict	consequently	folglich
Klosett	toilet (BrE), bathroom (AmE)	closet (AmE), cupboard (BrE)	Wandschrank
Lektüre	literature, book	lecture	Vorlesung
Mappe	folder	map	Landkarte, Stadtplan
ordinär	vulgar	ordinary	gewöhnlich
Pension	hotel	pension	Rente
Miete	rent		
Promotion	doctorate	promotion	Förderung
Prospekt	brochure	prospect	Aussicht
Provision	commission	provision	Versorgung
Residenz	castle	residence	Wohnort
sensibel	sensitive	sensible	vernünftig
sympathisch	likeable	sympathetic	verständnisvoll, mitfühlend
Zirkel	compass	circle	Kreis

//
7 What are the most commonly misspelt words in English?

Here is a list of the words that give bad spellers the most trouble. The typical mistake made by even educated native speakers of English is given in brackets.

accessible (~~accessable~~)
accidentally (~~accidently~~)
acclaim (~~aclaim~~)
aggravate (~~aggrevate~~)
alleged (~~aleged~~)
all right (~~alright~~)
auxiliary (~~auxillary~~)

basically (~~basicly~~)
beginning (~~begining~~)
believe (~~beleive~~)
biscuit (~~biscit~~)
broccoli (~~brocolli~~)

calendar (~~calender~~)
commitment (~~committment~~)
connoisseur (~~connisseur~~)
conscientious (~~conscientous~~)
consciousness (~~conscousness~~)
corroborate (~~corrobberate~~)

diarrhea (~~diarear~~)
disappearance (~~disappearence~~)
drunkenness (~~drunkeness~~)

embarrass (~~embarass~~)
entrepreneur (~~entreprenneur~~)
existence (~~existance~~)
exuberance (~~exuberence~~)

fascinate (~~fasinate~~)
February (~~Febuary~~)
fictitious (~~fictitous~~)
forfeit (~~forfit~~)

fulfilment (~~fulfillment~~)
goodbye (~~good bye~~)
guarantee (~~garantee~~)

hello (~~hallo, hullo~~)
hindrance (~~hinderance~~)

idiosyncrasy (~~idiosincracy~~)
immediately (~~immediatly~~)
independent (~~independant~~)
indispensable (~~indispensible~~)
inevitable (~~inevitible~~)
intelligence (~~intelligance~~)
interesting (~~interessting~~)

mediocre (~~midiocer~~)
mischievous (~~mischevous~~)
misspelled (~~misspeled~~)

necessary (~~necessarry~~)

obsolescent (~~obslescent~~)
omelette (~~ommlette~~)

parallel (~~paralell~~)
pastime (~~pasttime~~)
perseverance (~~perseverence~~)
procedure (~~proceedure~~)
pursue (~~persue~~)

realistically (~~realisticly~~)
receive (~~recieve~~)
recommend (~~reccommend~~)
remembrance (~~rememberence~~)
roommate (~~roomate~~)

sacriligious (sacreligious)
salary (salery)
separate (seperate)
shining (shineing)
soliloquy (soliloquy)
stubbornness (stubborness)
subtle (suttle)
success (sucess)
suddenness (suddeness)
surreptitious (sureptitous)

temperamental (tempremental)
tendency (tendancy)

tomorrow (tomorow)
transferred (transfered)
truly (truely)
twelfth (twelth)
tyranny (tyrany)

unnecessary (unecessary)
until (untill)
usage (useage)

vacuum (vacume)
welcome (wellcome)

8 What is the English equivalent of *nichts anbrennen lassen* and similar idiomatic expressions?

The English equivalent of *nichts anbrennen lassen* is 'to not miss out on anything' or 'to not let the grass grow under one's feet'. Here is a list of further such expressions, first from German into English then the other way round.

The English equivalents or meaning of common German idiomatic expressions

German	English
das A und O	the be-all and end-all
jmdn. abblitzen lassen	give sb the brush-off, snub sb
abgebrüht sein	be thick-skinned
ein Abklatsch von etwas sein	be a rehash of sth
aufs Abstellgleis geschoben werden	be put out to grass/in a backwater
etwas in einem Abwasch machen	do sth in one go
ständig auf Achse sein	always be on the go/move

Idiomatic expressions (German → English)

German	English
jmdn. achtkantig hinauswerfen	chuck/throw sb out
sich aus der Affäre ziehen	wriggle out of one's responsibilities
affengeil sein	to be cool/magic/wicked
so sicher wie das Amen in der Kirche sein	be as sure as eggs are eggs
nichts anbrennen lassen	not miss out on anything, not let the grass grow under one's feet
etwas auf Anhieb tun	do sth at first attempt/shot
jmdn. anpumpen	cadge money off sb
jmdn. anschwärzen	put the finger on sb, to tell tales on sb
schnell/sofort beleidigt sein	easily/immediately take offence
jmdn. zu etwas anstiften	put sb up to sth
etwas für nen'Appel und n'Ei kaufen/verkaufen	buy/sell sth for a song
sich den Arsch aufreißen	work one's balls off
ein Arschkriecher sein	be a bootlicker/brown nose
zu dick auftragen	be/go over the top
etwas ausbaden müssen	have to face the music/take the rap
sich wie die Axt im Walde benehmen	behave like a bull in a china shop
aus der Bahn geworfen werden	lose one's way, to be thrown off balance
nur Bahnhof verstehen	it's Greek to sb
mit harten Bandagen kämpfen	fight with no holds barred
etwas auf die lange Bank schieben	to put sth on the back burner
jmdm. einen Bärendienst leisten	be more of a hindrance than a help to sb
schwer von Begriff sein	be slow on the uptake
mit dem falschen Bein aufstehen	get out of bed on the wrong side
über den Berg sein	be out of the woods
eine schöne Bescherung sein	be a fine (old) mess
ein Bild für die Götter sein	be a sight for sore eyes
von der Bildfläche verschwinden	vanish into thin air
auf einem anderen Blatt stehen	be a different story
kein Blatt vor den Mund nehmen	not pull one's punches, call a spade a spade
ein Blitz aus heiterem Himmel sein	be a bolt out of the blue
null Bock auf etwas haben	not fancy doing sth

dumm wie Stroh sein	be as thick as two short planks
ein Bombengeschäft machen	do a roaring trade
ein Brett vorm Kopf haben	have a mental blockage
ein harter Brocken sein	be a tough nut to crack
die Bude auf den Kopf stellen	turn the place upside down
der Buhmann sein	be the scapegoat/whipping-boy
etwas unter Dach und Fach bringen	get sth sown up
einen Dachschaden haben	have a loose screw
die Decke fällt jmdm. auf den Kopf	be sick of these four walls
mit jmdm. unter einer Decke stecken	be hand in glove with sb
einen Dickkopf haben	be pig-headed
böhmische Dörfer sein	be double Dutch
auf Draht sein	be on one's toes
sich einen Dreck um etwas scheren	not give a damn about sth
Dreck am Stecken haben	have a skeleton in the cupboard
jmdn. wie den letzten Dreck behandeln	treat sb like the lowest of the low
aus dem gröbsten Dreck heraus sein	be over the hill/the worst
sich wegen jedes Drecks aufregen	get worked up over every little thing
sich um jeden Dreck kümmern müssen	have to do every last little thing
etwas auf den letzten Drücker machen	do sth at the very last minute
mit allem Drum und Dran	with all the trimmings
ein Duckmäuser sein	be a moral coward
keinen blassen Dunst haben	not have the faintest/slightest idea
wie eine kalte Dusche sein	be like a slap in the face
an allen Ecken und Kanten	right down the line, at every turn
jmdn. wie ein rohes Ei behandeln	treat sb with kid gloves
sich gleichen wie ein Ei dem anderen	be as like two peas in the pod
im Eimer sein	be down the drain
sich etwas einbrocken	let oneself in for sth, have only oneself to blame
ein heißes Eisen sein	be a hot potato
das Ende der Fahnenstange erreichen	be at the end of one's tether

Idiomatic expressions (German → English)

erstunken und erlogen sein	be a pack of lies
keinen guten Faden an jmdm. lassen	not have a good word to say for sb
ins Fadenkreuz geraten	take the flack, get stick
eine Fahne haben	reek of alcohol/liquor
die Fahne nach dem Wind drehen	trim one's sails to the wind
auf der falschen Fährte sein	get hold of the wrong end of the stick
jmdn. aus der Fassung bringen	throw sb for a loop
etwas auf eigene Faust machen	do sth off one's own bat
nicht mehr feierlich sein	be beyond a joke
seine Felle davon schwimmen sehen	see all one's hopes go up in smoke
ins Fettnäpfchen treten	put one's foot in it, drop a clanger
etwas an allen fünf Fingern abzählen können	be as clear as daylight
stumm wie ein Fisch sein	be as quiet as a mouse
gesund wie ein Fisch im Wasser sein	be as fit as a fiddle
zwei Fliegen mit einer Klappe schlagen	kill two birds with one stone
platt wie eine Flunder sein	be as flat as a pancake
keinen Funken Verstand haben	not have a grain of sense
gang und gäbe sein	be the usual thing
jmdm. ins Gehege kommen	cross sb
gehupft wie gesprungen sein	be six of one and half a dozen of the other
von allen guten Geistern verlassen	have taken leave of one's senses, be off one's head
im Geld schwimmen	be rolling in money/it
Geld zum Fenster hinauswerfen	put/throw money down the drain
etwas aufs Geratewohl tun	do sth on the off chance
sich zum Gespött der Leute machen	make oneself a laughing stock
auf etwas Gift nehmen	bet one's sweet life on sth
sich in ausgefahrenen Gleisen bewegen	be stuck in a rut
etwas an die große Glocke hängen	shout/trumpet sth from the rooftops
Glück im Unglück haben	be lucky in the circumstances
bei jmdm. auf Granit beißen	beat one's head against a brick wall

ins Gras beißen	bite the dust
die Gretchenfrage stellen	ask the $64,000 question
jmdm. nicht grün sein	be on bad terms with sb
einen grünen Daumen haben	have green fingers
ein Haar in der Suppe finden	find a fly in the ointment
an den Haaren herbeigezogen sein	be far-fetched
sich in den Haaren liegen	be at daggers drawn with sb, be at loggerheads with sb
jmdm. die Haare vom Kopf fressen	eat sb out of house and home
sich keine grauen Haare wachsen lassen	lose no sleep over sth
zum Hals heraushängen	be sick and tired of sth
zwei linke Hände haben	be all thumbs
etwas im Handumdrehen machen	do sth in less than no time
um etwas herumreden	beat about the bush
sein Herz an etwas hängen	set one's heart on sth.
das Herz auf der Zunge haben	have one's heart on one's sleeve
jmdm. etwas ans Herz legen	drum sth into sb's head
jmdn./etwas auf Herz und Nieren prüfen	put sb/sth through his/her/its paces
ein Herz und eine Seele sein	be soulmates
etwas auf dem Herzen haben	have sth on one's mind
jmdm. den Himmel auf Erden versprechen	promise sb the moon
sich ein Hintertürchen offen halten	leave oneself a loophole/way out
mit jmdm. ein Hühnchen zu rupfen haben	have a bone to pick with sb
bekannt sein wie ein bunter Hund	be known far and wide
kalter Kaffee sein	be old hat
jmdn. durch den Kakao ziehen	take the mickey out of sb
nicht alles über einen Kamm scheren	judge everybody/everything on its/his/her own merits
das Kind beim Namen nennen	call a spade a spade
mit Kind und Kegel reisen	travel with everything but the kitchen sink

Idiomatic expressions (German → English)

auf der Kippe stehen	be balanced on a knife edge
die Kirche im Dorf lassen	keep things in proportion
in der Klemme sein	be in a fix/on the spot
jmdm. ein Klotz am Bein sein	be a millstone round sb's neck
etwas nicht übers Knie brechen	not give way to a knee-jerk reaction over sth
nicht wissen, wo einem der Kopf steht	not know if one's coming or going
jmdn. vor den Kopf stoßen	turn sb down flat
sich den Kopf zerbrechen	rack one's brains
zum Kotzen sein	make one want to throw up
die Kurve nicht kriegen können	not be able to manage to do sth
den Kürzeren ziehen	come off worst
den ganzen Laden schmeißen	run the whole show alone
ein Ladenhüter sein	become part of the shop fixtures
etwas lang und breit erzählen	go on and on about sth
durch die Lappen gehen	slip through one's fingers
viel Lärm um nichts machen	kick up a fuss about nothing
Lehrgeld zahlen müssen	have to learn the hard way
jmdn./etwas gut leiden können	be fond of sb/sth
sich einen Lenz machen	sit back and have an easy time
sein Licht unter den Scheffel stellen	hide one's light under a bushel
jmdn. ein Loch in den Bauch fragen	drive sb up the wall with questions
etwas mit jmdm. wieder ins Lot bringen	mend fences/patch things up with sb
alles Mache sein	be all show
wie die Made im Speck leben	live like a pig in clover
etwas an den Mann bringen	find a market for sth
mit zweierlei Maß messen	apply double standards
jmdm. das Maul/den Mund stopfen	shut sb up
sich das Maul über etwas zerreißen	sound off about sth
Mäuschen spielen wollen	want to be a fly on the wall
über etwas nichts zu melden haben	have absolutely no say in sth
gute Miene zu bösem Spiel machen	make the best of a bad job
die halbe Miete sein	be half the battle

jmdn. auf den Mond schießen wollen	want to send sb to the devil
aus einer Mücke einen Elefanten machen	make a mountain out of a molehill
die Mücke machen	make oneself scarce
sich den Mund fusselig reden	talk oneself blue in the face
in aller Munde sein	be on everybody's lips
sich den Mund verbrennen	burn one's fingers
den Mund zu voll nehmen	bite off more than one can chew
etwas für bare Münze nehmen	take sth at face value
schlafen wie ein Murmeltier	sleep like a log
den Nagel auf den Kopf treffen	hit the nail on the head
der Nagel zum Sarg sein	be another nail in one's coffin
Nägel mit Köpfen machen	do the job properly
aus dem Nähkästchen plaudern	tell the inside story
sich an seine eigene Nase fassen	put one's own house in order
jmdn. an der Nase herumführen	pull the wool over sb's eyes
jmdm. auf der Nase herumtanzen	play sb up
die Nase voll haben	be fed up with sb/sth
Nerven wie Drahtseile haben	have nerves of steel
auf dem Nullpunkt angekommen sein	have hit the bottom
auf Nummer Sicher gehen	be on the safe side
frech wie Oskar sein	have the cheek of the devil
päpstlicher als der Papst sein	be a stickler for detail
wie angegossen passen	fit like a glove
wie Pech und Schwefel zusammenhalten	be as thick as thieves
etwas um jeden Preis machen	do sth at whatever the cost
den Punkt aufs i setzen	put the finishing touch(es) to sth
ohne Punkt und Komma reden	talk non-stop
jmdm. in die Quere kommen	cross sb
die Quittung für etwas bekommen	pay the price for sth
unter die Räder kommen	sink out of sight, go to the dogs
außer Rand und Band sein	go berserk
sich rar machen	go out of circulation

Idiomatic expressions (German → English)

gesundheitlichen Raubbau treiben	burn the candle at both ends
eine alte Rechnung begleichen	pay off old scores
nach dem Rechten sehen	see that everything is all right
langer Rede kurzer Sinn	to put it in a nutshell
etwas nach allen Regeln der Kunst tun	do sth according to all the tricks of the trade
aus der Reihe tanzen	step out of line
etwas ins Reine bringen	straighten sth out
mit sich selbst nicht im Reinen sein	be at odds with oneself
jmdn. hereinlegen	do the dirty on sb, play dirty tricks on sb
über etwas hin und her gerissen sein	be in two minds about sth
nicht mehr zu retten sein	be beyond help
jmdn. nicht mehr riechen können	no longer be able to bear/stand sb
einer Sache einen Riegel vorschieben	put an end to sth
aus der Rolle fallen	forget oneself
keine Rolle spielen	be of no importance
Rosinen im Kopf haben	have big/unrealistic ideas
etwas rundweg ablehnen	turn sth down out of hand
über die Runden kommen	get by
jmdm. Sand in die Augen streuen	pull the wool over sb's eyes
Sand ins Getriebe streuen	put a spanner in the works
Geld in den Sand setzen	throw money down the drain
etwas/jmdn. satt haben	be fed up with sth/sb
in Saus und Braus leben	live in the lap of luxury
aus Schaden klug werden	learn from one's own mistakes
sein Schäfchen ins Trockene bringen	take care of number one
alles in den Schatten stellen	put everybody/everything in the shade
mehr Schein als Sein sein	be nothing but show
etwas nach Schema F tun	do sth according to routine
von etwas keinen blassen Schimmer haben	not have the faintest clue about sth
ein Schlag ins Wasser sein	be a flop/wash-out

aus etwas nicht schlau werden	not be able to make head or tail of sth
jmdn./etwas schlecht machen	badmouth sb/sth
den Kopf aus der Schlinge ziehen	get onself out of a hole
ein Schnäppchen machen	get a real bargain
eine große Schnauze haben	be a big-mouth
einen Seitensprung machen	have a bit on the side
Spaß muss sein	There's no harm in a joke.
kein Sterbenswörtchen sagen	not breathe a word
jmdn. in die Tasche stecken	run rings round sb
rot wie eine Tomate werden	go as red as a beetroot
etwas kurz vor Toresschluss machen	do sth in the nick of time
treu und brav sein	be as good as gold
den Trick raushaben	have the knack of doing sth
nur ein Tropfen auf einen heißen Stein	just a drop in the ocean
das Tüpfelchen aufs i setzen	put the icing on the cake
eine offene Tür einrennen	knock at an open door
von Tuten und Blasen keine Ahnung haben	not have the first clue about how to do sth
die nackte Wahrheit sagen	tell the unvarnished truth
ein(e) waschechte(r) Bayer(in)/... sein	be a dyed-in-the-wool Bavarian/...
ein Waschlappen sein	be a wimp
jmdm. auf den Wecker gehen	get on sb's nerves
neue Wege beschreiten	break new ground
sich selbst im Wege stehen	be one's own worst enemy
jmdm. nicht über den Weg trauen	not trust sb an inch
ein Wort gab das andere	one thing led to another
etwas/jmdm. wurscht sein	be all the same to sb
etwas zum x-ten Mal tun	do sth for the umpteenth time
jmdn. den Zahn ziehen	knock sb's idea/intention on the head
jmdn. in die Zange nehmen	give sb a good grilling
die Zeche bezahlen müssen	have to foot the bill, take the rap for sth
in einer Zwickmühle sein	be caught between a rock and a hard place

The German equivalents or meaning of common English idiomatic expressions

English	German
bark up the wrong tree	auf dem Holzweg sein
be a flash in the pan	ein Strohfeuer sein
be against the odds	unwahrscheinlich sein
be all the rage	der letzte Schrei sein
be a pain in the neck/arse	jmdm. auf die Nerven gehen
to be a sight for sore eyes	eine Augenweide sein
be between a rock and a hard place	in einer Zwickmühle sein
be dead beat	erschöpft sein
be fed up with sb/sth	von etwas/jmdm. die Nase voll haben
be hand in glove with sb	mit jmdm. unter einer Decke stecken
be left holding the baby	mit der Verantwortung allein gelassen sein
be off the record	nicht für die Öffentlichkeit sein
be on the make	sich die eigenen Taschen füllen
be on the rocks	am Ende sein
be on the safe side	ganz sicher gehen
be on the waggon	das Alkoholtrinken aufgegeben haben
be out of one's depth	überfordert sein
be right up one's street	genau nach dem Geschmack von jmdm. sein
be sitting pretty	gut dran sein
be too big for one's boots	größenwahnsinnig sein
be unable get a word in edgeways/edgewise	überhaupt nicht zu Wort kommen
be upfront with sb	mit jmdm. offen und ehrlich sein
be up the creek without a paddle	in der Klemme sein
bite off more than one can chew	sich zu viel zumuten
catch sb doing sth red-handed	jmdn. auf frischer Tat erwischen
come in handy for sth	für etwas nützlich sein
come to the point	zur Sache kommen
cut down on sth	etwas einschränken
do sb a good turn	jmdm. einen Gefallen tun

do sth for kicks	etwas aus Vergnügen tun
do sth just for laughs	etwas zum Spaß machen
eat one's words	eine Äußerung kleinlaut zurücknehmen
fall into line with sb/sth	mit etwas/jmdm. einverstanden sein
find sth out by trial and error	etwas durch Versuch und Irrtum herausfinden
fly off the handle	ausrasten
get a piece/slice of the action	am geschäftlichen Erfolg teilhaben
get away with sth	ungestraft davonkommen
get hold of the wrong end of the stick	etwas völlig falsch verstehen
get one's act together	das Leben besser regeln/organisieren
get on sb's nerves	jmdm. auf die Nerven gehen
get real	(etwas) realistisch betrachten/sehen
get up sb's/one's nose	jmdm. auf die Nerven gehen
give a straight answer	eine klare Antwort geben
give sb a hand to do sth	jmdm. helfen, etwas zu tun
give sb a piece of one's mind	jmdm. ungeschminkt sagen, was man denkt
go off the deep end	aus der Haut fahren
go incandescent/spare	völlig ausrasten
go to the dogs	vor die Hunde gehen
have a bee in one's bonnet	einen Tick haben
have a chip on one's shoulder	sich unfair behandelt/benachteiligt fühlen
have a close shave	einer Gefahr knapp entkommen
have a soft spot for sb	eine Schwäche für jmdn. haben
have egg on one's face	wie ein Depp erscheinen
have green fingers	einen grünen Daumen haben
have one's back against the wall	in die Enge getrieben sein
have one's feet on the ground	eine handfeste Natur haben
have sb over a barrel	jmdn. in der Zange haben
have the gift of the gab	sehr redegewandt sein
hit it off with sb	sich mit jmdm. gut verstehen
hit the ceiling/roof	ausrasten
keep an eye on sb/sth	ein Auge auf jmdn./etwas haben

Idiomatic expressions (English → German)

keep a straight face	ein ausdrucksloses Gesicht/ein Pokerface aufsetzen/behalten
keep one's fingers crossed	die Daumen drücken
keep one's hair on	ruhig bleiben
kick up a fuss	sich lauthals beschweren
leave sb in the lurch	jmdn. im Stich lassen
let the cat out of the bag	etwas preisgeben
make a go of sth	etwas erfolgreich tun
make tracks	sich auf die Socken machen
pick a fight/quarrel with sb	Streit mit jmdm. anfangen
pick sb's brains	jmdn. zum eigenen Vorteil ausfragen
play it safe	sichergehen
play sth down	etwas verharmlosen
poke fun at sb/sth	sich über jmdn./etwas lustig machen
pour oil on troubled water	die Wogen glätten
pull sb's leg	jmdn. auf den Arm nehmen
pull strings	etwas durch Beziehungen erreichen
pull the wool over sb's eyes	jmdn. hinters Licht führen
put all one's eggs in one basket	alles auf eine Karte setzen
put the cart before the horse	eine Sache falsch herum betrachten/ das Pferd von hinten aufzäumen
put the cat among the pigeons	für Unruhe sorgen
put sb's back up	jmdn. verärgern
put sb's on the spot	jmdn. in Verlegenheit bringen
screw sth up	etwas vermasseln
see eye to eye with sb	mit jmdm. einverstanden sein
sell like hot cakes	wie warme Semmeln weggehen
serve sb right	jmdm. recht geschehen
smell a rat	Verdacht schöpfen
try to keep up with the Joneses	mit jmdm. finanziell Schritt halten
turn a blind eye to sth	etwas bewusst ignorieren
not turn a hair	absolut ruhig bleiben, nicht mit der Wimper zucken
turn sb/sth down	jmdn./etwas ablehnen
wash one's hands of sb/sth	mit jmdm./etwas nichts mehr zu tun haben wollen

9 What are the differences between American English (AmE) and British English (BrE)?

This is a huge area with thousands of differences in pronunciation, spelling, vocabulary and usage. Here we can only deal with the most obvious differences between the two forms of English. However, with the occasional exception of a word like 'faucet', which some BrE-speakers do not recognise as 'tap', it's worth saying in advance that such differences seldom cause problems of understanding.

Pronunciation

(1) An [r] after a vowel, e. g. *hair*, *turn*, *rare*, is silent in BrE, but can usually be heard in AmE.

(2) A [t] or double **t** after a vowel or diphthong, e. g. *bottle*, *dirty*, *tomato*, is pronounced as a [d] in AmE, i. e. 'boddle', 'dirdy', 'tomaydo' etc.

(3) When an [a] stands before a fricative ([s], [f], th [ð] or [θ]) or a nasal ([n], [m]) followed by a consonant as in *after*, *aunt*, *can't*, *dance*, *example*, *fast*, *half*, *laugh*, *pass*, *past* etc., it is pronounced long in BrE as the [aː] in 'father' and short in AmE as the [æ] in 'cat'.

(4) The **-ary**-ending in such words as *necessary*, *military* and *secretary* are stressed and fully pronounced in AmE, e. g. BrE ['nesəsəri], ['mɪlətri], ['sekrətri] versus AmE ['nesəseri], ['mɪləteri] ['sekrəteri].

(5) The **-ile**-ending is often shortened or not pronounced at all in AmE, e. g. *docile* as ['daːsl], *missile* as ['mɪsl] and *fertile* as ['fɜːrtl]. However, here there are big regional differences within the USA. For example, *meanwhile*, *tile* and *infantile* are usually pronounced as in BrE.

(6) Many, mostly longer, words are differently stressed in AmE, e. g. *advertisement* [ˌædvərˈtaɪzmənt] *laboratory* [ˈlæbrətɔːri], *research* [rɪˈsɜːrtʃ].

(7) A number of words of foreign origin are differently pronounced in AmE, e. g. *depot* [ˈdiːpoʊ], *theatre/theater* [ˈθiːətər] and *herbs* [(h)ɜːrbs].

Spelling

American spelling is often simpler and more regular than the British style. Many AmE forms can be traced back to the work of Noah Webster (1758–1843) and appeared in his first dictionary of American English, published in 1828. These changes can be categorized as follows.

(1) **-or for -our**

English words ending in **-our** derive from Norman-French. Most common:

AmE	BrE	AmE	BrE
color	colour	labor	labour
favor	favour	neighbor	neighbour
favorite	favourite	odor	odour
harbor	harbour	tumor	tumour
humor	humour	valor	valour
glamor	glamour	vigor	vigour

(2) **-er for -re**

AmE	BrE	AmE	BrE
center	centre	meter	metre
fiber	fibre	somber	sombre
liter	litre	theater	theatre
meager	meagre		

However, please note that many words ending in **-re** retain this form in AmE because an -er-ending would lead to faulty pronunciation. Examples are *acre*, *massacre*, *mediocre* and *ogre*.

(3) **-e for the diphthongs -æ/-œ**

This group comprises mostly medical terms of Greek and Latin origin and the simpler AmE spelling is becoming more and more popular in BrE as well. Most common are:

AmE	BrE	AmE	BrE
anemia	anæmia	ether	æther
anesthetic	anæsthetic	gynecology	gynæcology
diarrhea	diarrhoea	hemoglobin	hæmoglobin
esophagus	œasophagus	hemorrhage	hæmorrhage
esthetic	æsthetic	hemophilia	hæmophilia
estrogen	œstrogen	homeopathy	homœpathy

(4) *-ll* for *-l*

Most words ending with a vowel followed by a single -l in BrE usually end in a double -l in AmE, for example:

AmE	BrE	AmE	BrE
appall	appal	enthrall	enthral
distill	distil	fulfill	fulfil
enroll	enrol	instill	instil

(5) *-lyze* for *-lyse*

Some verbs ending in -yse in BrE are written -yze in AmE to reflect the pronunciation more accurately, for example analyze (BrE **analyse**), paralyze (BrE **paralyse**).

(6) *-og* for *-ogue*

BrE words with an **-ogue**-ending are mostly written in AmE with an **-og**-ending:

AmE	BrE	AmE	BrE
analog	analogue	monolog	monologue
catalog	catalogue	pedagog	pedagogue
dialog	dialogue		

Please note, however, that **analog** and **catalog** are now becoming more common in BrE as well.

(7) *-se* for *-ce*

The **-se**-ending is preferred in AmE, e. g. **defense** (BrE defence), **pretense** (BrE pretence), even in those cases when a distinction is made in BrE between a verb and a noun form, most importantly **practise** (BrE practice [noun], practise [verb] and **license** (BrE licence [noun], license [verb]).

Important note

In addition to these main groups, there are many general simplifications that cannot be categorised, for example:

AmE	BrE	AmE	BrE
ax	axe	mold	mould
check	cheque	nite	night
disk	disc*	plow	plough
jewelry	jewellery	program	programme*

* **Program** und **disk** are also used in BrE for **computer program** and **computer disk**.

Vocabulary

(1) **Same word, different meaning**
There are a number of words that are used in both AmE and BrE, but with different meanings, for example:

Word	AmE	BrE
biscuits	weiches Brötchen	Kekse
chips	Kartoffelchips	Pommes Frites
corn	Mais	Getreidekorn
depot	Bahnhof	Lagerhaus, Magazin
gas	Benzin	Gas
jelly	Marmelade	Wackelpeter
pants	Hosen	Unterhosen
subway	U-Bahn	Fußgängertunnel
vest	Weste	Unterhemd

(2) **Same meaning, slightly different form**
There are also a number of words and expressions that share the same meaning in AmE and BrE, but have a slightly different form:

AmE	BrE
aluminum	aluminium
baby bottle	baby's bottle
beach chair	deck chair
cookbook	cookery book
crawfish	crayfish
dollhouse	doll's house
driver's license	driving licence
driver's test	driving test
mail box	letter box
math	Maths (school subject)
pajamas	pyjamas
railroad	railway
rowboat	rowing boat
sailboat	sailing boat
sanitarium	sanatorium
sled	sledge
windshield	windscreen
zipper	zip
zip code	post code

(3) Different words

A third group of words are completely different. Most important are:

AmE	BrE
apartment[2]	flat
apartment building	block of flats
automobile	car[1]
bathrobe	dressing gown
cab[2]	taxi[1]
candy	sweets
cookie	biscuit
diaper	nappy
drapes	curtains
elevator[2]	lift
eraser	rubber
fall	autumn
flashlight[2]	torch
garbage	rubbish
garbage can	dustbin
gas	petrol
hood	bonnet (*Motorhaube*)
movie[2]	film[1]
rest room	toilet
row house	terraced house
rummage sale	jumble sale
sidewalk	pavement
single family house	detached house
thumb tack	drawing pin
trailer	caravan, mobile home
truck[2]	lorry
trunk	boot (*Kofferraum*)
tub	bath[1]
two-family house	semi-detached house
undershirt	vest
vacation[2]	holiday(s)
vest	waistcoat

[1] These BrE words also occur in AmE, though more rarely.
[2] These AmE words are becoming increasingly common in BrE as well.

Usage

There is some variation in the use of prepositions in AmE and BrE. For example, Americans live '**on** a street', Brits '**in** a street'; Americans go out '**on** weekends', Brits '**at** weekends'; American students are '**in** a course', British students '**on** a course'. Americans can say 'I'm leaving Thursday' and 'The cat went out the window', while Brits must say 'I'm leaving **on** Thursday' and 'The cat went out **of** the window'.

Further such variations in the use of prepositions are:

AmE	BrE
back of/in back of	behind
Monday through Friday	Monday to Friday
a quarter of three	a quarter to three
a quarter after five	a quarter past five
ten of seven	ten (minutes) to seven
in school	at school
different than	different to/from
in the hospital	in hospital
wash up	have a wash
wash/do the dishes	wash up/do the washing up

Grammar

As the grammar of English is identical in both AmE and BrE, it is as nonsensical to write *Aus dem Amerikanischen von ...* as to say 'Translated from the Austrian by ...'. However, there are a few 'preferences' that affect the use of grammar.

(1) **The use of *would* for *should***

Just as **shall** has been largely replaced by **will** in both AmE and BrE, so there is a distinct preference in AmE for the use of **would** rather than **should**:

▶ BrE I **should** be happy to lend it to you.
   AmE I **would** be happy to lend it to you.

   BrE I **shouldn't** do that if I were you!
   AmE I **wouldn't** do that if I were you!

However, **should** continues to be used in AmE in certain rather fixed idiomatic expressions such as 'You **should** be shamed of yourself!'.

(2) **The use of *have* as a full verb for *have got***
The old claim that **have got** is preferred in BrE and **have** in AmE no longer holds good. In modern usage, **have** is as often used in BrE as it always has been in AmE, for example:

> I have a new car.   for   I've got a new car.
> I don't have any money.   I haven't got any money.

(3) **Past form of certain verbs**
A few verbs have retained an earlier form in AmE, or have taken on a simplified form, as follows:

AmE	BrE
dive – dove – dove	dive – dived – dived
fit – fit – fit	fit – fitted – fitted
get – got – gotten	get – got – got
ring – rung – rung	ring – rang – rung
sew – sewed – sewed	sew – sewed – sewn
sing – sung – sung	sing – sang – sung
sink – sunk – sunk	sink – sank – sunk
sow – sowed – sowed	sow – sowed – sown
swim – swum – swum	swim – swam – swum

(4) **Use of *want* to express wishes**
When using **want** to express a wish that somebody does something, the German structure *Ich möchte, dass ...* is preferred in AmE:

> AmE   I **want that you go** to bed now, kids.
> BrE   I **want you to go** to bed now, kids.

(5) **The use of *going to* for *will***
There seems to be a greater willingness to use **going to** rather than **will** for thoughts, hopes and forecasts in AmE:

> AmE   I think Jason **is going to fail** his driver's test.
> BrE   I think Jason **will fail** his driving test.

> AmE   We hope they'**re going to visit** us in the summer.
> BrE   We hope they'**ll visit** us in the summer.

> AmE   It said on TV that we'**re going to have** a white Christmas.
> BrE   It said on TV that we'**ll have** a white Christmas.

7 Übungsbausteine

Dieses Kapitel soll dem Lehrer praktische Hilfe bei der Erstellung von Klassenarbeiten und Übungsmaterialien leisten. Es ist hier nicht unser Ziel, fertige „Arbeitsblätter" zum sofortigen Einsatz anzubieten. Wegen der Vielfalt der Zielgruppen ist es kaum realistisch, Übungsblätter zu entwerfen, die unverändert übernommen werden können. Statt dessen haben wir versucht, „Bausteine" zur Verfügung zu stellen, die von dem Lehrer in einer für seine Zwecke und Lerngruppe geeigneten Kombination zusammengestellt werden können.

Alle Bausteine sind ready for use. Abgesehen von der Erstellung einer Fotokopiervorlage benötigen sie also keine weitere Bearbeitung durch den Lehrer. Wie bei Kapitel 2 *(Games and Activities)* sind die Übungen den Anforderungen der Richtlinien, dem Themenbereichen und dem Wortschatz der gängigen Kursbücher sowie dem Wissensstand der entsprechenden Lerngruppe angepasst. Da die Bausteine zur Verwendung im schriftlichen Bereich gedacht sind, spielen situativ-kommunikative Übungen im mündlichen Bereich einen untergeordnete Rolle. Wir haben meist Schreibblöcken und -zeilen vorgegeben; diese sind eher für Klassenarbeiten gedacht. Im Unterricht ist es wegen der Kosten von Fotokopien vielleicht sinnvoller, die Schüler die Lösungen in ihr Heft, also nicht in die Lücken, schreiben zu lassen, und die Fotokopien weitere Male zu verwenden. Die Übungen sind nach Lernjahren – also Lernjahr 1/2, Lernjahr 3/4 und Lernjahr 5/6 – geordnet. Die Übungen innerhalb eines Lernjahres sind wiederum in drei Kategorien unterteilt, nämlich Grammatik, Wortschatz und Syntax.

Außerdem finden Sie die Übungsbausteine in editierbarer Form unter www.cornelsen-fundgruben.de/fundgruben. Sie können sie als Dokumente im WORD-Format herunterladen, gemäß Ihren Bedürfnissen bearbeiten (editieren) und anschließend ausdrucken sowie kopieren. Ihren Webcode finden Sie auf S. 1 dieses Bandes.

Lernjahr 1/2

A Grammatik

A1 I don't like school!

Fill in the gaps. Use do, does, don't or doesn't.

(1) I _____ like him. Neither _____ I.

(2) I need a drink. So _____ I.

(3) She doesn't eat meat, _____ she? What _____ she eat?

(4) He lives in Berlin, _____ he? Yes and so _____ Simon.

(5) _____ sit down on that chair. The paint is wet!

(6) Janet's husband _____ most of the housework. I _____ remember much about him. _____ he have a job? No, he _____ .

(7) You remember me, _____ you?

(8) We _____ think you are good enough for the team. I'm very sorry.

(9) I _____ think that this is a good idea.

(10) You don't want to go to the party, _____ you?

(11) They _____ seem very happy. I wonder what the problem is.

(12) I _____ feel like doing this exercise.

(13) What _____ you think I should do?

© Cornelsen Verlag Scriptor, Berlin • Fundgrube Englisch

Lösungen: (1) don't, do (2) do (3) Doesn't, does (4) doesn't, does (5) Don't (6) does, don't, Does, doesn't (7) don't (8) don't (9) don't (10) do (11) don't (12) don't (13) do

A2 What are they doing?

Simple present *or* present progressive? *Choose the right tense.*

(1) Look! Bob _____ into the water. (jumps/is jumping)

(2) I _____ lunch in the cafeteria every day. (have/am having)

(3) I _____ to the cinema next Thursday. Do you want to come? (go/am going)

(4) Don't give Tim any cheese. He _____ it! (hates/is hating)

(5) Robert _____ for his exam in the library at the moment. (studies/is studying)

(6) Once a week I _____ to an art class at the college. (go/am going)

(7) I _____ you're crazy! (think/am thinking)

(8) Mr Brown is very rich – he _____ a Mercedes. (drives/is driving)

(9) Look! It _____ . Perhaps we can make a snowman tomorrow. (snows/is snowing)

© Cornelsen Verlag Scriptor, Berlin • Fundgrube Englisch

Lösungen: (1) is jumping (2) have (3) am going (4) hates (5) is studying (6) go (7) think (8) drives (9) is snowing

A3 A terrible day!

Choose the right verb and write it in the simple past.

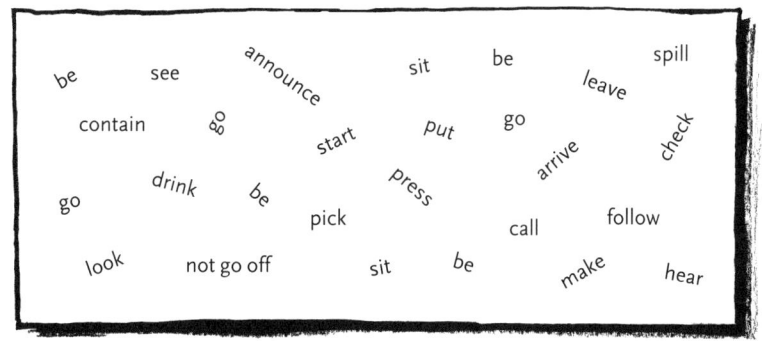

The day _____ (1) terribly. My alarm _____ (2) and I _____ (3) the house with only one hour to spare before the plane _____ (4) due to take off. Luckily there _____ (5) very little traffic and I _____ (6) at the airport with 30 minutes to spare. I _____ (7) in at the gate and _____ (8) for a coffee. Just as I _____ (9) down, the announcer _____ (10) my flight. I _____ (11) my coffee quickly, too quickly in fact as I _____ (12) some on my shirt. I _____ (13) the sign to the departure gate and _____ (14) through passport control. I _____ (15) down in the departure lounge. It _____ (16) full of teenagers, obviously a school trip. They _____ (17) a terrible noise. And then I _____ (18) that terrible announcement, the one you don't want to hear. There _____ (19) a problem with the engine. I _____ (20) around for a place to get another coffee. I _____ (21) a drinks machine so I _____ (22) over to get some. I _____ (23) in my money and _____ (24) the button for black coffee. When I _____ (25) up the cup, it _____ (26) only water. At that moment, the hostess _____ (27) that the plane was delayed because of bad weather.

© Cornelsen Verlag Scriptor, Berlin • Fundgrube Englisch

Lösungen: (1) started (2) didn't go off (3) left (4) was (5) was (6) arrived (7) checked (8) went (9) sat (10) called (11) drank (12) spilt (13) followed (14) went (15) sat (16) was (17) made (18) heard (19) was (20) looked (21) saw (22) went (23) put (24) pressed (25) picked (26) contained (27) announced

A4 This is easy, isn't it?

Add the right question tag. Remember the rule: When the sentence is positive you need a negative question tag. When the sentence is negative you need a positive question tag.

(1) You're new here, _____?
(2) You don't think he is ill, _____?
(3) He isn't going to Spain again this year, _____?
(4) You don't remember me, _____?
(5) You wanted that, _____?
(6) He saw that, _____?
(7) You know that's right, _____?
(8) We've spoken about that, _____?
(9) He will be coming, _____?
(10) He won't be unhappy _____?
(11) You're not going to bed, _____?
(12) He needs to learn more vocabulary, _____?
(13) You think you know the answer but you don't, _____?
(14) He didn't fail the exam, _____?
(15) The colour of classrooms has changed, _____?
(16) I don't need to say any more, _____?
(17) John doesn't know how much work he has made for us, _____?
(18) You wouldn't report me, _____?
(19) After all this time you would think he would have forgotten, _____?
(20) You wouldn't eat at that restaurant again, _____?

© Cornelsen Verlag Scriptor, Berlin • Fundgrube Englisch

Lösungen: (1) aren't you? (2) do you? (3) is he? (4) do you? (5) didn't you? (6) didn't he? (7) don't you? (8) haven't we? (9) won't he? (10) will he? (11) are you? (12) doesn't he? (13) do you? (14) did he? (15) hasn't it? (16) do I? (17) does he? (18) would you? (19) wouldn't you? (20) would you

A5 Pam goes to school by bike

Use the words to form positive statements (+), negative statements (–) or questions (?). Look at the example sentences first.

Examples:
+ Pam/go/to/school/by bike: *Pam goes to school by bike.*
– Pam/go/to/school/by bike: *Pam doesn't go to school by bike.*
? Pam/go/to/school/by bike: *Does Pam go to school by bike?*

(1) – Jane/eat/cornflakes/for breakfast

(2) ? the children/learn/French/at school

(3) + yesterday/the boys/break/a window

(4) ? you/often/write/stories/for homework

(5) – we/go/to school/on Saturdays

(6) ? why/Janet/come/to school/by taxi/yesterday

(7) + at the moment the girls/play/hockey/and/the boys/read comics

(8) – the children/have/Biology/at present/./ + the teacher/be/ill

(9) ? you/like/reading/animal books

(10) – Ben/play/very well/in the match/last week

(11) ? Mr Gregg/live/in Castle Street

(12) + The Greens/buy/a new car/last year

© Cornelsen Verlag Scriptor, Berlin • Fundgrube Englisch

Lösungen: (1) Jane does not/doesn't eat cornflakes for breakfast. (2) Do the children learn French at school? (3) Yesterday the boys broke a window. (4) Do you often write stories for homework? (5) We do not/don't go to school on Saturdays. (6) Why did Janet come to school by taxi yesterday? (7) At the moment the girls are playing hockey and the boys are reading comics. (8) The children do not/don't have Biology at present. The teacher is ill. (9) Do you like reading animal books? (10) Ben did not/didn't play very well in the match last week. (11) Does Mr Gregg live in Castle Street? (12) The Greens bought a new car last year.

A6 *for* or *since*?

*Do you use **for** or **since** with these expressions of time?*

(1) _____ three weeks		(2) _____ last Easter	
(3) _____ 10 o'clock		(4) _____ an hour	
(5) _____ I was a child		(6) _____ a long time	
(7) _____ we first met		(8) _____ several weeks	
(9) _____ the beginning		(10) _____ 31st May 1990	
(11) _____ ages		(12) _____ she scored a goal	

Lösungen: (1) for (2) since (3) since (4) for (5) since (6) for (7) since (8) for (9) since (10) since (11) for (12) since

A7 some, somebody, something, somewhere

Put in some, somebody, something *or* somewhere.

(1) I've got _____ money. Would you like _____ to eat?
(2) Don't lock the door. I think there's still _____ inside.
(3) I don't know the way. We'll have to ask _____.
(4) There have been _____ very good films on TV lately.
(5) – I can't find my purse.– Well, it must be _____, mustn't it?
(6) There's _____ wrong with my torch. I think I probably need _____ new batteries for it.
(7) Mum gave me _____ tickets to a pop concert for my birthday.
(8) Is _____ wrong? You look quite ill.

© Cornelsen Verlag Scriptor, Berlin • Fundgrube Englisch

Lösungen: (1) some, something (2) somebody (3) somebody (4) some (5) somewhere (6) something, some (7) some (8) something

A8 any, anybody, anything, anywhere

Put in any, anybody, anything *or* anywhere.

(1) Our team hasn't scored _____ goals in their last four matches.
(2) – Listen! Did you hear something then? – No, I didn't hear _____.
(3) We always stay at home. We haven't been _____ interesting for weeks.
(4) You can't ask just _____ questions like that. You must ask an expert.
(5) Have you got _____ money? I need 30p for the bus.
(6) – Keep quiet, Bob. You haven't done _____ yet in this lesson.
   – I didn't say _____, sir. It was Jack.
(7) I want a pink T-shirt but I can't find one at _____ of the shops.
(8) Where are you going on holiday? _____ exciting?

© Cornelsen Verlag Scriptor, Berlin • Fundgrube Englisch

Lösungen: (1) any (2) anything (3) anywhere (4) anyone (5) any (6) anything, anything (7) any (8) anywhere

B Wortschatz

B1 What an awful mess!

Pick out and list words about school.

When Mr Gregg went into 3G's classroom he was not pleased. What an awful mess! The blackboard was dirty and there was chalk all over the floor. The duster was in the wastepaper basket and the desks were all over the place. A lot of pupils had not put their exercisebooks and writing things into their schoolbags. The atlases from the Geography lesson were still on the teacher's desk. No one had put them in the cupboard. One of the History posters was lying on the floor, too. Mr Gregg went out into the playground to find some of the children. "You have got just ten minutes to tidy up the classroom," he told them. "And I am not going to show you a nature film in the lunch break today. You are going to have a Biology test instead."

© Cornelsen Verlag Scriptor, Berlin • Fundgrube Englisch

Lösungen: 3G's classroom; blackboard; chalk; duster; wastepaper basket; desks; pupils; exercisebooks; writing things; schoolbags; atlases; Geography lesson; teacher's desk; cupboard; History poster; playground; children; tidy up the classroom; show a nature film; lunch break; have a Biology test

B2 That silly computer

Mr Floppy asked his computer to make three list of words: (a) one about clothes, (b) one about traffic and transport and a last one (c) about food and drink, but the silly computer made a mistake. It put lots of words in one list.
Look at the words and mark them correctly with (a), (b) or (c).

__ apple	__ bus	__ T-shirt	__ hamburger
__ hat	__ bike	__ road	__ banana
__ sweatshirt	__ bread	__ train	__ lemonade
__ coke	__ station	__ coat	__ tram
__ socks	__ shirt	__ boat	__ cake
__ blouse	__ biscuits	__ steak	__ driver
__ bus stop	__ pullover	__ sandwiches	__ ferry
__ pear	__ canoe	__ shorts	__ pavement
__ jeans	__ sausages	__ wheel	__ bathing costume
__ sweets	__ scarf	__ lorry	__ gloves
__ van	__ meat pie	__ soft drink	__ whisky
__ trousers	__ plane	__ harbour	__ ticket
__ shoes	__ bacon	__ jacket	__ traffic
__ eggs	__ raincoat	__ strawberries	__ platform
__ police car	__ suit	__ yoghurt	__ milk
__ anorak	__ ice cream	__ ship	

© Cornelsen Verlag Scriptor, Berlin • Fundgrube Englisch

Lösungen:

(a) *clothes*: T-shirt – hat – sweatshirt – coat – socks – shirt – blouse – pullover – shorts – jeans – bathing costume – scarf – gloves – trousers – shoes – jacket – raincoat – suit – anorak

(b) *traffic and transport*: bus – bike – road – train – station – tram – boat – driver – bus stop – ferry – canoe – pavement – wheel – lorry – van – plane – harbour – ticket – traffic – platform – police car – ship

(c) *food and drink*: apple – hamburger – banana – bread – coke – cake – biscuits – steak – sandwiches – pear – sausages – sweets – meat pie – soft drink – whisky – bacon – eggs – strawberries – yoghurt – milk – ice cream – lemonade

Lernjahr 1/2 (Wortschatz)

B3 Compound nouns

What are these words in English? Choose a word from list A and a word from list B. The first one is done for you. Use an exercise-book.

(1)	Briefkasten	= letter box
(2)	Brotmesser	
(3)	Dosenöffner	
(4)	Eierbecher	
(5)	Kaffeekanne	
(6)	Kochbuch	
(7)	Mikrowellenherd	
(8)	Küchenschrank	
(9)	Seifenschale	
(10)	Tiefkühltruhe	
(11)	Computerprogramm	
(12)	Fernsehprogramm	
(13)	Bushaltestelle	
(14)	Geburtstagskarte	
(15)	Farbfilm	
(16)	Hintertür	
(17)	Lastwagenfahrer	
(18)	Notausgang	
(19)	Abendkleid	
(20)	Hundefutter	

List A: back, birthday, bread, bus, coffee, colour, cookery, computer, deep, dog, emergency, evening, kitchen, ~~letter~~, lorry, microwave, soap, tin, TV

List B: book, ~~box~~, card, cup, cupboard, dish, door, dress, driver, exit, film, food, freeze, knife, opener, oven, pot, program, programme, stop

© Cornelsen Verlag Scriptor, Berlin • Fundgrube Englisch

Lösungen: (2) bread knife (3) tin opener (4) egg cup (5) coffee pot (6) cookery book (7) microwave oven (8) kitchen cupboard (9) soap dish (10) deep freeze (11) computer program (12) TV programme (13) bus stop (14) birthday card (15) colour film (16) back door (17) lorry driver (18) emergency exit (19) evening dress (20) dog food

B4 A trip to Aberdeen

Complete the sentences with the words from the list. Use an exercisebook.

List: at, for, in, in, in front of, into, near, next to, of, of, to, to, to, on, under

Dave wanted ____ (1) visit his old friend Alistair ____ (2) Aberdeen. Alistair lived ____ (3) a farm ____ (4) Aberdeen. It was a nice day, so Dave walked ____ (5) the station. He didn't have a ticket, so he looked ____ (6) the ticket office. It was ____ (7) a newspaper shop. Before he bought his ticket he looked ____ (8) the timetable. The next train ____ (9) Aberdeen was half an hour later, so he had lots ____ (10) time. He went ____ (11) the ticket office. There were only three people ____ (12) him. When his train arrived ____ (13) Aberdeen it was ten minutes late. The station was also full ____ (14) football fans and Dave couldn't see his friend Alistair anywhere. But everything was OK. He found their meetingplace – a big clock – and Alistair was standing ____ (15) it.

© Cornelsen Verlag Scriptor, Berlin • Fundgrube Englisch

Lösungen: (1) to (2) in (3) on (4) near (5) to (6) for (7) next to (8) at (9) to (10) of (11) into (12) in front of (13) in (14) of (15) under

B5 Anybody and nobody

Complete these sentences with a word from the list. Use an exercisebook.

List: anybody, anything, anywhere, nobody, nothing, somebody, something, somewhere

(1) I don't know who it was, but I heard ____ talking.
(2) I knocked on the door, but ____ answered.
(3) I'd like to help, but there's ____ I can do.
(4) I don't know where we are. We could be ____ .
(5) Ellen saw him put ____ into his bag.
(6) His house is ____ near the station.
(7) Did ____ see Mr Thomas yesterday morning?
(8) I'm sorry, but I don't know ____ about last night.

© Cornelsen Verlag Scriptor, Berlin • Fundgrube Englisch

Lösungen: (1) somebody (2) nobody (3) nothing (4) anywhere (5) something (6) somewhere (7) anybody (8) anything

C Syntax (*word order*)

C1 Easy English sentences

Put the words of the sentences in the right order.

(1) very like I English much

(2) very German friend speak not good my does

(3) hates bananas Peter

(4) children songs like to sing

(5) supermarket the sell flowers they in

(6) Thursday you see doctor can next the

(7) buy cat milk he his wants to for some

(8) feed you my cat tomorrow can

(9) sister has my got a dog

(10) must school the book read you for

© Cornelsen Verlag Scriptor, Berlin • Fundgrube Englisch

Lösungen: (1) I like English very much. (2) My friend does not speak very good German. (3) Peter hates bananas. (4) Children like to sing songs. (5) They sell flowers in the supermarket. (6) You can see the doctor next Thursday. (7) He wants to buy some milk for his cat. (8) You can feed my cat tomorrow. (9) My sister has got a dog. (10) You must read the book for school.

C2 More difficult sentences

Put the words of the sentences in the right order.

(1) chocolate makes mother dinner my pudding for often

_____

(2) on is late school for Mondays always John

_____

(3) Saturday never have the cinema we gone to on afternoon

_____

(4) always when it am I on holiday rains

_____

(5) is Susan in a good after mood always school

_____

(6) my having father was a bath rang the phone in the hall when

_____

(7) the dog playing bit the with man a leg who was the wooden piano

_____

© Cornelsen Verlag Scriptor, Berlin • Fundgrube Englisch

Lösungen: (1) My mother often makes chocolate pudding for dinner. (2) John is always late for school on Mondays. (3) We have never gone to the cinema on Saturday afternoon. (4) It always rains when I am on holiday. (5) Susan is always in a good mood after school. (6) My father was having a bath when the phone rang in the hall. (7) The dog bit the man with a wooden leg who was playing the piano.

Lernjahr 1/2 (Syntax)

C3 Questions, questions, questions

Put the words of the questions in the right order.

(1) your at tennis when lesson the is new club next?

_____

(2) you a of tea like would cup?

_____

(3) the evening you money Dad can give some cinema for this me?

_____

(4) homework your when the teacher check did?

_____

(5) my crashed has computer again why?

_____

(6) which we restaurant going to are?

_____

(7) girl dress is the name of the is wearing that red who what?

_____

(8) homework kitchen is Janet why doing her in the?

_____

(9) Dan are Amanda where and going on this year holiday?

_____

(10) has cleaned Catherine why the house?

_____

© Cornelsen Verlag Scriptor, Berlin • Fundgrube Englisch

🔍 **Lösungen:** (1) When is your next tennis lesson at the new club? (2) Would you like a cup of tea? (3) Can you give me some money for the cinema this evening Dad? (4) When did the teacher check your homework? (5) Why has my computer crashed again? (6) Which restaurant are we going to? (7) What is the name of the girl who is wearing that red dress? (8) Why is Janet doing her homework in the kitchen? (9) Where are Amanda and Dan going on holiday this year? (10) Why has Catherine cleaned the house?

Lernjahr 3/4

A Grammatik

A1 That's not your English book. It's mine.

Fill in the possessive pronouns: mine, yours, his, hers, ours, theirs.

(1) I don't think this is Henry's book. _____ is newer. I think it is Helen's. _____ has a red cover and this book has a red cover, too.

(2) Is this your test? No, it's not _____. I wrote _____ on a piece of lined paper. Is it Jane's? No, Jane has _____.

(3) – Hello, Mr and Mrs Jones. That's a nice car you've got.
 – Oh, it's not _____. It's a rental car. _____ is in the garage. But where is _____?
 – Oh, I sold _____ yesterday. It was too old and expensive to run.

(4) – Oh, look, an accident! Isn't that the Greens' car – the blue one?
 – No, _____ is newer. That is the Smiths' car.
 – No, it isn't. _____ isn't blue, it's red.
 – Oh, yes, you're right.

(5) – Where is Peter, Miss Brown?
 – He went home. He's not feeling well. Now who can take his things home for him?
 – I can, Miss Brown. Is this his school bag?
 – No, that's _____! _____ is over there beside his desk.
 – I thought that was Betty's.
 – No, _____ is red and black. Peter's bag is black and yellow.

(6) – So, Johnny, is this your classroom?
 – No, this is 7b's classroom. – _____ is room 35.

(7) Whose walkman is this?
 – It's _____, Miss.
 – Tommy! It isn't _____. You don't have two walkmen. I can see _____ in your bag.
 – Oh, sorry. No, it isn't _____.

(8) – Paul, can you help me? I'm new here.
 – Sure, Betty, what's your problem?
 – I want to go to the toilet. Is that the girl's toilet over there?
 – No, that is _____. _____ is over there beside the stairs.

Lösungen: (1) his, hers (2) mine, mine, hers (3) ours, ours, yours, mine (4) theirs, theirs (5) mine, his, hers (6) mine (7) mine, yours, yours, mine (8) ours, yours

A2 Relative pronouns

Make one sentence from the two. Only use a relative pronoun where necessary.

(1) The boy answered the teacher's question. He was very clever.

(2) The test was very difficult. I wrote it yesterday.

(3) What was the name of the boy? He sat beside me yesterday.

(4) The books fell on the floor. They were mine.

(5) The school was over 400 years old. My father went to it.

(6) The class was very noisy. It was the worst class in the school.

(7) London is the capital of England. It has a very old underground system.

(8) Columbus discovered America. He was born in Italy in 1451.

(9) My computer has got a sound card. I got my computer for my birthday last year.

(10) My personal stereo is broken. It is called "walkman" in Germany.

© Cornelsen Verlag Scriptor, Berlin • Fundgrube Englisch

Lösungen: (1) The boy who answered the teacher's question was very clever. (2) The test I wrote yesterday was very difficult. (3) What was the name of the boy who sat beside me yesterday? (4) The books which fell in the floor were mine. (5) The school my father went to was over 400 years old. (6) The class which was very noisy was the worst class in the school. (7) London, which is the capital of England, has a very old underground system. (8) Columbus, who discovered America, was born in Italy in 1451. (9) My computer which I got for my birthday last year has got a sound card. (10) My personal stereo which is called "walkman" in German is broken.

A3 More relative pronouns

Put in who, which, *or* that *only where necessary.*

(1) Mrs Peterson gives Sally, her daughter, everything _____ she asks for.

(2) John is the only boy in our class _____ can understand maths.

(3) Why do you always argue with everything _____ your mother says?

(4) I didn't buy the pullover _____ I saw in the shop window because it was too expensive.

(5) The pullover _____ I bought was a lot cheaper.

(6) Who is the girl _____ is talking to Tom?

(7) The pizza _____ we had for dinner yesterday was not very good.

(8) The boy _____ sits next to Janet has red hair.

(9) Have you found the library book _____ you lost?

(10) The boys _____ go to our school are very loud.

(11) I like the boy _____ I see every day in my bus.

(12) If you tell me _____ ice-cream you would like then I can buy some for you.

© Cornelsen Verlag Scriptor, Berlin • Fundgrube Englisch

Lösungen: (1) – (2) who (3) – (4) – (5) – (6) who (7) – (8) who (9) which (10) who (11) who (12) which

A4 Active to passive

Change these active sentences into passive sentences.

(1) In Britain we celebrate Christmas on Christmas Day.

(2) We often decorate the tree at the beginning of December.

(3) We use coloured lights.

(4) We make paper-chains and hang them up over the room.

(5) We sing carols in the streets.

(6) We open our presents on Christmas Day.

(7) We eat turkey on Christmas Day.

(8) We pull Christmas crackers.

(9) We wear the funny hats from the crackers.

(10) We listen to the Queen's speech on TV.

(11) On Boxing Day we visit relatives.

(12) In Germany the people celebrate Christmas on Christmas Eve.

© Cornelsen Verlag Scriptor, Berlin • Fundgrube Englisch

Lösungen: (1) In Britain Christmas is celebrated on Christmas Day. (2) The tree is often decorated at the beginning of December. (3) Coloured lights are used. (4) Paper-chains are made and hung up over the room. (5) Carols are sung in the streets. (6) Our presents are opened on Christmas Day. (7) Turkey is eaten on Christmas Day. (8) Christmas crackers are pulled. (9) The funny hats from the crackers are worn. (10) The Queen's speech is listened to on TV. (11) Relatives are visited on Boxing Day. (12) In Germany Christmas is celebrated on Christmas Eve.

A5 More passive sentences

Complete these passive sentences by putting the verb in brackets in the correct tense.

(1) Cornflakes (invent) in 1898 by William Kellog and today they (buy/eat) by millions of people.

(2) Jeans (invent) in 1850 by Oscar Levi-Strauss and today they (buy/wear) by millions of people.

(3) The coffee filter (invent) in 1908 by Melitta Benz and it (use) by millions of people.

(4) Tomato ketchup (invent) in 1876 by Oscar Heinz and today it (eat) on chips all over the world.

(5) Tonic water (invent) by Jakob Schweppes in 1840 and today it (drink) by millions.

(6) The electric drill (invent) in 1917 by Duncan Black and Alonso Decker and today it (use) in millions of homes.

(7) The rubber tyre (invent) in 1888 by John Dunlop and today they (put) on cars everywhere.

(8) The safety razor (invent) in 1895 by King Camp Gillette and today it (use) by men everywhere.

(9) The ball-point pen (invent) in 1938 by Laszlo Biro and today they (use) in millions of schools.

(10) The sewing machine (invent) in 1851 by Isaac Singer and today they (sell) in shops everywhere.

© Cornelsen Verlag Scriptor, Berlin • Fundgrube Englisch

Lösungen: (1) were invented, are bought, are eaten (2) were invented, are bought, are worn (3) was invented, is used (4) was invented, is eaten (5) was invented, is drunk (6) was invented, is used (7) was invented, are put (8) was invented, is used (9) was invented, are used (10) was invented, are sold

A6 Wrong sentences

There is a mistake in each sentence. Correct it, please.

(1) I have forgot to post the letter.

(2) There is four books on the table.

(3) I want that you learn your vocabulary for tomorrow.

(4) The best team won the football match.

(5) I saw a dog with his master with a long tail in the park.

(6) He couldn't remember nothing.

(7) One of the horses were tired.

(8) The man learnt him to swim.

(9) When started school yesterday?

(10) Do you sport?

(11) Did you went to the cinema yesterday?

(12) The train comes now so I'll have to run.

(13) Do you have got any questions about the homework?

© Cornelsen Verlag Scriptor, Berlin • Fundgrube Englisch

Lösungen: (1) I have **forgotten** to post the letter. (2) There **are** four books on the table. (3) I **want you to** learn your vocabulary for tomorrow. (4) The **better** team won the football match. (5) I saw a **dog with a long tail** with his master in the park. (6) He couldn't remember **anything**. (7) One of the horses **was** tired. (8) The man **taught** him to swim. (9) When **did school start** yesterday? (10) Do you **do** sport? (11) Did you **go** to the cinema yesterday? (12) The train **is coming** now so I'll have to run. (13) Do you **have any** questions about the homework?

A7 Mixed tenses

Put the verb in brackets in the correct tense.

(1) My aunt (give) _____ € 50 to me yesterday afternoon.

(2) What does Tim do after school? He (play) _____ baseball.

(3) Every country (have) _____ good people and bad people.

(4) My uncle (live) _____ in the centre of town.

(5) He (be) _____ very busy all day yesterday so he (not go) _____ to the party.

(6) Look! Bruce (swim) _____ in the cold lake.

(7) The headmaster (give) _____ a speech now.

(8) The dog (run) _____ after the cat when he (run over) _____ by the bus.

(9) I (meet) _____ him at the station yesterday afternoon but I (not recognise) _____ him.

(10) Mary? I (not know) _____ who she is.

(11) George (go) _____ to school every morning by bicycle.

(12) Both my sister and my brother (know) _____ how to bake bread.

(13) They (run) _____ as fast as they could, but they (miss) _____ the bus and (have to) _____ wait for the next one.

(14) I (write) _____ a test last Friday and because I (learn) _____ a lot for it, I think I (get) _____ a good mark.

© Cornelsen Verlag Scriptor, Berlin • Fundgrube Englisch

Lösungen: (1) gave (2) plays (3) has (4) lives (5) was; did not go (6) is swimming (7) is giving (8) was running; was run over (9) met; didn't recognise (10) I don't know (11) goes (12) know (13) ran; missed; had to (14) wrote; had learnt; will get

A8 Possessives

Rewrite the following sentences by replacing the of-forms where possible with 's and s'.

(1) The father of the boy is very tall.

(2) The friends of mother and father are coming to dinner.

(3) They usually travel to school in the car of a friend.

(4) They usually sit in the back of the bus.

(5) There are always some pets of the children in the house.

(6) The teeth of the dog are beginning to fall out.

(7) Tomorrow Peter will get his pocket money of a month.

(8) The house of my grandfather was a big one.

(9) The books of Peter Charles are very interesting.

(10) At the moment he is having a holiday of two months.

Lösungen: (1) boy's father (2) mother and father's friends (3) friend's car (4) no change (5) children's pets (6) the dog's teeth (7) month's pocket money (8) grandfather's house (9) Peter Charles' books (10) a two month holiday

A9 -ed-ending or -ing-ending?

Decide if you need an adjective or a participle in these sentences.

(1) My dad is leaving his job. He says he's _____ with his present job. He wants something more _____ . (boring/bored; stimulating/stimulated)

(2) Hey, my mum's job's _____ too, but that's no reason to leave. It's not easy to find a new job. (boring/bored)

I think he's leaving for another reason. He didn't get the promotion you told me about and perhaps he's really _____. (disappointing/disappointed)

(3) Yes, that's true. He works hard and his boss is very _____ with his work, so he deserves promotion. (satisfying/satisfied)

(4) Well I hope he changes his mind. It's difficult to find _____ work with a good salary. (satisfied/satisfying)

(5) How about your friend Kate? I hear that she won a prize for her school project. She must be _____. (thrilling/thrilled)

(6) Yes, I'm really happy for her. She worked so hard. It's a photography project and it's full of _____ photos. (fascinating/fascinated)

(7) You know, she invited me to see the photo exhibition. I planned to go, but when the day came, I completely forgot. It was so _____. (embarrassing/embarrassed)

(8) Yes, she said you were really _____ when she mentioned it. (surprising/surprised)

(9) By the way, there's a documentary on TV this evening about climate change, and some of its predictions are quite _____. (terrifying/terrified)

(10) Climate change! Future disasters! It sounds very _____. (depressing/depressed)

(11) Well I'm very _____ in that type of documentary. (interesting/interested)

(12) When I come home, I just want to relax because I find school _____ _____ . (exhausting/exhausted)

(13) Me, too, but I find these things quite _____. (fascinating/ fascinated)

(14) I think you're like those people who go to see horror movies. You love to be _____. You find it very exciting. (frightening/frightened)

(15) You're right. I'm _____ to see that you know me so well. (pleasing/ pleased)

© Cornelsen Verlag Scriptor, Berlin • Fundgrube Englisch

Lösungen: (1) bored; stimulating (2) boring; disappointed (3) satisfied/ satisfying (4) satisfying (5) thrilled (6) fascinating (7) embarrassing (8) surprised (9) terrifying (10) depressing (11) interested (12) exhausting (13) fascinating (14) frightened (15) pleased

A10 The right place for the word

Mark the right place for the adverbs with an arrow.

(1) We went to the cinema (yesterday).

(2) We go to the cinema (often).

(3) I will go to the cinema (next Tuesday).

(4) They go to the cinema (never).

(5) She goes to the cinema (every Sunday).

(6) I am at the cinema (seldom).

(7) I don't go to the cinema (every week).

(8) Francis does not go to the cinema (always).

(9) Do you go to the cinema (frequently)?

(10) My friends didn't go to the cinema (on Friday).

© Cornelsen Verlag Scriptor, Berlin • Fundgrube Englisch

Lösungen: (1) letztes Wort (erstes, abgetrennt mit Komma, nur bei besonderer Betonungsabsicht), (2) zweites Wort (3) vorletztes und letztes Wort (4) zweites Wort (5) vorletztes und letztes Wort (6) drittes Wort (7) vorletztes und letztes Wort (8) viertes Wort (9) entweder drittes oder letztes Wort (10) vorletztes und letztes Wort

B Wortschatz

B1 Find the opposites

Write down the opposites (antonyms) of these words. Use the following words:

answer, close, come, dirty, early, found, future, giant, leave, lies, lose, morning, nowhere, rich, sell, senior, strange, terrible, top, wet

(1) arrive _____   (2) wonderful _____

(3) evening _____   (4) lost _____

(5) past _____   (6) win _____

(7) buy _____   (8) open _____

(9) everywhere _____   (10) clean _____

(11) junior _____   (12) poor _____

(13) go _____   (14) dry _____

(15) late _____   (16) truth _____

(17) question _____   (18) dwarf _____

(19) familiar _____   (20) bottom _____

© Cornelsen Verlag Scriptor, Berlin • Fundgrube Englisch

Lösungen: (1) leave (2) terrible (3) morning (4) found (5) future (6) lose (7) sell (8) close (9) nowhere (10) dirty (11) senior (12) rich (13) come (14) wet (15) early (16) lies (17) answer (18) giant (19) strange (20) top

Lernjahr 3/4 (Wortschatz)

B2 Words of similar meaning

Find a word of similar meaning (synonym) for each word in the list.

List: afraid, begin, drop, funny, home, inside, large, leave, loud, new, nice, outside, popular, quiet, sad, terrible

(1) kind _____   (2) start _____

(3) enormous _____ (4) exterior _____

(5) interior _____ (6) fall _____

(7) well-liked _____ (8) unhappy _____

(9) frightened _____ (10) modern _____

(11) noisy _____   (12) strange _____

(13) house _____   (14) bad _____

(15) peaceful _____ (16) go away _____

© Cornelsen Verlag Scriptor, Berlin • Fundgrube Englisch

Lösungen: (1) nice (2) begin (3) large (4) outside (5) inside (6) drop (7) popular (8) sad (9) afraid (10) new (11) loud (12) funny (13) home (14) terrible (15) quiet (16) leave

B3 Can you tell me the way to the bus-station, please?

Underline the right preposition.

− Can you tell me the way (1) for/into/to the bus-station, please?

− Of course. It's (2) in/next to/on Surrey Street. Now you go (3) along/in/to this road until you come (4) at/through/to the second traffic lights. (5) At/In/Under those lights you must turn left (6) at/in/into Norfolk Street. Walk (7) along/in/over Norfolk Street (8) from/for/of about a hundred yards. Then go (9) along/over/ through the bridge and straight (10) down/in/through the park. Go out (11) for/ from/of the park (12) over/through/under the big gate and you are (13) in/into/on Olga Road. Go right (14) down/into/to Olga Road (15) at/from/to the end. You'll see a big supermarket (16) at/on/onto your right. The supermarket is (17) along/ in/on the corner of Olga Road and Surrey Street. Go straight (18) for/into/up Surrey Street and the bus-station is (19) at/down/on the right. Okay?

− Fine. Thank you very much (20) from/for/of your help.

© Cornelsen Verlag Scriptor, Berlin • Fundgrube Englisch

Lösungen: (1) to (2) in (3) along (4) to (5) At (6) into (7) along (8) for (9) over (10) through (11) of (12) through (13) in (14) down (15) to (16) on (17) on (18) up (19) on (20) for

B4 Choosing the best word

Look at the alternatives and underline the preferred word. Be careful. Sometimes the other alternatives are completely wrong, and sometimes they are possible but not as good as the preferred one.

(1) There was a big/great crowd/mass of people hearing/listening to the commentators/speakers at the political meeting/rally in Hyde Park.

(2) When I arrive/get home, I eat/have lunch and then I do/make my homework. When I am ready with/have finished my homework, my mum allows me to do/lets me do/makes me do whatever/whichever I like/want.

(3) (teacher talking to class) Please don't forget to bring/take your exam books home and have/let/make them signed by your parents.

(4) Can you borrow/lend me some money, please?

(5) You can't miss/overlook our house. It's the one with the high/tall hedge and the high/tall trees in the garden.

(6) Mary is the captain/head/leader of the basketball team.

(7) Don't be so loud/noisy.

(8) I'm nervous. I am doing/taking/writing an important exam/test tomorrow.

(9) Must we travel altogether/all together, or can we go alone/separately?

(10) Jack is very lazy. He never gets up/stands up before 10.

(11) We always buy/purchase our food at a supermarket. We find it more economic/economical than going to a corner shop/small shop.

(12) Come on, Sally. You've been looking at/watching TV all afternoon. Let's go for/make a walk.

(13) I can't like/stand Mr Grubb. He's such a nasty little/small man.

(14) Can you say/tell me the road/way to the station, please? I'm a foreigner/stranger here.

(15) "Should we have a barbecue/grill at the weekend?" "Well, I mean/think we should look/see what the weather's like."

(16) Where do you hold/keep/preserve the dog food?

(17) What/Which road/street do I need/take to drive/get from Bristol to Gloucester?

(18) Look at/See that funny/humourous wife/woman! She's carrying/wearing a frightful/frightening hat.

© Cornelsen Verlag Scriptor, Berlin • Fundgrube Englisch

Lösungen: (1) big, crowd, listening to, speakers, political rally (2) get, have, do, have finished, lets me do, whatever, like (3) take, have (4) lend (5) miss, high, tall (6) captain (7) noisy (8) taking, exam (9) all together, separately (10) gets up (11) buy, more economical, corner shop (12) watching, go for (13) stand, little (14) tell, way, stranger (15) barbecue, think, see (16) keep (17) Which, road, take, get (18) Look at, funny, woman, wearing, frightful

C Syntax (*word order*)

C1 Relative clauses

Put the parts of these relative clauses in the right place.

(1) Peter is in our football team with whom I go to school.

(2) Your information is very helpful for which I am very glad.

(3) The owner of the restaurant gave us our money back to whom we complained.

(4) John lives in Main Street to whose party we are invited.

(5) Mum's cooking is great which everybody likes.

(6) The oldest man was ninety eight who lived in our town.

(7) Mr Brown knows my father who is my maths teacher.

(8) The cat sat on the chair which was a black one.

(9) Mum's birthday is tomorrow which I almost forgot.

(10) In February we will go on holiday which is always the shortest month.

(11) My birthday is in July which was on a Monday last year.

(12) John's brother plays cricket who studies at Cambridge.

© Cornelsen Verlag Scriptor, Berlin • Fundgrube Englisch

Lösungen: (1) Peter, with whom I go to school, is in our football team (2) Your information, for which I am very glad, is very helpful. (3) The owner of the restaurant, to whom we complained, gave us our money back. (4) John, to whose party we are invited, lives in Main Street. (5) Mum's cooking, which everybody likes, is great. (6) The oldest man, who lived in our town, was ninety eight. (7) Mr Brown, who is my maths teacher, knows my father. (8) The cat, which was a black one, sat on the chair. (9) Mum's birthday, which I almost forgot, is tomorrow. (10) In February, which is always the shortest month, we will go on holiday. (11) My birthday, which was on a Monday last year, is in July. (12) John's brother, who studies at Cambridge, plays cricket.

C2 Subordinate clauses

Complete the sentences with the words in brackets. Place time expressions at the end of the sentences.

(1) My mother is very fit because (every week/goes/she to the gym)

_____

(2) I think (likes/Bob/you)

_____

(3) I can't talk to you because (time/do not have/I/now)

_____

(4) Look at that rain! We are really happy that (at home/did not leave/we/our umbrella)

_____

(5) We will all miss you when (to Berlin/next month/move/you)

_____

(6) The boys don't remember where (after the game/left/the football/they)

_____

(7) Ring me tonight if (have/you/maths homework/a problem/your/with)

_____

(8) If she wants to improve her English I wonder why (her holiday/does not spend/she/in England)

_____

(9) They told him that (wanted to play/in the garden/they/football)

_____

(10) He was reading the paper while (she/in the garden/was working)

_____

© Cornelsen Verlag Scriptor, Berlin • Fundgrube Englisch

Lösungen: (1) ... she goes to the gym every week. (2) ... Bob likes you. (3) ... I do not have time now. (4) ... we did not leave our umbrella at home. (5) ... you move to Berlin next month. (6) ... they left the football after the game. (7) ... you have a problem with your maths homework. (8) ... she does not spend her holiday in England. (9) ... they wanted to play football in the garden. (10) ... she was working in the garden.

Lernjahr 5/6

A Grammatik

A1 Connectors

Join the sentences with a word from the list.

List: although, and, but, if, or, so, when

(1) They rushed the lorry driver to hospital. He died in the helicopter.

(2) It was raining. The taxi arrived.

(3) You can go out. You must promise to be back before 11 o'clock.

(4) We saw the accident. We were waiting for a bus.

(5) Jim is mad about snooker. He travels to games all over Britain.

(6) Tom will never be a top tennis player. He always tries very hard.

(7) Jill likes dancing. She often goes to the disco.

(8) I always read my horoscope. I don't believe in it.

(9) I hide. I see Barbara coming.

(10) We didn't win the match. We trained twice a week.

© Cornelsen Verlag Scriptor, Berlin • Fundgrube Englisch

Lösungen: (1) They rushed the lorry driver to hospital, but he died in the helicopter. (2) It was raining when the taxi arrived. (3) You can go out if you promise to be back before 11 o'clock./You can go out, but you must promise to be back before 11 o'clock. (4) We saw the accident when we were waiting for the bus. (5) Jim is mad about snooker and/,so he travels to games all over Britain. (6) Tom will never be a top tennis player although he tries very hard./Tom will never be a top tennis player, but he tries very hard. (7) Jill likes dancing and she often goes to the disco./Jill likes dancing, so she often goes to the disco. (8) I always read my horoscope, although I don't believe in it. (9) I hide when I see Barbara coming. (10) We didn't win the match although we trained twice a week.

A2 Zero article

Use the definite article only when necessary. Put in xxx when this is not the case.

Women in Indian Society

Is it right that _____ (1) rich, aid-giving countries of _____ (2) industrialised world use their economic power to force _____ (3) poor countries of _____ (4) developing world to introduce _____ (5) social reform?

Before you answer 'no' to this question, look at _____ (6) example of India or, better, at _____ (7) example of _____ (8) status of _____ (9) women in _____ (10) Indian society. Even _____ (11) country's very best friends cannot deny that _____ (12) sexist discrimination and _____ (13) oppression in India is an international scandal. Particularly in _____ (14) rural communities, _____ (15) women are treated more like _____ (16) domestic animals than _____ (17) human-beings. They live a life of _____ (18) drudgery (*Plackerei*) and _____ (19) toil (*Schwerstarbeit*) wholly under _____ (20) control of _____ (21) men.

© Cornelsen Verlag Scriptor, Berlin • Fundgrube Englisch

Lösungen: (1) the (2) the (3) xxx (4) the (5) xxx (6) the (7) the (8) the (9) xxx (10) xxx (11) the (12) xxx (13) xxx (14) xxx (15) xxx (16) xxx (17) xxx (18) xxx (19) xxx (20) the (21) xxx

(xxx = zero article)

A3 Present perfect, present perfect progressive or simple past?

Put the verb into the present perfect, the present perfect progressive or the simple past.

(1) **A:** How long (you /work) _____ (1) as a bricklayer?
B: Well, I (start) _____ (2) in 1998 and I (do) _____ (3) the job ever since.

(2) **A:** I (not see) _____ (1) the paper anywhere. (it/be delivered) _____ (2) yet?
B: No, and it (arrive) _____ (3) very late yesterday as well.

(3) **A:** The garage (still + not finish) _____ (1) my car. Yesterday they (tell) _____ (2) me that it just (need) _____ (3) a new battery.
B: Well, perhaps they (find) _____ (4) something else wrong with it when they (start) _____ (5) work on it.

(4) Julie (clean) _____ (1) the house for hours and she (not have) _____ (2) a rest all day.

(5) **A:** What (you/do) _____ (1) all morning?
B: Well, first I (write) _____ (2) to my sister, then I (make) _____ (3) a few phone calls and after that I (go) _____ (4) shopping.

(6) **Enquirer:** How many accidents (your pupils/have) _____
_____ (1) while learning to drive, Mr Sutton?
Sutton: Well, we (never have) _____ (2) an accident in the 15 years that I (teach) _____ (3) pupils to drive, but I admit that we (have) _____ (4) a number of near-misses in that time.

© Cornelsen Verlag Scriptor, Berlin • Fundgrube Englisch

Lösungen: (1) 1 have you been working, 2 started, 3 have been doing (2) 1 have not seen, 2 Has it been delivered, 3 arrived (3) 1 has still not finished, 2 told, 3 needed, 4 found, 5 started (4) 1 has been cleaning, 2 has not had (5) 1 have you been doing, 2 wrote, 3 made, 4 went (6) 1 have your pupils had, 2 have never had, 3 have been teaching, 4 have had

A4 Mixed tenses

Put the verb in brackets in the correct tense.

(1) I only hope there (not be) _____ (1) too much traffic on the motorway tomorrow because our plane (take off) _____ (2) at eight.

(2) Tom (just + buy) _____ (1) a camcorder. (you/see) _____ (2) it? It (be) ___ (3) great!

(3) The immigration officer who (check) _____ (1) passengers' passports (look) _____ (2) at Ranjit's for a very long time before he (hand) _____ (3) it back to him. It (be) ___ (4) very unfair. It (be) ___ (5) just because he (have) _____ (6) black hair and brown eyes.

(4) While I (fetch) _____ (1) some water to clean my car, somebody (steal) _____ (2) it. Now the insurance company (refuse) _____ (3) to pay because I (leave) _____ (4) the key in the ignition.

(5) The Browns (come) _____ (1) to Sheringham on holiday ever since 1970. In that time they (see) _____ (2) the town change so much that you (no longer + can recognise) _____ (3) it for what it once (be) ___ (4). It (change) _____ (5) into Las Vegas!

(6) Poor Jack (buy) _____ (1) a new surfboard last summer but he (never + be able to use) _____ (2) it. The winds (be) _____ (3) so strong when he (be) _____ (4) on holiday in Brittany last year that he (can + not surf) _____ (5) once. Now he (try) _____ (6) to sell it on ebay.

(7) **Pat:** Hi, Josh. What (you/do) _____ (1)?
Josh: Oh, hello, Pat. I (pack) _____ (2) my suitcase. We (go) _____ (3) on holiday in the morning.
Pat: Really? Where (you/go) _____ (4) to?
Josh: We (go) _____ (5) to my aunt's. She (live) _____ (6) in Jersey so we always (go) ___ (7) there for a month in the summer.

(8) While dad (put) _____ (1) petrol in the car before the family (start) _____ (2) their holiday journey, mum (go) _____ (3) into the petrol station to buy some magazines. Josie (go) _____ (4) with her. She (want) _____ (5) to buy a map because she (not know) _____ (6) where Bergen aan Zee (be) ___ (7).

© Cornelsen Verlag Scriptor, Berlin • Fundgrube Englisch

🔎 **Lösungen:** (1) 1 won't be, 2 takes off (2) 1 has just bought, 2 Have you seen, 3 is (3) 1 was checking, 2 looked, 3 handed, 4 is, 5 is, 6 has (4) 1 was fetching, 2 stole, 3 is refusing, 4 had left (5) 1 have been coming, 2 have seen, 3 can no longer recognise, 4 was, 5 has changed (6) 1 bought, 2 has never been able to use, 3 were, 4 was, 5 couldn't surf, 6 is trying (7) 1 are you doing, 2 am packing, 3 are going, 4 are you going, 5 are going, 6 lives, 7 go (8) 1 was putting, 2 started, 3 went, 4 went, 5 wanted, 6 didn't know, 7 is

A8 Modals

Fill in the space in the sentences with a suitable modal. Be careful that you choose the correct tense.

(1) You _____ (1) forget to fill up the car with petrol and check the oil. This is the last petrol station before the border.

(2) John realised that he was on the wrong train but he _____ (1) wait until Glasgow before he _____ (2) get off. It didn't stop before then.

(3) When you go walking in the hills in Scotland you _____ (1) take a rain jacket, even in summer because the weather _____ (2) change very quickly.

(4) You _____ (1) take a chair with you to the beach at Brighton. You _____ (2) get one there. But you _____ (3) pay. The chairs are not free.

(5) Before they built that new block of flats you _____ see (1) the church from my bedroom window. Now you _____ (2) see anything except the flats!

(6) **A:** _____ (1) I change trains to get from Manchester to London?

B: No, Madam. It's direct so you _____ (2) change. But you _____ (3) book a seat as the trains are always full on Fridays.

© Cornelsen Verlag Scriptor, Berlin • Fundgrube Englisch

🔎 **Lösungen:** (1) mustn't (2) 1 had to, 2 could (3) 1 should, 2 can (4) 1 needn't, 2 can, 3 have to (5) 1 could, 2 cannot (6) 1 Must, 2 don't have to, 3 should

A9 The Passive

Make passive sentences using the verbs in the brackets.

(1) The government says that 20 new hospitals (build) _____ _____ in the next ten years. The old hospital cannot cope any more.

(2) The pyramids (build) _____ by thousands of slaves.

(3) This newspaper (read) _____ by millions of people every day.

(4) The company (sell) _____ (1) to a French firm in 1994 and several hundred people (sack) _____ (2) by the new owners.

(5) Diamonds (find) _____ (1) mainly in South Africa, but big deposits (also + discover) _____ (2) in Russia.

(6) Gold (find) _____ (1) in California in 1849 and it started what (come + call) _____ (2) the 'Great Gold Rush'.

(7) Nowadays, a lot of newspapers and magazines (sell) _____ in supermarkets.

(8) Snooker and darts (watch) _____ (1) by millions of viewers in Britain and these sports (now + transmit) _____ _____ (2) to all parts of the world by satellite TV.

(9) It (estimate) _____ (1) that last week's championship matches (see) _____ (2) by 10 million people in Britain alone.

(10) Is it true that a new gold mine (just/discover) _____ _____ in Canada?

(11) A new hospital (open) _____ (1) by Prince Charles yesterday but the builders (disappoint) _____ (2) by the small crowd of onlookers. They say that their next hospital (open) _____ _____ (3) by a pop star.

(12) Fifty people (already + fire) _____ (1) by the new production manager and they (likely + follow) _____ _____ (2) by many more.

(13) Many convicts (send) _____ (1) to Georgia in America by the British until the colonies (lose) _____ (2) in the War of Independence. After that, new convicts' colonies (must set up) _____ _____ (3) in New South Wales in Australia.

(14) Over ten thousand people (kill) _____ since the war started.

Lösungen: (1) will have to be built (2) were built (3) is read (4) 1 was sold, 2 were sacked (5) 1 are found, 2 have also been discovered (6) 1 was found, 2 came to be called (7) are sold (8) 1 are watched, 2 are now being transmitted (9) 1 is estimated, 2 were seen (10) has just been discovered (11) 1 was opened, 2 were disappointed, 3 will be opened (12) 1 have already been fired, 2 are likely to be followed (13) 1 were sent, 2 were lost, 3 had to be set up (14) have been killed

A10 If Christopher Columbus ...

Let's think what the world would be like if history was different.
First, join up the two parts of the if-sentences that belong together and then put the verbs into the correct tense. Use an exercisebook.

(1) If Amerigo Vespucci (never be) to America,
(2) If Bell (not invent) the telephone,
(3) If France (not give) America the Statue of Liberty in 1884,
(4) If Harold Godwinson (win) the Battle of Hastings,
(5) If John Lennon (not be killed),
(6) If the Chinese communists (not put down) the democracy movement,
(7) If the snake (not give) Eve an apple,
(8) Some say that if atomic bombs (not be used) against Japan,

– we (be able + see) it in France today.
– she and Adam (not have to + leave) Paradise.
– he (write) a lot of new songs.
– we (not be able to + speak) to people in the USA for years.
– it (not be called) 'America'.
– the war in Asia (last) much longer.
– the English language (develop) quite differently.
– China (be) the world's biggest democracy today.

© Cornelsen Verlag Scriptor, Berlin • Fundgrube Englisch

Lösungen: (1) If Amerigo Vespucci had never been to America, it would not have been called 'America'. (2) If Bell had not invented the telephone, we would not have been able to speak to people in the USA for years. (3) If France had not given America the Statue of Liberty in 1884, we would have been able to see it in France today. (4) If Harold Godwinson had won the Battle of Hastings, the English language would have developed very differently. (5) If John Lennon had not been killed, he would have written a lot of new songs. (6) If the Chinese Communists had not put down the democracy movement, China would have been the world's biggest democracy today. (7) If the snake had not given Eve an apple, she and Adam would not have had to leave Paradise. (8) Some say that if atomic bombs not been used against Japan, the war in Asia would have lasted much longer.

A11 The Strike

Some of the workers at ABC Chemicals Ltd have gone on strike. Jim Bradley, a manager, is talking to Ben Cobham, a striker.

Look at the parts of if-sentences given below, and use the words in brackets to complete them. Note that you must add some other words such as articles and prepositions.

Jim: This strike is mad. If you had listened to me, we (arrive/fair agreement) _____ (1).

Ben: Nonsense. If you really want to end the strike, you (just + have to pay/better wages) _____ (2).

Jim: But we can't afford it, Ben. The fact is that if we did that, we (go) _____ (3) bankrupt and then nobody (have/job) _____ (4). We can only pay higher wages if there (be/big improvent/productivity) _____ _____ (5) to cover the additional costs.

Ben: That's not fair, Jim. If you were honest, you (agree/me) _____ _____ (6) that (productivity/improve) _____ _____ (7) over the last two years.

Jim: But our material costs and taxes have risen, too, Ben. If they hadn't gone up, the firm (be able to + pay) _____ (8) better wages long ago.

Ben: I've heard that old story a hundred times, Jim. If things go well, it (be/because/ good management) _____ (9), but if they go badly, it (be/fault/workers) _____ (10).

Jim: I'm sorry, Ben. If you can't recognise the facts, there (be/no point/my talking/ you) _____ (11).

© Cornelsen Verlag Scriptor, Berlin • Fundgrube Englisch

Lösungen: (1) would have arrived at a fair agreement (2) will just have to pay better wages (3) would go (4) would have a job (5) is a big improvement in productivity (6) would agree with me (7) productivity has improved (8) would have been able to pay (9) is because of good management (10) is the fault of the workers (11) is no point in my talking to you

A12 Question tags

Put in the missing question tag.

(1) You collect old cars, _____ ?

(2) That's a Harley-Davidson motorbike, _____ ?

(3) She shouldn't be so rude, _____ ?

(4) He was a teacher at your last school, _____ ?

(5) I'm not very good at this, _____ ?

(6) You haven't seen Tom today, _____ ?

(7) There isn't anybody at home, _____ ?

(8) Let's go to the movies tonight, _____ ?

(9) You still work for Carr & Co, _____ ?

(10) I can't be expected to do everything, _____ ?

(11) You don't think he's the thief, _____ ?

(12) Things aren't always what they seem, _____ ?

(13) You'll have time to the shopping, _____ ?

(14) You haven't been too well lately, _____ ?

(15) There aren't many people here tonight, _____ ?

© Cornelsen Verlag Scriptor, Berlin • Fundgrube Englisch

Lösungen: (1) don't you? (2) isn't it? (3) should she? (4) wasn't he? (5) am I? (6) have you? (7) is there? (8) shall we? (9) don't you? (10) can I? (11) do you? (12) are they? (13) won't you? (14) have you? (15) are there?

A13 Gerund or infinitive?

Translate these sentences. Use either a gerund or an infinitive, as necessary.

(1) Links fahren ist nicht schwer. → ***Driving on the left is not difficult.***

(2) Es ist nicht schwierig, links zu fahren.

(3) Museen zu besichtigen ist für mich im Urlaub sehr wichtig.

(4) Zu viele Zigaretten nach England mitzunehmen kann teuer sein.

(5) Mein Vater liebt es, in guten Restaurants zu essen.

(6) Im Grand Canyon hielt er das Auto jeweils nach fünf Kilometern an, um Fotos von den Sehenswürdigkeiten zu machen.

(7) Er fährt nicht gern durch Tunnel, weil er Angst vor dem unterirdischen Fahren hat.

(8) Sie hörte nicht auf, Postkarten aus Singapore zu schreiben. Am Schluss hatte sie 106 Postkarten geschrieben.

(9) Es ist nicht mehr gefährlich, in Nordirland zu leben.

(10) Ich hasse es, Hosen zu kaufen. Ich habe große Schwierigkeiten, eine zu finden, die ich mag.

© Cornelsen Verlag Scriptor, Berlin • Fundgrube Englisch

Lösungen: (2) It is not difficult to drive on the left. (3) Visiting museums is very important for me on holiday. (4) Taking too many cigarettes into England can be expensive. (5) My father loves eating in good restaurants. (6) In the Grand Canyon he stopped the car every five kilometres to take photos of the sights. (7) He doesn't like driving through tunnels because he is frightened of travelling underground. (8) She didn't stop writing postcards from Singapore. In the end she had written 106 postcards. (9) It is no longer dangerous to live in Northern Ireland. (10) I hate buying trousers. I have great difficulty finding ones that I like.

A14 Writing sentences with sentence elements

Use these elements to make sentences. The elements are in the right order, but you must put the verbs, nouns and pronouns in the right form, and also put in the missing articles, prepositions, etc., as necessary.

(1) Mr Green/work/Carr & Co, but/lose/job/yesterday/so now/he/look for/ work. →
Mr Green worked for Carr & Co but he lost his job yesterday so now he is looking for work.

(2) **A:** that/poor old woman/wait/bus/over/hour.

B: why/ you + give/her/lift/home? I/think/she/live/little house/end/your street.

(3) we/live/my parents/moment/(but)/hope/have/house/our own/end/year.

(4) by/time/Sally/arrive/party, everything/already + be eaten/(and)/there be/only/ coke/drink.

(5) thousands/book/be stolen/public libraries/each year/(but)/nobody/seem/ treat/people/(who)/ take/them/(as)/criminal.

(6) it/be/big mistake/buy/this old house. repairs/cost/much money/moment/ (that)/we/not have/penny/spend/anything else.

© Cornelsen Verlag Scriptor, Berlin • Fundgrube Englisch

Lösungen: (2) A: That poor old woman has been waiting for the bus for over an hour. B: Why don't you give her a lift home? I think she lives in the little house at the end of your street. (3) We are living with my parents at the moment, but we hope to have a house of our own by the end of the year. (4) By the time Sally arrived at the party, everything had already been eaten, and there was only coke to drink. (5) Thousands of books are stolen from public libraries each year but nobody seems to treat the people who take them as criminals. (6) It was a big mistake to buy this old house. The repairs are costing so much money at the moment that we don't have a penny to spend on anything else.

B Wortschatz

B1 Does automation destroy or create jobs?

Complete the text with words or expressions from the box.

> taken over — assembly-line operatives — unskilled workers — humans — jobs — automation — different — software programmers — productivity — workers — factory — problem — companies — robots

Many workers are afraid of _____ (1) because they think that they will lose their _____ (2). But the _____ (3) is not that simple. In fact, automation has made it possible for _____ (4) to increase _____ (5) so much that they need more, not less, _____ (6).

In Japan, the home of the fully automated _____ (7), managers have found that even the most modern _____ (8) need a lot of help from _____ (9).

But the human workers themselves are _____ (10). Most are highly-trained _____ (11) and computer technicians. There are not many jobs for _____ (12) or even for traditional _____ (13) any more. Their jobs have indeed been _____ (14) by robots.

Lösungen: (1) automation (2) jobs (3) problem (4) companies (5) productivity (6) workers (7) factory (8) robots (9) humans (10) different (11) software programmers (12) unskilled workers (13) assembly-line operatives (14) taken over

B2 Tourist pollution

Complete the text. The first letter of the missing word will help you to do this.

Every country likes to attract as many tourists as p_____ (1) In Britain, for e_____ (2), tourism is the country's second biggest i_____ (3) But unfortunately g_____ (4) are better at counting the m_____ (5) that the tourists spend than counting up the cost of the d_____ (6) that the feet of m_____ (7) of tourists do. Westminster Abbey in L_____ (8) is just one of h_____ (9) of examples in B_____ (10) alone. The Abbey is nearly 1000 y_____ (11) old. It has survived bombing during the Second World W___ (12) and the effects of air p_____ (13), but the question now is whether it can s_____ (14) the hundreds of thousands of tourists that v_____ (15) it during the tourist s_____ (16) each summer. The answer to this q_____ (17) is 'No, it can't!'. The same goes for thousands of historic b_____ (18) all over the w_____ (19). Soon we may have to restrict the number of p_____ (20) visiting some sites or even c_____ (21) them to the public altogether.

© Cornelsen Verlag Scriptor, Berlin • Fundgrube Englisch

Lösungen: (1) possible (2) example (3) industry (4) governments (5) money (6) damage (7) millions (8) London (9) hundreds (10) Britain (11) years (12) War (13) pollution (14) survive (15) visit (16) season (17) question (18) buildings (19) world (20) people (21) close

B3 Antonyms

Find antonyms *(words of opposite meaning)* for the following words. You can use your dictionary if necessary.

(1)	aggressive	peaceful	(2)	ashamed	_____
(3)	conscientious	_____	(4)	attractive	_____
(5)	sad	_____	(6)	kind	_____
(7)	disappointed	_____	(8)	fed up	_____
(9)	cheeky	_____	(10)	helpful	_____
(11)	quiet	_____	(12)	self-confident	_____
(13)	tolerant	_____	(14)	understanding	_____
(15)	strong	_____	(16)	sympathetic	_____
(17)	fit	_____	(18)	clumsy	_____
(19)	greedy	_____	(20)	miserly	_____

© Cornelsen Verlag Scriptor, Berlin • Fundgrube Englisch

Lösungen: (2) proud (3) lazy (4) unattractive, repellent (5) happy (6) cruel (7) satisfied (8) satisfied (9) polite (10) unhelpful (11) loud (12) diffident (13) intolerant (14) dismissive (15) weak (16) unsympathetic (17) unhealthy, out of condition (18) skilful, elegant (19) generous (20) generous

B4 Synonyms

Find synonyms *(word of similar meaning)* for the following words. You can use a dictionary if necessary.

(1)	interested	keen	(2)	reliable	_____
(3)	skilful	_____	(4)	aggressive	_____
(5)	afraid	_____	(6)	cheerful	_____
(7)	satisfied	_____	(8)	angry	_____
(9)	insulting	_____	(10)	co-operative	_____
(11)	good-looking	_____	(12)	sociable	_____
(13)	tolerant	_____	(14)	isolated	_____
(15)	imaginative	_____			

© Cornelsen Verlag Scriptor, Berlin • Fundgrube Englisch

Lösungen: (1) keen, involved (2) trustworthy (3) clever (4) violent (5) frightened (6) happy, merry (7) pleased (8) irritated, furious (9) rude, cheeky (10) helpful (11) handsome (12) friendly, gregarious (13) understanding, sympathetic (14) lonely (15) creative

B5 Verb forms

Write down the verb forms of theses nouns.

(1) analyst   (to) *analyse*

(2) circulation   (to) _____

(3) collection   (to) _____

(4) controller   (to) _____

(5) delivery   (to) _____

(6) development   (to) _____

(7) disappointment   (to) _____

(8) enjoyment   (to) _____

(9) information   (to) _____

(10) intention   (to) _____

(11) invention   (to) _____

(12) laughter   (to) _____

(13) organization   (to) _____

(14) printer   (to) _____

(15) repair   (to) _____

(16) report   (to) _____

(17) solution   (to) _____

(18) success   (to) _____

(19) thought   (to) _____

(20) transmission   (to) _____

© Cornelsen Verlag Scriptor, Berlin • Fundgrube Englisch

Lösungen: (2) circulate (3) collect (4) control (5) deliver (6) develop (7) disappoint (8) enjoy (9) inform (10) intend (11) invent (12) laugh (13) organize (14) print (15) repair (16) report (17) solve (18) succeed (19) think (20) transmit

Lernjahr 5/6 (Wortschatz)

B6 Books, books, books

Use the material in the box to say which book or other publication you need.

> a maintenance manual
> a history book
> an encyclopedia
> a dictionary
> a novel
> a map
> instructions for use
> a calendar
> a diary
> a newspaper
> an autobiography
> a phone book
> a catalogue
> a timetable
> a street plan

You want to find information on or read about ...

(1) ... a person's telephone number. _____
(2) ... the meaning of a word. _____
(3) ... a person's life story written by himself or herself. _____
(4) ... how to operate (e.g.) a camcorder. _____
(5) ... how to repair (e.g.) a motorbike. _____
(6) ... the arrival/departure time of a train. _____
(7) ... a longer fictional story. _____
(8) ... the exact position of a place in a town. _____
(9) ... reports and comments about current events. _____
(10) ... the day and date of a month. _____
(11) ... a record of personal daily happenings. _____
(12) ... a list of products with order numbers/prices. _____
(13) ... the position of a place in a country. _____
(14) ... shorter articles on anything and everything. _____
(15) ... the past. _____

© Cornelsen Verlag Scriptor, Berlin • Fundgrube Englisch

Lösungen: (1) a phone book (2) a dictionary (3) an autobiography (4) instructions for use (5) a maintenance manual (6) a timetable (7) a novel (8) a street plan (9) a newspaper (10) a calendar (11) a diary (12) a catalogue (13) a map (14) an encyclopedia (15) a history book

C Syntax (*word order*)

a) Use numbers to put the jumbled words into the correct order.

(1) [6] developed [5] first [7] in China [2] mass-production [3] methods [1] Modern [4] were.

(2) [ ] as early as [ ] clothing [ ] There [ ] the 16th century [ ] they [ ] to produce [ ] used [ ] were.

(3) [ ] adapted [ ] by [ ] car [ ] Henry Ford [ ] mass-produced [ ] the first [ ] The technique [ ] to build [ ] was.

(4) [ ] an assembly-line [ ] cars [ ] designed [ ] Ford [ ] on which [ ] put together [ ] the [ ] were.

(5) [ ] along it [ ] assembly-line [ ] but [ ] did not [ ] first [ ] moved [ ] move itself [ ] The [ ] workers.

(6) [ ] an assembly-line [ ] designing [ ] Ford [ ] groups of workers [ ] had [ ] of [ ] moved [ ] past [ ] slowly [ ] the idea [ ] Then [ ] which.

(7) [ ] assembly-line [ ] cars [ ] greatly [ ] increased [ ] moving [ ] per day [ ] produced [ ] The [ ] the number [ ] of.

(8) [ ] by humans [ ] by robots [ ] car plants [ ] done [ ] In [ ] is done [ ] modern [ ] once [ ] some of [ ] the work.

© Cornelsen Verlag Scriptor, Berlin • Fundgrube Englisch

Lösungen a):

(2) [7] as early as [6] clothing [1] There [8] the 16th century [2] they [5] to produce [4] used [3] were.

(3) [3] adapted [4] by [9] car [5] Henry Ford [8] mass-produced [7] the first [1] The technique [6] to build [2] was.

(4) [3] an assembly-line [6] cars [2] designed [1] Ford [4] on which [8] put together [5] the [7] were.

(5) [8] along it [2] assembly-line [5] but [3] did not [9] first [7] moved [4] move itself [1] The [6] workers.

(6) [7] an assembly-line [6] designing [2] Ford [12] groups of workers [3] had [5] of [9] moved [11] past [10] slowly [4] the idea [1] Then [8] which.

(7) [3] assembly-line [8] cars [4] greatly [5] increased [2] moving [10] per day [9] produced [1] The [6] the number [7] of.

(8) [8] by humans [10] by robots [3] car plants [7] done [1] In [9] is done [2] modern [6] once [4] some of [5] the work.

b) *Form sentences with the elements. Add any missing words and use the adverb(s) in brackets.*

(1) most Europeans/go/holiday/summer months. (usually)

   Most Europeans usually go on holiday in the summer months.

(2) surprising number/people/go away/holiday (never)

(3) it/be claimed/tourists/destroy/very place/want/visit (often)

(4) a lot/West German/go/Dutch coast/sunny weekends (normally)

(5) safari traffic/drive/animal/away/their feeding grounds (at the moment; unfortunately)

(6) environmentalist/call for/stricter control/tourism (always)

(7) much/coast/Spain/destroyed/building boom (in the 1990s; sadly)

(8) but/Spanish government/point out/tourism/biggest/be/Spain's/industry (currently; quickly)

© Cornelsen Verlag Scriptor, Berlin • Fundgrube Englisch

Lösungen b): (2) A surprising number of people never go away from home on holiday. (3) It is often claimed that tourists are destroying the very places they want to visit. (4) A lot of West Germans normally go to the Dutch coast on sunny weekends. (5) Unfortunately safari traffic is driving animals away from their feeding grounds at the moment. (6) Environmentalists are always calling for stricter controls on tourism. (7) Sadly, much of the coast of Spain was destroyed by a building boom in the 1990s. (8) But the Spanish government quickly points out that tourism is currently Spain's biggest industry.

Oberstufe

A Prüfungsfertigkeiten

A1 Expanding headlines

Write out these headlines in full. Be creative. You must add missing words/information and change tenses as necessary. Often more than one solution is possible.

Example: ROAD RAGE KILLS BABY?
→ Did road rage kill a baby?   → Was a baby killed by road rage?

(1) Mother of 4 wins £1 million

(2) Government to increase tax soon

(3) Picasso sold for $10 by mistake

(4) Nurses offered 2%, managers 7.5%

(5) US to leave Iraq early?

(6) Dogs best protection against crime say police

(7) UEFA: No security problems at WM 2006

(8) Laser drill painless

(9) Doctors slam govt's health policy

(10) Olympics 2012 triumph or disaster for London?

© Cornelsen Verlag Scriptor, Berlin • Fundgrube Englisch

Lösungen: (1) A mother of four children has won £1 million. (2) The government will increase tax(es) soon. (3) A Picasso was sold for $10 by mistake. (4) Nurses have been offered a 2% pay rise while managers (have been offered) 7.5%. (5) Is the USA going to leave Iraq early?; Is the USA intending/planning to leave Iraq early? (6) The police says (that) dogs are the best protection against crime. (7) UEFA says (that) there will be no security problems at WM 2006. (8) Laser drills are painless. (9) Doctors have slammed/severely criticised the government's health policy. (10) Will the Olympics 2012 be a triumph or a disaster for London?

A2 Summarising

Summarise these sentences by cutting out all unnecessary information. Use an exercise book.

Example:
The president returned to Washington last night after having a short holiday at his ranch in Crawford, Texas and called an immediate meeting of the security council at the White House.
→ The president called a meeting of the security council yesterday.

(1) In power stations, in factories and in our cars, we are burning more and more fossil fuels (coal, oil and natural gas) and this produces huge quantities of carbon dioxide – it is calculated that 18 billion (that's 18 thousand million!) tonnes of the stuff enter our atmosphere every year.

(2) To defend the sea-route from Europe to India, the British built up colonies, which were in fact often little more than coaling stations and docks to repair ships, round the coast of Africa and, after the opening of the Suez Canal in 1868, in Egypt and the Middle East as well.

(3) The East India Company, originally licensed by Elizabeth I (1558–1603) as a private company trading in Asian goods like cotton, silk and, of course, spices, suddenly found itself responsible for the civil and military administration of the whole Indian sub-continent from the Himalayas in the north to the island Ceylon – today Sri Lanka – in the south, an area no less than 18 times the size of Britain.

(4) Although all white Americans were themselves immigrants, or were at least descended from immigrants, many of them had little understanding or sympathy for the waves of new immigrants flooding into Ellis Island, New York, from eastern European countries like Poland, Russia and Romania – increasing social problems such as the slum developments in fast-growing cities like New York, Chicago and Pittsburgh. Overcrowded schools where a growing number of pupils could not even understand English, the rise in crime and vagrancy, the growth of of ghettos, the fear of unemployment and falling living standards all were blamed on the newcomers.

© Cornelsen Verlag Scriptor, Berlin • Fundgrube Englisch

Lösungen: (1) In power stations, factories and cars, we are burning more fossil fuels and this produces huge quantities of carbon dioxide every year. (2) To defend the sea-route to India, the British built up colonies round the coast of Africa and later in Egypt and the Middle East. (3) The East India Company found itself responsible for the administration of the whole of the Indian sub-continent. (4) Although all white Americans were themselves immigrants, many of them had little sympathy for the new immigrants flooding into Ellis Island from eastern European countries – increasing social problems were blamed on the newcomers.

A3 Using the question to start the answer

Here are 10 questions from exam papers. Use the question to write an opening to the answer.

Example: What is the kid in the cartoon complaining about?
→ The kid (in the cartoon) is complaining about ...

(1) How does the incident at the bar influence our opinion of Charles Lumley?

(2) Why has the author devoted so much space to the car chase?

(3) What does the description of the shop tell us about the antique dealer as a person?

(4) Why was Molly so disturbed by Simon's treatment of the dog?

(5) Why do some commentators claim that "there is no such thing as 'society'"?

(6) By what means does Hemingway make the nature of the wife's relationship to her husband clear to the reader?

(7) Which reason for the declining popularity of the monarchy do you find most convincing, and why?

(8) How do we know right from the beginning of the story how the narrator will probably react to Helen's visit?

(9) What do you understand by the term "virtual community"?

(10) Do you agree with the author's argument that "despite what liberals say, the state owes no one a living"?

© Cornelsen Verlag Scriptor, Berlin • Fundgrube Englisch

Lösungen: (1) The incident (at the bar) influences our opinion of Charles Lumley in that ... (2) The author devoted so much space to the car chase because ... (3) The description of the shop tells us that the antique dealer is ... (4) Molly is disturbed by Simon's treatment of the dog because ... (5) Some commentators claim that there is no such thing as society because ... (6) Hemingway makes the nature of the wife's relationship to her husband clear by ... (7) The reason for the declining popularity of the monarchy that I find most convincing is ... because ... (8) We know how the narrator is likely to react to Helen's visit because/by the fact that ... (9) By the term "virtual community" I understand ... (10) I agree/do not agree with the author's argument that the state owes no one a living because in my opinion ...

A4 Finding verb synonyms

Look at the verbs in the list 1–25. Find a synonym *(word of similar meaning) for each verb in the box. The* synonym *you are looking for rhymes with the word in brackets. Look at the two answers provided first.*

advertise	alter	assist	attack	attempt
build	buy	deceive	defend	discuss
escort	express	grow	make	mix
~~own~~	pollute	preserve	prevent	remember
repair	row	sell	show	~~test~~

Verb		Rhyming word	Synonym
(1)	examine	(nest)	test
(2)	possess	(phone)	own
(3)	purchase	(lie)	_____
(4)	market	(bell)	_____
(5)	change	(falter)	_____
(6)	try	(contempt)	_____
(7)	help	(insist)	_____
(8)	promote	(computerise)	_____
(9)	assault	(back)	_____
(10)	blend	(kicks)	_____
(11)	increase	(throw)	_____
(12)	construct	(filled)	_____
(13)	manufacture	(bake)	_____
(14)	debate	(bus)	_____
(15)	cheat	(receive)	_____
(16)	protect	(offend)	_____
(17)	accompany	(thought)	_____
(18)	exhibit	(though)	_____
(19)	stop	(lent)	_____
(20)	recall	(November)	_____
(21)	articulate	(distress)	_____
(22)	quarrel	(cow)	_____
(23)	mend	(pear)	_____
(24)	keep	(serve)	_____
(25)	contaminate	(loot)	_____

© Cornelsen Verlag Scriptor, Berlin • Fundgrube Englisch

Lösungen: (3) buy (4) sell (5) alter (6) attempt (7) assist (8) advertise (9) attack (10) mix (11) grow (12) build (13) make (14) discuss (15) deceive (16) defend (17) escort (18) show (19) prevent (20) remember (21) express (22) row (23) repair (24) preserve (25) pollute

A5 Human characteristics: Finding *antonyms*

Look at the adjectives in the list 1–24 and find their antonyms *(words of opposite meaning)* in the box:

aggressive	boring	brutal	cheeky
cold-hearted	critical	disappointed	extreme
horrible	hostile	lazy	mean
noisy	~~passive~~	repulsive	sad
stupid	unhelpful	unjust	unpleasant
unsympathetic	violent	weak	withdrawn

(1) active	*passive*	(2) amusing	_____
(3) attractive	_____	(4) charming	_____
(5) civilised	_____	(6) determined	_____
(7) fair	_____	(8) friendly	_____
(9) generous	_____	(10) gentle	_____
(11) happy	_____	(12) hardworking	_____
(13) helpful	_____	(14) intelligent	_____
(15) moderate	_____	(16) nice	_____
(17) peaceful	_____	(18) polite	_____
(19) quiet	_____	(20) satisfied	_____
(21) sociable	_____	(22) tolerant	_____
(23) understanding	_____	(24) warm-hearted	_____

© Cornelsen Verlag Scriptor, Berlin • Fundgrube Englisch

Lösungen: (2) boring (3) repulsive (4) unpleasant (5) brutal (6) weak (7) unjust (8) hostile (9) mean (10) violent (11) sad (12) lazy (13) unhelpful (14) stupid (15) extreme (16) horrible (17) aggressive (18) cheeky (19) noisy (20) disappointed (21) withdrawn (22) critical (23) unsympathetic (24) cold-hearted

A6 Talking about texts: Definitions

Link the words 1–20 with the definitions A–T. The first two solutions have been provided for you.

Words

(1)	fictional text	[E]	(2)	song	[P]
(3)	pie chart	[ ]	(4)	playwright	[ ]
(5)	copywriter	[ ]	(6)	journalist	[ ]
(7)	simile	[ ]	(8)	autobiography	[ ]
(9)	case study	[ ]	(10)	protagonist	[ ]
(11)	characterisation	[ ]	(12)	contrast	[ ]
(13)	enumeration	[ ]	(14)	climax	[ ]
(15)	turning point	[ ]	(16)	exposition	[ ]
(17)	hyperbole	[ ]	(18)	rhetorical question	[ ]
(19)	stylistic device	[ ]	(20)	comic	[ ]

Definitions

[A] account of a person's life told by the person himself or herself
[B] another name for "dramatist"
[C] any device used by a writer to make his or her intention and meaning clear to the reader or spectator
[D] any means used by a writer to describe a character
[E] any text that could be real, but is in fact produced by the writer's imagination
[F] common stylistic device that lists three or more items applying to people, things or ideas
[G] descriptive technique which concentrates on the differences between people, things or ideas
[H] factual description of a real-life situation in which the people concerned speak for themselves with a minimum of interference by the reporter
[I] highly significant development in a character's life after which nothing will be quite the same ever again
[J] introduction to a fictional work in which the characters are introduced and the scene is set
[K] most important single character in a story
[L] person producing reports, interviews etc. for press or radio/TV
[M] person who writes texts for advertisements
[N] point of maximum tension in a story followed by a phase of falling action
[O] representation of statistical information as a circle divided into segments of appropriate
[P] rhyming text set to music
[Q] series of cartoon-like drawing that tell a story and are intended simply to entertain
[R] statement form of a question asked for effect and hence not expecting an answer
[S] stylistic device which points up the similarities between apparently dissimilar people, things or ideas
[T] technical term – from the Greek – for "exaggeration"

© Cornelsen Verlag Scriptor, Berlin • Fundgrube Englisch

Lösungen: (3) O (4) B (5) M (6) L (7) S (8) A (9) H (10) K (11) D (12) G (13) F (14) N (15) I (16) J (17) T (18) R (19) C (20) Q

A7 Dealing with unknown words (a)

Here are some ways of working out the meaning of unknown words without the help of a dictionary.

a) International words
There are an enormous number of English words, particularly in such areas as business, information technology (IT), transport, the media, youth culture and sport, that have become 'international'. These words – for example 'manager', 'advertising spot', 'jeans', 'car', 'biker', 'camera', 'video', 'camping', 'tourist', 'stewardess' and 'golf' – are used in many languages.
Here is a mixed list of international words. Draw a table like the one below and complete it by putting words from the box into the correct word field.

~~advertising~~
aquaplaning
boom
cap (Mütze)
check-in desk
corporate image
deo-spray
discount store
fax
flight recorder
hovercraft
investment portfolio
jogger
know-how
link
marketing
pullover
shampoo
software
sweatshirt
workstation

~~after shave~~
~~badminton~~
boots
champion
city-hopper
crew
design
email
fitness training
hair style
inline skates
jacket
just-in-time delivery
league
mailbox
match
satellite
shareware
sponsoring
ticket

~~airbag~~
~~bite~~
business school
charter flight
coach
cup (Pokal)
digital technology
fashion
flight attendant
hardware
interface
jeans
kicker
leggings
manager
navigator
score
shuttle bus
squash
virtual reality

Clothing, cosmetics	Transport	IT	Sport	Business
after shave	airbag	bite	badminton	advertising

© Cornelsen Verlag Scriptor, Berlin • Fundgrube Englisch

Lösungen a): Clothing, cosmetics: after-shave, boots, cap, deo-spray, fashion, hair style, jacket, jeans, leggings, pullover, shampoo, sweatshirt **Transport:** airbag, aquaplaning, charter flight, check-in desk, city-hopper, crew, flight attendant, flight recorder, hovercraft, navigator, shuttle bus, ticket **IT:** bite, digital technology, email, fax, hardware, interface, link, mailbox, satellite, shareware, software, virtual reality **Sport:** badminton, champion, coach, cup, fitness training, inline skates, jogger, kicker league, match, score, squash **Business:** advertising, boom, business school, corporate image, design, discount store, just-in-time delivery, know-how, manager, marketing, investment portfolio, sponsoring, workstation

A7 Dealing with unknown words (b)

b) Similarity to German
A great many English words, particularly concrete nouns and verbs from everyday life – for example 'bread', 'bring', 'come', 'family', 'field', 'fish', 'garden', 'house', 'make', 'sing', 'street' and so on – come from an old form of German. Such English words are generally differently spelt and pronounced than in German, but German-speakers can normally easily recognise them.
Just as important as these Germanic words are so-called *Fremdwörter* (words of foreign origin) such as, for example, the German words *aggressiv, Demokratie, Diplomatie, Politik, Sozialismus, telefonieren* and so on. These words are based mainly on Latin or Greek and are also used – again with small changes – in English. Hence the English equivalents of the examples given above are 'aggressive', 'democracy', 'diplomacy', 'politics', 'socialism', '(to) telephone'.

Read the sentences and translate the underlined parts into German.

(1) Services like health and care for old people are <u>based on the idea of social solidarity</u>.

(2) Islam is <u>worried by the spread of Western cultural and religious ideas</u>. Muslims are particularly <u>anxious about materialism and sexual morals</u>.

(3) The USA wants <u>to hinder illegal immigration</u> by guarding its frontiers more strictly.

(4) The British <u>established the first tobacco plantations</u> in their American colonies and <u>imported slaves from West Africa</u> to work on them.

(5) The US government plans to stop smuggling, if necessary by military intervention.

(6) One person argued that European integration would take generations.

(7) Economists say that more firms went bankrupt during the last recession than during the Great Depression of the 1930s.

(8) Most people accept immigration as long as the immigrants do not establish ghettos with an individual identity that is different from the rest of society.

(9) Some pessimistic experts say we will have critical energy problems unless something is done now to conserve the energy we've got and to invest in new forms of energy for the future.

(10) Bill Gates thinks there will soon be no transport problems because we will all communicate in cyberspace.

Lösungen b): (1) ... sind auf der Idee von sozialer Solidarität gegründet./ ... basieren auf der Idee von sozialer/gesellschaftlicher Solidarität. (2) ... von westlichen kulturellen und religiösen Traditionen; ... besorgt über Materialismus und Sexualmoral. (3) ... illegale Immigration zu verhindern. (4) ... etablierten die ersten Tabakplantagen in ihren amerikanischen Kolonien und importierten Sklaven aus Westafrika ... (5) ... plant, das Schmuggeln zu stoppen, ... durch militärische Intervention. (6) Eine Person argumentierte, ... europäische Integration Generationen ... (7) Ökonomen sagen, dass mehr Firmen während der letzten Rezession Bankrott machten ... (8) ... akzeptieren Immigration ... die Immigranten keine Ghettos mit einer individuellen Identität ... etablieren. (9) Einige pessimistische Experten sagen, dass wir ernste Energieprobleme haben werden ..., um die Energie, die wir haben, zu konservieren und in neue Energieformen ... zu investieren. (10) ... keine Transportprobleme, da wir alle miteinander im Cyberspace kommunizieren werden.

B Wortschatz

B1 Word families

Complete the table with the missing forms. In some cases there is more than one. XXX means there is no word.

	Verb	Noun	Adjective
(1)	advertise	advertisement	advertising
(2)	broadcast	1 broadcaster 2 broadcast	1 broadcasting 2 broadcasted
(3)		1 discoverer 2	XXX
(4)	persuade		
(5)		1 arguer 2	
(6)		1 informer 2	
(7)	1 compute 2		XXX
(8)	automate		
(9)			exaggerated
(10)			accommodating
(11)			embarrassing
(12)		1 critic 2	
(13)		1 2	immigrant
(14)		marriage	
(15)	industrialise	1 2	
(16)	discuss		XXX
(17)	decide		
(18)			expressive
(19)	differ		
(20)			analytical
(21)			complaining
(22)		damage	1 2
(23)		1 2	accusative
(24)	destroy		1 2
(25)		1 2 report	XXX
(26)			agreeable
(27)	educate		
(28)		reliance	
(29)			growing
(30)			isolated

Lösungen: (3) discover, discovery (4) persuasion, persuasive (5) argue, argument, argumentative (6) inform, information, informative (7) computerise, computer (8) automation, automatic (9) exaggerate, exaggeration (10) accommodate, accommodation (11) embarrass, embarrassment (12) criticise, criticism, critical (13) immigrate, immigrant, immigration (14) marry, married (15) industry, industrialisation, industrialised (16) discussion (17) decision, decisive (18) express, expression (19) difference, different (20) analyse, analysis (21) complain, complaint (22) damage, damaging, damaged (23) accuse, accuser, accusation (24) destruction, destructive (25) report, reporter (26) agree, agreement (27) education, educational (28) rely, reliable (29) grow, growth (30) isolate, isolation.

B2 Collocations

Some pairs of words fit together – or 'collocate' – and some do not. For example, we say 'team captain', not 'team head' or 'team leader', although 'captain', 'head' and 'leader' are very similar in meaning. Again, when we want the English equivalent of the German expression *Briefkasten*, we find that in this sense the noun 'post' collates with the 'box', but not with 'container' or 'case'.

Look at the words 1–25 in the list. Choose a word from the box to make collocations.

officer	ticket	centre	analysis	professor
report	letter	software	terminal	terrace
post	broadcast	teacher	machine	receiver
number	hall	interview	assistant	~~pollution~~
van	park	court	club	agency

(1) air   *pollution*   (2) bus   _____
(3) business _____   (4) car   _____
(5) computer _____   (6) concert _____
(7) delivery _____   (8) employment _____
(9) frontier _____   (10) head _____
(11) job _____   (12) news _____
(13) newspaper _____   (14) night _____
(15) observation _____   (16) passenger _____
(17) police _____   (18) satellite _____
(19) shop _____   (20) shopping _____
(21) telephone _____   (22) tennis _____
(23) text _____   (24) university _____
(25) washing _____

© Cornelsen Verlag Scriptor, Berlin • Fundgrube Englisch

Lösungen: (2) bus ticket (3) business letter (4) car park (5) computer software (6) concert hall (7) delivery van (8) employment agency (9) frontier post (10) head teacher (11) job interview (12) news broadcast (13) newspaper report (14) night club (15) observation terrace (16) passenger terminal (17) police officer (18) satellite receiver (19) shop assistant (20) shopping centre (21) telephone number (22) tennis court (23) text analysis (24) university professor (25) washing machine

B3 False friends (a)

a) Just English
Cross out the incorrect alternative. Only one solution is possible.

(1) Don't you ~~mean~~/think Barbara is right to leave her husband?
(2) Foreigners/Strangers from out of town have problems finding somewhere to park.
(3) Sarah is popular. Everybody finds her very likeable/sympathetic .
(4) I only did so well in the test because the teacher overlooked/oversaw several mistakes.
(5) The government's policy/politics towards the Middle East is crazy.
(6) Bobby Hunt is 16 but his mother still brings/takes him to school each day.
(7) For heaven's sake hurry up. Our plane starts/takes off in a few minutes.
(8) I'm not paying for this steak. It's absolutely awful/miserable .
(9) Sorry. You can't have this medicine without a doctor's prescription/receipt .
(10) You needn't wear black but please wear something decent/quiet .
(11) Can you tell me what the menu/set meal is today, please?
(12) The policeman stopped me because I didn't notice/remark a No Entry sign.
(13) It's very dangerous to distract/irritate a driver in heavy traffic.
(14) Let's not waste time on this problem. It won't be actual/current until 2020.
(15) Wendy always donates/spends money to the dogs' home at Christmas.
(16) I haven't decided yet but eventually/maybe I'll come to the party after all.
(17) Have you heard the latest/newest news? The firm has been taken over.
(18) Bob was so disinterested/uninterested in his work that he lost his job.
(19) Patterson, Jackson & Snibbs is a very reputable/serious New York law firm.
(20) Some short men are extremely sensible/sensitive about their height.

© Cornelsen Verlag Scriptor, Berlin • Fundgrube Englisch

Lösungen a): Die folgenden Wörter sind richtig, sollen also übrigbleiben:
(2) Strangers (3) likeable (4) overlooked (5) policy (6) takes (7) takes off (8) awful (9) prescription (10) quiet (11) set meal (12) notice (13) distract (14) current (15) donates (16) maybe (17) latest (18) uninterested (19) reputable (20) sensitive

B3 False friends (b)

b) German-English
Complete the sentences with the correct form of the English equivalent of the German word given on the left.

aktuell	(1)	_____ developments in Iran are very worrying.
aufstehen	(2)	Lucy didn't _____ at all on Sunday.
bringen	(3)	My father always _____ me from home to school.
Chips	(4)	A lot of children just eat some _____ for lunch.
konsequent	(5)	Always be _____ when training dogs.
dezent	(6)	This isn't a disco. Wear _____ clothes to the office in future.
Fremde	(7)	You can't expect _____ to know the way to the village.
irritieren	(8)	It's not fair to _____ the players by shouting insults at them.
Land	(9)	How many _____ are there in Germany now?
machen	(10)	We haven't got time to _____ the washing-up now.
meinen	(11)	Do you _____ we should invite the Browns to our party, too?
Menü	(12)	The _____ today is pork, cabbage and potatoes.
merken	(13)	A driver didn't _____ a red light.
miserabel	(14)	I thought the prize-winning film was simply _____.
neu	(15)	My _____ information is that the match will be called off.
Pension	(16)	We only had to pay £10 a night at the _____.
Politik	(17)	The opposition's education _____ will cost a fortune.
Rente	(18)	Many old people live on a _____ of less than £20 a week.
Rezept	(19)	Don't trouble the doctor. I just need a new _____.
sensibel	(20)	Be careful what you say. Ann can be very _____ about her children.
seriös	(21)	I'm afraid a lot of car salesmen are not very _____.
spenden	(22)	I only _____ money to local charities.
starten	(23)	What time does our plane _____?
sympathisch	(24)	Eva is much more _____ than her pompous husband.
übersehen	(25)	We got lost when we _____ the signpost to Riga.

© Cornelsen Verlag Scriptor, Berlin • Fundgrube Englisch

Lösungen b): (1) Current (2) get up (3) takes (4) crisps (5) consistent (6) quiet (7) strangers (8) distract (9) states (10) do (11) think (12) set meal (13) notice (14) awful (15) latest (16) guest house (17) policy (18) pension (19) prescription (20) sensitive (21) reputable (22) donate (23) take off (24) likeable (25) overlooked

B4 Confusibles

We call words that often get mixed up – or confused – confusibles. Cross out the incorrect alternative of the two confusibles given.

(1) I had to ~~lay~~/lie down because my back hurt.
(2) Jack will have money problems unless he becomes more economic/economical.
(3) A principal/principle result of the industrial revolution was new attitudes to work.
(4) Some say that Europeans are less industrial/industrious than Asians.
(5) Do you think that's a practical/practicable idea in the present situation?
(6) Happily/Luckily nobody was hurt in the accident.
(7) I'm afraid that a lot of people are better in theory than in practice/practise.
(8) I need some postcards. Is there a stationary/stationery shop near here?
(9) You can't expect to become/get a good job without qualifications.
(10) Does Jane always drive/go to work by bike?
(11) The English meaning of *Domstadt* was once just city/town.
(12) Mum needs another ten minutes and then she'll be finished/ready.
(13) I don't think these curtains a very tasteful/tasty, do you?
(14) It is against the law to avoid/evade taxes.
(15) Are you inferring/implying that the president lied to Congress?
(16) Nothing you say will convince/persuade Sally not to marry that awful man.
(17) Surely you're not saying that smoking does not affect/effect your health?
(18) Child abuse/misuse hasn't increased; people are just more willing to talk about it.
(19) In Germany there are biannual/biennial school reports.
(20) We had an awful holiday. It rained continually/continuously. It never stopped once.
(21) Our neighbours are very sociable/social. They're always inviting people in for drinks.
(22) The EU should prescribe/proscribe stricter rules to control factory farming.
(23) The army could not repel/repulse the enemy's attack.
(24) Jane must drive. Harry has lost his licence/license because of dangerous driving.
(25) Don't forget to get a recipe/receipt for the office supplies, will you?

© Cornelsen Verlag Scriptor, Berlin • Fundgrube Englisch

Lösungen: Die folgenden Wörter sind richtig, sollen also übrigbleiben: (2) economical (3) principal (4) industrious (5) practicable (6) Luckily (7) practice (8) stationery (9) get (10) go (11) city (12) ready (13) tasteful (14) evade (15) implying (16) persuade (17) affect (18) abuse (19) biennial (20) continuously (21) sociable (22) proscribe (23) repulse (24) licence (25) receipt

B5 Phrasal verbs (a)

a) Look at the German on the left and complete the sentences with the equivalent English phrasal verb from the list. They are already in the correct form.

brought up	built up	call in	called out
calm down	clear away	find out	gave away
give in	give up	growing up	looking forward to
looks down on	make out	~~pick up~~	stay up
takes off	try on	Watch out	work out

abholen	(1)	Can you <u>pick up</u> the children from school today?
anprobieren	(2)	You should always _____ shoes before buying them.
aufbauen	(3)	A long queue of cars had _____ at the frontier.
aufbleiben	(4)	Most parents let children _____ longer on Saturdays.
aufgeben	(5)	The doctor told me to _____ smoking and drinking.
aufpassen	(6)	_____ when you cross the road.
aufwachsen	(7)	Millions of children in Africa are _____ up in poverty.
ausrechnen	(8)	Can you _____ how much the bill will be?
ausrufen	(9)	Our flight will be _____ in a few minutes.
erkennen	(10)	I can't _____ what some modern poems are trying to say.
erziehen	(11)	A lot of children are being _____ in one-parent families.
herabsehen auf	(12)	Henry always _____ people poorer than himself.
herausfinden	(13)	You can _____ about last-minute holidays on the internet.
nachgeben	(14)	I don't think Iran will _____ to the USA's demands.
sich beruhigen	(15)	Look, _____, okay? Shouting won't solve the problem.
sich freuen auf	(16)	We are _____ Jim Parker's party at the weekend.
starten	(17)	Our plane _____ from Düsseldorf at 10.30 a.m. tomorrow.
verschenken	(18)	Our team _____ certain victory last night.
vorbeischauen	(19)	Can you _____ at Ann's on your way home from work?
wegräumen	(20)	Please _____ the dishes before you go to bed.

© Cornelsen Verlag Scriptor, Berlin • Fundgrube Englisch

Lösungen a): (2) try on (3) built up (4) stay up (5) give up (6) Watch out (7) growing up (8) work out (9) called out (10) make out (11) brought up (12) looks down on (13) find out (14) give in (15) calm down (16) looking forward to (17) takes off (18) gave away (19) call in (20) clear away

B5 Phrasal verbs (b)

b) Complete the phrasal verbs with the correct particle.

> up   on   around   off   up   off   out   off   out   up
> off   up   out   off   out   out   on   around   up   on
> in   up   out   up

(1) Some young people spend a lot of their time just hanging _____.
(2) Can you stick _____ for a few minutes after work? The boss wants to see you.
(3) I can't stand those phones that play music to you while you're hanging ___.
(4) Caroline goes to bed so late that she can't get ___ in the morning.
(5) Cheap tyres wear _____ quicker than more expensive ones.
(6) Cheer ___! Life can't be that bad.
(7) Have you settled ___ to your new job now?
(8) Julie and Sam fell _____ with each other about where to go on holiday.
(9) If Tim doesn't watch _____, Sarah will leave him.
(10) If you don't work harder, they'll throw you _____.
(11) I hate the way you show _____ in front of people.
(12) It's very rude just to go _____ without even saying goodbye.
(13) It's very unfair to point _____ people's mistakes in public.
(14) Miss Havers was hurt because I dropped _____ during her lesson.
(15) Sally is always turning ___ late for work.
(16) The film turned _____ to be much better than I expected.
(17) The firm is laying _____ 50 more workers at the end of the month.
(18) The girl who waited ___ our table was a German student from Berlin.
(19) The Smiths don't get ___ very well with their neighbours.
(20) A terrorist blew ___ a bus last week.
(21) Three dangerous criminals broke _____ of prison last night.
(22) We are staying at home this summer because we are doing ___ our flat.
(23) We can put ___ two of your visitors if you like.
(24) We had to call _____ the match because of snow.
(25) We will end ___ bankrupt unless business improves soon.
(26) Why are you always making ___ silly stories about other people?

© Cornelsen Verlag Scriptor, Berlin • Fundgrube Englisch

Lösungen b): (1) around (2) around (3) on (4) up (5) out (6) up (7) in (8) out (9) out (10) out (11) off (12) off (13) out (14) off (15) up (16) out (17) off (18) on (19) on (20) up (21) out (22) up (23) up (24) off (25) up (26) up

B5 Phrasal verbs (c)

c) Replace the verbs with a phrasal verb of similar meaning from the list.

breathed in	broken off	carrying out	cleared up
fill in	fix up	give back	~~got away~~
knocked down	left out	looking into	put on
put up	put up with	set out	show off
stood up	take off	take on	tore up

(1) Alec Carr escaped <u>got away</u> from the police as he was being taken to court.
(2) A lot of people inhaled _____ the gas that escaped from the chemical factory.
(3) Ann destroyed _____ all Tony's letters when he left her.
(4) Everybody rose _____ when the boss came into the room.
(5) I couldn't give you a better grade because you omitted _____ the last question.
(6) Inspector Morse hasn't solved _____ the murder yet.
(7) It is illegal to hire _____ people who are not properly qualified.
(8) Please return _____ the dictionaries at the end of the exam.
(9) Some unpleasant men boast _____ in front of pretty women.
(10) The concert was discontinued _____ when the conductor became ill.
(11) The doctors are performing _____ the operation next week.
(12) The firm has increased _____ its prices by 5% this year.
(13) The police are investigating _____ the crime.
(14) The power lines were demolished _____ when a plane crashed.
(15) Tourists must complete _____ a special form at the frontier.
(16) I'm afraid we weren't able to arrange _____ an interview with Robbie Williams.
(17) We left _____ at 3 a.m. because of the holiday traffic.
(18) You can't expect me to tolerate _____ your drinking any longer.
(19) You must wear _____ a hard hat when you are on the building site.
(20) You shouldn't remove _____ all your clothes in public.

© Cornelsen Verlag Scriptor, Berlin • Fundgrube Englisch

Lösungen c): (2) breathed in (3) tore up (4) stood up (5) left out (6) cleared up (7) take on (8) give back (9) show off (10) broken off (11) carrying out (12) put up (13) looking into (14) knocked down (15) fill in (16) fix up (17) set out (18) put up with (19) put on (20) take off

B6 Verb/noun + preposition combinations (a)

a) Complete the sentences by putting the correct preposition after the verb.

(1) Banks seem to only lend <u>to</u> people who already have money.

(2) Does Norway belong _____ the EU?

(3) Don't ask _____ a day off. We have too much work to do.

(4) Don't run _____ the road against the lights.

(5) Have you looked _____ the postbox yet?

(6) It's a crime to borrow _____ banks if you don't intend to repay the money.

(7) It's a scandal to throw _____ food when people are starving.

(8) It's unhealthy just to dream _____ winning the lottery.

(9) Minette Walters often writes _____ women in modern society.

(10) Please stop playing _____ that biro all the time.

(11) The Green Party will definitely vote _____ building more motorways.

(12) The mechanics have been working _____ my car all day.

(13) We have been waiting _____ the bus for almost an hour.

(14) What did you wish _____ when you saw the black cat?

(15) You shouldn't laugh _____ things that mean a lot to others.

© Cornelsen Verlag Scriptor, Berlin • Fundgrube Englisch

Lösungen a): (2) to (3) for (4) across or over (5) into (6) from (7) away (8) about or of (9) about or on (10) with (11) against (12) on (13) for (14) for (15) at

B6 Verb/noun + preposition combinations (b)

b) Complete the sentences with the correct verb. Only one solution is possible.

| advise | agree | approve | believe | ~~differ~~ |
| insisted | object | relied | report | succeed |

(1) Does Austrian German <u>differ</u> from High German much?
(2) Don't ask Jack to do the job. He just can't be _____ on to do it on time.
(3) Most doctors _____ against eating too many animal fats.
(4) Many non-smokers strongly _____ to people smoking in restaurants.
(5) The policeman _____ on seeing my driving licence.
(6) The British will never _____ to an all-Ireland referendum on the future of Northern Ireland.
(7) The tabloids only _____ on crime, sex and sport.
(8) Do all religions _____ in the survival of the spirit after death?
(9) Few commentators thought that BVB would _____ in winning the cup.
(10) Many doctors _____ of the legalisation of some drugs.

| ~~aiming~~ | apologised | began | choose | deals |
| depends | distinguish | identify | refer | sympathise |

(11) The firm is <u>aiming</u> at increasing its profits by at least 15% this year.
(12) Have you _____ to the Harpers for damaging their new car?
(13) The speaker _____ by introducing herself to the audience.
(14) Bill and Ben are twins. Unless you know them well, you can't _____ between them.
(15) Can I speak to the person who _____ with customer enquiries, please?
(16) We might barbecue at the weekend. It _____ on the weather, of course.
(17) Idealistic young people find it easy to _____ with good causes.
(18) We _____ to your fax about our new prices.
(19) You can't marry both of them, Sally. You must _____ between them, I'm afraid.
(20) It's hard to _____ with people who are too lazy to help themselves.

© Cornelsen Verlag Scriptor, Berlin • Fundgrube Englisch

Lösungen b): (2) relied (3) advise (4) object (5) insisted (6) agree (7) report (8) believe (9) succeed (10) approve (12) apologised (13) began (14) distinguish (15) deals (16) depends (17) identify (18) refer (19) choose (20) sympathise

B6 Verb/noun + preposition combinations (c)

c) Use an English prepositional noun for the German expressions on the left.

Freiheit von	(1)	Morphine has given us almost complete <u>freedom from</u> pain.
Sicherheit vor	(2)	The UN safe areas were designed to give civilians _____ attack.
Interesse (dar)an	(3)	The West has little _____ helping Africa to industrialise.
Angst (da)vor	(4)	Some people live in _____ what others think of them.
Bewusstsein (dar)über	(5)	Few governments show any _____ what it means to be poor.
Scham angesichts	(6)	The EU ought to express _____ what happened in Bosnia.
Erstaunen über	(7)	The audience showed its _____ the child's talent.
Sorge um	(8)	Our elderly neighbours have a lot of _____ their health.
Freundlichkeit gegenüber	(9)	_____ animals is said to be 'very British'.
Eheschließung mit	(10)	Brian has changed completely since his _____ Sally.

© Cornelsen Verlag Scriptor, Berlin • Fundgrube Englisch

Lösungen c): (2) safety from (3) interest in (4) fear of (5) awareness of (6) shame at (7) astonishment at (8) worry about (9) Kindness to (10) marriage to

B7 Common prepositional idioms (a)

a) Complete the sentences with the correct preposition(s).

(1) Everyone was there with the exception _of_ Ruth, who is on holiday.

(2) You can't make important decisions like that just _____ hand.

(3) Please get in touch with me _____ delay.

(4) This report is too general. I want an ___-depth study of the project.

(5) We met Werner and Birgit in St Malo purely ___ chance.

(6) My boss is _____ suspicion ___ having stolen some money from the firm.

(7) I agree with your arguments _____ a point but you are far too emotional.

(8) Of course journalists concentrate on events that are _____ the ordinary.

(9) I liked the idea ___ first sight but now I am less sure.

(10) Film stars are asked to write books ___ virtue ___ their popularity.

(11) ___ the circumstances it would be best if you left the firm voluntarily.

(12) This was not an accident. Our car was damaged ___ purpose.

(13) There's no hurry. Read the report ___ leisure and tell me what you think.

(14) ___ view ___ the economic situation, we can't offer a better price.

(15) I only know Brenda ___ a limited extent.

(16) It's surprising how many things happen simply ___ mistake.

(17) ___ addition ___ stealing money, he also tried to blackmail us.

(18) _____ average, wages are higher in the EU than in the USA.

(19) I don't want to cook. Let's eat out _____ a change.

(20) There's no improvement at all. In fact, things are going _____ bad ___ worse.

© Cornelsen Verlag Scriptor, Berlin • Fundgrube Englisch

Lösungen: a) (2) out of hand (3) without delay (4) in-depth study (5) by chance (6) under suspicion of (7) up to a point (8) out of the ordinary (9) at first sight (10) by virtue of (11) In the circumstances (12) on purpose (13) at leisure (14) in view of (15) to a limited extent (16) by mistake (17) In addition to (18) On average (19) for a change (20) from bad to worse

B7 Common prepositional idioms (b)

b) *Finish translating the sentences into English. Use prepositional expressions.*

(1) Wir können uns bei meinem Onkel in London treffen.
→ We can meet at my uncle's in London.

(2) War Boris Becker mit 17 Wimbledon-Sieger?
→ Was Boris Becker Wimbledon champion _____?

(3) Der Arzt lachte nur über mich.
→ The doctor just laughed _____.

(4) Der Journalist hat um ein Interview gebeten.
→ The journalist asked _____.

(5) Du sollst dich wegen deines schlechten Benehmens entschuldigen.
→ You should apologise _____.

(6) Der Angeklagte hat den Banküberfall immer noch nicht gestanden.
→ The accused has still not _____ the bank robbery.

(7) Ich bestehe auf Ihrer Anwesenheit bei der Sitzung.
→ I _____ your presence _____.

(8) Wir beziehen uns auf Ihr Schreiben vom 23. August.
→ We _____ your letter _____ 23 August.

(9) Angesichts deiner Einstellung habe ich wenig Mitleid mit dir.
→ _____ your attitude I have little _____.

(10) Natürlich hat die Gesellschaft Verpflichtungen älteren Menschen gegenüber.
→ _____ society has a duty _____.

(11) Du brauchst nicht alles so ausführlich zu erzählen.
→ You needn't narrate everything _____.

(12) In der Praxis sind solche Ideen sehr schwierig umzusetzen.
→ _____, such ideas are very difficult to translate _____.

© Cornelsen Verlag Scriptor, Berlin • Fundgrube Englisch

Lösungen b): (2) at 17 (3) at me (4) for an interview (5) for your bad behaviour (6) confessed to (7) insist on, at the meeting (8) refer to, of (9) In view of, sympathy for you (10) Of course, towards elderly/older people (11) at such length (12) In practice, into action

B8 Verb + *infinitive* or verb + *-ing-form*?

Put the verbs on the left into the sentences. Use the -ing-form or the to-infinitive.

arrange	(1)	My bank suggested <u>arranging</u> another loan.
arrest	(2)	The policeman tried _____ the two men.
build	(3)	We are planning _____ a factory in Estonia.
buy	(4)	Jane wants _____ a flat in Camden Town.
visit	(5)	I'll never forget _____ Paris for the first time.
change	(6)	Do you really mean _____ your job?
decorate	(7)	I haven't finished _____ my room yet.
bring	(8)	I'm sorry I forgot _____ my homework to school.
pay	(9)	The boss has promised _____ us more money.
go	(10)	A lot of people can never afford _____ on holiday.
have	(11)	We very much regret _____ to refuse your request.
invest	(12)	We cannot risk _____ money in such an unstable country.
lose	(13)	Can you imagine _____ your whole family in a plane crash?
marry	(14)	A lot of modern women prefer _____ later than their mothers did.
move	(15)	The Snows are considering _____ out of London.
pay	(16)	People won't mind _____ higher taxes if they get something for them.
see	(17)	Don't miss _____ the Niagara Falls when you're in Canada.
smoke	(18)	Sarah stopped _____ when she was ill.
spend	(19)	Don't tell me you forgot _____ over £ 200 on one meal!
tolerate	(20)	Teachers must refuse _____ such violent behaviour.
get	(21)	We are a little late because we stopped _____ some petrol.

© Cornelsen Verlag Scriptor, Berlin • Fundgrube Englisch

Lösungen: (2) to arrest (3) to build (4) to buy (5) visiting (6) to change (7) decorating (8) to bring (9) to pay (10) to go (11) having (12) investing (13) losing (14) marrying (15) moving (16) paying (17) seeing (18) smoking (19) spending (20) to tolerate (21) to get

B9 Watch the spelling!

Cross out and correct the misspelt word.

(1) The price of ~~accomodation~~ in London is very high. *accommodation*

(2) When did India get its ~~independance~~? *independence*

(3) Be careful with Alan. He's a real mischieous maker. _____

(4) Who assasinated Abraham Lincoln? _____

(5) People aren't embarrased by nudity nowadays. _____

(6) I have several acquaintences in France. _____

(7) There are computer programmes for just about everything. _____

(8) How many stories does your house have? _____

(9) It's terrible but sexual harrasment is still common. _____

(10) Germany has 17 parlaments! _____

(11) The books were despatched last week. _____

(12) I'm going to swop my car for a bike. _____

(13) Sales representetives often say anything to get a sale. _____

(14) The goverment is planning to raise taxes. _____

(15) Most of the audiance left early. _____

© Cornelsen Verlag Scriptor, Berlin • Fundgrube Englisch

Lösungen: (3) mischievous (4) assassinated (5) embarrassed (6) acquaintances (7) programs (8) storeys (9) harassment (10) parliaments (11) dispatched (12) swap (13) representatives (14) government (15) audience

Using commas

Put in the missing commas only when necessary. Use a tick ✔ if you think a sentence is already correct.

(1) The headmaster said "We will however be offering more courses in Biology, Chemistry and Physics in the new school year."

(2) Don't forget to tell Ann that we'll wait for her in the bar.

(3) The UN which is a purely representative assembly cannot possibly be expected to police the world because it has no money or army of its own.

(4) Aldous Huxley who was born and brought up in England spent his later years in California.

(5) The article is about discrimination because of sex and social class.

(6) BP is a big British oil company isn't it?

(7) The Open University was only founded in the 1960s but it already has an international reputation.

(8) I'm afraid you won't find the road that Joan lives in marked on that map.

(9) The director told the actors to do the scene again or they would all be sacked.

(10) If the government loses the vote the prime minister will call an election.

(11) The people who called in last night are our new neighbours.

(12) The last world environment conference which was held in Brazil has had little real effect on governments who continue to look after purely national interests.

(13) You needn't work late tomorrow if you finish the job in time.

(14) The music was so loud that you couldn't talk without shouting into the other person's ear.

(15) I'm taking the car to the garage in order to have its brakes looked at.

© Cornelsen Verlag Scriptor, Berlin • Fundgrube Englisch

Lösungen: (Correct) 2; 5; 7; 8; 9; 11; 13; 14; 15
(Missing commas) (1) The headmaster said, "We will, however, be offering more courses in Biology, Chemistry and Physics in the new school year." (3) The UN, which is a purely representative assembly, cannot possibly be expected to police the world because it has no money or army of its own. (4) Aldous Huxley, who was born and brought up in England, spent his later years in California. (6) BP is a big British oil company, isn't it? (10) If the government loses the vote, the prime minister will call an election. (12) The last world environment conference, which was held in Brazil, has had little real effect on governments, who continue to look after purely national interests.

8 Lob und Kritik – Sprache des Klassenzimmers

Der folgende Katalog von Ausdrücken soll Lehrerinnen und Lehrern helfen, sich in alltäglichen Klassenzimmersituationen zeitgemäß und angemessen auf Englisch auszudrücken.

1 Simple Instructions (*einfache Anweisungen*)

a) **Books, writing materials etc.** (*Bücher, Schreibzeug usw.*)
- Get out your books/workbooks/exercise books/homework/reader.
- Get out the handout I gave you/something to write with/...
- Turn to page .../section... on page .../the vocab list/the grammar section/...
- Look at page ... the background information/footnote/infobox/text on page ...
- Look at the cartoon/comic strip/diagram/drawing/graph/illustration/picture/photo on page ...
- Find/Look at line ... on page .../at the top of/in the middle of/at the bottom of page ...
- Let's/I want/I'd like to go on/continue with the text/exercise on page ...
- I'd like to look at the text we started last time/week/lesson again.

b) **Homework, exercises, assignments etc.**
(*Hausaufgaben, Übungen, Ausgaben usw.*)
- (name), please read out your homework/what you have written/prepared/...
- (name), can you answer question (number)/the question, please?
- (name), start reading, please.
- Okay/All right, stop there. (name), go on, please.

- Is that right/correct? What do you think, (name)?
- What must/should we say there, (name)/someone?
- What should (name) have said there?
- Can you add anything to that, (name)?

c) The blackboard (*Die Tafel*)
- (name), please come/go to the (black)board and complete the sentence/write down the English word for .../show us what you've written/...
- Use the middle/centre section/the left flap (*Flügel, Seitenteil*)/ the right flap/the back of the left flap/...
- Clean the board/middle section/... first, (please).
- Have you got some chalk?/Can you find some/a bit of chalk?
- Here's a bit of chalk.
- We can't read that. Please write bigger/more clearly/more neatly.
- Push the board up a bit. It's too low.
- Are you sure that's right? Look at the spelling/the past form/...
- Is that right, (name)? Can you help him/her?

d) Auxiliary equipment (*Hilfsgeräte*)
CD/DVD player, cassette recorder
- Put the CD player/cassette recorder in the middle of the room/desk/...
- Plug it/the player/the recorder into this/that socket (*Steckdose*).
- Put the plug (*Stecker*) into this/that socket/the socket near/next to the board/door/window/...
- Start the CD at the beginning/at the first track/at track 6/...
- Go on to track 10/...

- Wind the tape back to the beginning/back to zero.
- Don't forget to set the counter (*Zählwerk*) at zero.
- Wind the tape back/forward to (a reading of) ... (on the counter).

- Turn up the volume. We can't hear it.
- Turn down the volume. It's (much) too loud.

- Press the pause button. Let's talk about what we've heard/seen so far.
- Let's listen to that part of the dialogue/.../watch that scene again.

- Switch off the recorder (first) and (then) unplug it/pull/take out the plug.

Overhead (projector)

- Put the overhead (projector) on my/the/(name's) desk/... so that everyone can see the picture/image.
- Plug it/the projector into this/that socket (*Steckdose*).
- Put the plug (*Stecker*) into this/that socket/the socket near the board/door/window/...
- Put the transparency on the projector properly. It's too high/too low/not straight.
- The transparency's the wrong way round/upside down.
- Raise/lower the picture/image. We can't see it properly.
- It's out of focus (*unscharf*). We can't read that/make that out.
- (name), come and fill in the (missing) words/complete the sentences/table/...
- Push up the transparency so we can see the last sentences.
- Change the transparency/Go on to the next transparency.
- Switch off the light but leave on the fan. The bulb is still hot.
- Don't knock the projector. The bulb is still hot.

Slide Projector

- Put the (slide) projector on my/the/(name's) desk/... so that everyone can see the picture/screen.
- Pull down the screen.
- Put the plug (*Stecker*) into this/that socket (*Steckdose*)/the socket near the board/door/window/...
- Let down the blinds/close the curtains.
- Switch on/off the lights, (name).

- You can start now.
- Put in the first slide.
- The slide is the wrong way round/upside down.
- Lift/Lower the picture. We can't see it properly.
- It's/The photo's out of focus (*unscharf*).
- Go on to the next slide/Let's see the next slide.

- Switch off the lamp but leave on the fan. The bulb ist still hot.
- Don't knock the projector. The bulb is still hot.
- Put up the screen.

Computer

- Go to the computer room and wait for me.
- Don't make a noise in the corridor while you're waiting (for me).

- Get into pairs and go to your computer/workstation.
- I'm turning on the computer now. Wait for it/the program to load, please.

- Press the start button and follow the instructions on the screen.

- I'm turning off the computer now.

General instructions

- Don't touch/play around/fiddle around (*herumfummeln*) with the computer/DVD player/equipment/..., (name).
- Leave the overhead (projector)/mouse/... alone, (name).
- If you break/damage the CD player/..., you know who'll pay for it, don't you, (name)?
- Can you see/hear all right/okay?
- (name), can you go and get an extension cable (*Verlängerungskabel*), please?
- (name), go and get the caretaker (*Hausmeister*)/Mr/Mrs ... This slide projector/... seems to be broken/doesn't work properly/isn't working (properly).
- Now, listen (to the CD/cassette) carefully.
- Look at this transparency (NOT 'folio')/slide/poster/...

e) In the language lab (*Im Sprachlabor*)

- Go to the language lab and wait for me.
- Don't make a noise in the corridor while you're waiting (for me).

- You can't sit anywhere you like.
- Sit in your usual places/in the places I told you.
- (name), you should be in place/booth (*Zelle*)/at desk number ...

- Can you all hear (now)?
- If you can't hear, press the call button (*Ruftaste*).
- If your machine's/tape recorder's not working, press the call button/put up your hand.
- (name), go to booth/place/desk (number) ... That's working all right.
- (name), (take your headphones and) go and work with (name).

- Everyone listen.
- You can work at your own speed now/on your own now.
- I'm afraid the equipment/the lab isn't working properly. We'll (have to) go back to the classroom/do normal work/play a game/get on with something else/…

2 Exams and tests (*Prüfungen und Tests*)

Wegen der unterschiedlichen Schul- und Prüfungssysteme lassen sich die deutschen Ausdrücke ‚Klassenarbeit', ‚Klausur', ‚Prüfung', ‚Test' usw. nicht eindeutig ins Englische übersetzen. ‚Klassenarbeit', ‚Klausur' und ‚Prüfung' werden hier *examination* oder einfach *exam* genannt. Der englische Begriff für ‚Übungsarbeit' lautet *mock exam*. Eine ‚Abschlussprüfung' nennt man *final exam*; eine ‚Zwischenprüfung' heißt nach diesem Muster *intermediate* oder *stage exam*.

Unserer Meinung nach entspricht die deutsche Verwendung von ‚Test' am ehesten dem englischen Begriff *placement test* oder *assessment test*, da dieser den diagnostischen Charakter, den solche Tests eigentlich haben sollten, zum Ausdruck bringt. Andere Möglichkeiten sind natürlich *vocab test*, *grammar test*, *verb test* usw.

Übrigens … Im Englischen ist es nicht möglich, eine Klassenarbeit zu schreiben oder schreiben zu lassen. Der Prüfer (*examiner*) erteilt/hält/gibt eine Prüfung. Der Prüfling (*examineer*) legt eine Prüfung ab oder ‚sitzt'/‚macht' eine Prüfung:

Der Prüfer: *hold an exam; give sb an exam/examine sb*
Der Prüfling: *sit an exam; take an exam; do an exam*

a) Fixing a date (*Terminierung*)
- I'm planning to hold/give you an exam/to hold/give you a written test at the end of the week/next week/the week after next/during/in the second/… lesson on Thursday/…
- I'd like/intend to examine you during/in the third/… lesson on Tuesday/…

- (VI Form) As you know, you will be examined in English on …/on this topic on …
- (VI Form), you must sit/take an exam on …
- What other exams have you got next week/during week ending (date)?
- I'm giving you an assessment/placement/vocab/… test on …

b) Place and materials (*Prüfungsort und Materialien*)
- I plan/hope/intend to use Room (number)/the assembly hall (*Aula*)/…
- Don't forget to bring your answer book (*Klassenarbeitsheft*)/writing materials/something to write with/dictionaries/readers/…

c) During exams and tests (*Während Klassenarbeiten und Tests*)
- Today's date is …/The date is …
- Don't forget to write your name on the answer sheet.
- Don't forget to leave a wide margin/one third of the page free for corrections.
- You can answer all the questions/questions … and …/questions … to … (directly) on the question paper.
- Answer question(s)/part(s) … in your answer book.
- Please write clearly/legibly.
- If I can't read something, then I'll have to count it as a mistake/ignore what you've written.
- You can't share dictionaries. You can use this one on my desk.
- Please don't forget to count your words.
- When you've finished give in your answer book and sit quietly/read/get on with something sensible/…
- You can give in your answer book/paper and leave the room.
- When you've given in your …, please leave the room immediately.

d) Seating arrangements (*Sitzplan*)
- (name), please sit here.
- (name), you can't sit there/next to (name).
- Please come and sit here/go and sit next to (name)/between (name) and (name)/behind (name)/in front of (name).
- Go and sit in the first/second/… row.

- Go and sit near the door/window/radiator (*Heizkörper*)/...
- Sit at the front/back of the room.
- (name), please move the desks further apart.
- (name), don't push the desks together. Put them back as they were.

e) Calming examinees down (*Wie man Prüflinge beruhigt*)
- Don't worry/get in a panic.
- There's nothing to worry about.

- Think about what we've done during the last three or four weeks/few weeks.
- There are no tricks or traps (*Fallen*). The exam is just like what we've done/practised in class.
- Do the questions you can answer easily first. Then go on to the harder ones.
- If you don't understand the question, just ask me.
- When you have finished, check what you have written.
- Calm down, stop chattering (*schwatzen, plappern*) and listen to me.
- You're wasting your own time. Stop chattering and we can start.
- You have plenty of time. Read through the questions carefully and then start to write.
- If you get stuck (*nicht weiter kommen*), put up your hand and I'll see what I can do.

f) Attempts at cheating (*Täuschungsversuche*)
Viele Kollegen meinen, dass es besser ist, Deutsch für formelle Warnungen über Täuschungsversuche zu verwenden. Andere benutzen Englisch oder Deutsch, entsprechend der Ernsthaftigkeit des Falles. Aus rechtlichen Gründen würden wir die Verwendung von Deutsch für formelle Warnungen mindestens bis Klasse 11 empfehlen.

- (name), stop talking and get on with your own work.
- (name), stop trying to look at (name)'s book/work.
- (name), put your book flat on the desk.
- (name), what have you got in your hand/under the desk/on your lap/in your shoe/stuck to your jeans/...?

- (name), (name) doesn't know either.
- (name), let (name) get on with his/her work, and you get on with yours.
- (name), come and sit here.

- Don't forget that helping others to cheat is as bad as/the same as cheating yourself.
- (name), you know (very well) that if I catch you cheating, I'll have to give you a 6.
- I'll have to take your paper/book and tell you to leave the room/have to ignore what you've written so far.

3 Achievement: praising and criticising (*Leistung: wie man Lob und Kritik erteilt*)

a) Giving mild praise (*mildes Lob*)
- That's was all right/okay.
- That was all right, but be careful about (your) pronunciation/intonation/(your use of) tenses/the definite article/…
- That seemed all right on the whole, but …
- It's/was all right as far as it goes/went, but you left out (some) important details/information/evidence.
- On the whole/In general, I'm satisfied with your work.

b) Being mildly critical (*geringfügige Kritik*)
- You (really) must start working more consistently/effectively/systematically/with greater concentration.
- Your work could be satisfactory, but you (tend to) work too erratically (*sprunghaft*)/in stops and starts/only as the mood takes you (*nach Lust und Laune*).
- You can't expect (to get) a good grade unless you're willing to work harder/pay attention during lessons/make a consistent contribution (*ständige Mitarbeit*)/do your homework (properly)/prepare for lessons/examinations.
- I'm sure you could do better if you worked harder.

- You've got to choose between working and playing. You can't expect both.
- You've got some good ideas, but you make (far) too many language mistakes. Don't forget that the subject is English, not (for example) Politics or Social Sciences (*Sozialwissenschaft*).

c) Unqualified praise (*uneingeschränktes Lob*)
- That was really good.
- I'm (very) satisfied with your work/contributions to lessons.
- You're obviously trying harder.
- You're making satisfactory/good progress. I'm very satisfied (with you).
- Your oral/written work's getting better (all the time).

- That was fine/very good/highly satisfactory. I'm (very) pleased/satisfied.
- You're making very good/excellent progress.
- I'm glad to see that you're working so well and showing such an improvement/so much interest.
- Well done, and keep it up (*weiter so*).
- Keep on as you are, and you'll do very well (indeed).
- Go on as you are, and I'll be glad/happy to give you a/an good/appropriate grade.
- I'm particularly pleased to see you making such a good contribution to lessons.

d) Being overtly critical (*offene Kritik*)
- Speak English. This is an English lesson.

- You must start working harder/stop being so lazy/do your homework/take part in lessons/...
- Your work has become disappointing/(increasingly) unsatisfactory/careless/slapdash (*schlampig*)/...
- What's happened? You can do (much) better than this!
- Unless you show a marked improvement, you'll have problems/get into difficulties/...
- (name), you won't be able to reach the required standard/a satisfactory standard.

- You write/say a lot, but you often repeat yourself/just read out bits of text.
- You make little/no effort to use your own language/express your own ideas.
- You make (far) too many basic language mistakes.

- Your vocabulary is (very) weak. You just haven't got enough words to express yourself.
- You won't get off a 4 unless you stop making so many basic grammar/vocab mistakes.
- I regard oral performance (*mündliche Leistung*) as being just as important as written work.
- Your written work is more or less acceptable, but you must contribute more to lessons.
- I'm very/extremely dissatisfied/disappointed with your work this term/year.
- You show no interest whatsoever in English/this subject.
- Get this clear/Understand this. If you go on as you are/like this, you'll (definitely) get a 5/ fail.
- You (never/seldom) do your homework/prepare for lessons, and you contribute nothing to discussions/oral sessions/lessons.
- You don't do anything yourself, and you do your best to distract (*ablenken*) others/disturb the lessons/stop others from working.

4 Behaviour: Reprimanding somebody (*Benehmen: wie man jemanden zurechtweist*)

a) Lateness (*Verspätung*)
- Don't just go to your place/seat without saying anything. Why are you late?
- This is the second/... time you've been late this week/during the last few weeks/recently. In future, make sure you're here on time.
- You're always late. Come and see me at the end of the lesson.
- It's all right this time, but in future you'll just have to get up earlier.

b) Without book etc. (*Vergessene Arbeitsmittel*)
- (Name), where is your book/workbook/homework/reader?
- I told you to bring your ... Why haven't you got it?
- You'll have to/can share with (name) this time, but don't forget your ... again.

- You can use my/this copy this time, but …
- Do you mean you've forgotten your homework or you haven't done your homework (at all)?
- You are always forgetting something. Come and see me at the end of the lesson, please.
- If you forget your book/… again, I'll have to write your name in the register (*Klassenbuch*)/ speak to your form teacher/your tutor/your parents about it.

c) **Disturbing lessons** (*Störung des Unterrichts*)
- (name), stop talking/chattering (*schwatzen*)/gossiping and get on with your work/listen to me/pay attention.
- (name), you're talking too much/making too much noise.
- (name), this is your last/final warning. If you don't stop talking/… and get on with your work, I'll have to put your name in the register (*Klassenbuch*).
- (name), stop talking to (name) so much, or you'll have to go and sit somewhere else/come and sit here.
- (name), sit down/go back to your place/seat/desk and get on with your (own) work.
- (name), please don't leave your place/… without asking.
- Please don't just shout out. Put up your hand.
- Stop pushing and shoving.
- (name), stop playing around with/fiddling around with your pen/that toy/…
- (name), give me that mobile phone/… You can come/go and get it at the end of the lesson/ when you go home/from the school office (*Sekretariat*).
- (name), go and sit there/near the window/by the door/next to (name)/ between (name) and (name).
- There's (far) too much noise. I can't hear what (name)'s trying to say.

d) **Distracting** (*Ablenkung*)
- (name), leave (name)/your neighbour alone.
- (name), leave (name)'s things alone.
- (name), stop interfering with (name) and let her/him get on with her/his work.

- (name), stop distracting (*ablenken*) (name) and get on with your work.
- (name), do you think it's fair to stop other people from working?
- (name), in the end you've got to decide yourself whether you work or not, but don't stop others from working/but you have no right to stop others from working.

e) Doing other work (*Anderweitige Beschäftigungen*)
- This is an English lesson. Put your Maths/Latin/German/... book(s)/things away, please.
- You should do your German/Biology/... homework at home. Get out your English book(s)/things.
- Give me that book/comic/magazine/toy/... You can come and get it from me at the end of the lesson/day/week/...

f) Packing up early (*Zu früh zusammenpacken*)
- The bell hasn't rung/gone yet. Stop putting your things away.
- Sit down until I've finished speaking.
- The bell's for me, not for you.

g) Cheek (*Frechheit*)
- (name), listen to/look at me when I'm talking to you.
- (name), I'm talking to you. Listen!
- Don't interrupt me when I'm speaking. I haven't finished yet.
- Don't be cheeky/rude/impolite.
- I'm not rude to you, and I don't expect you to be rude to me.
- If you want trouble, I can deliver – express.

9 Deutschland auf Englisch

Die folgende reduzierte Themenliste basiert auf einer Befragung von Ausländern, die in Deutschland leben, gelebt haben bzw. Deutschland einigermaßen gut kennen.

Interessanterweise ist diese Liste viel kürzer geworden, als es bei der letzten Ausgabe der Fundgrube der Fall war. Dies ist gewiss eine Auswirkung des Zusammenwachsens Europas und der zunehmenden Globalisierung der Wirtschaft und der Unterhaltungsindustrie, die dazu tendieren ‚nationale Besonderheiten' abzubauen.

Gemäß unserer Befragung sind vor allem die folgenden Themen von Bedeutung (in alphabetischer Reihenfolge):

1 A tendency towards pessimism? (*Neigung zum Pessimismus?*)

A: It is sometimes said in the American and British press that Germans always look on the black side. You know, the glass is always half empty, never half full. Is there any truth in that?

B: Well, as with all generalisations, you need to be careful with this one, too. In my opinion, it is certainly true that many Germans – like, I imagine, many Americans – show a healthy scepticism when it comes to politicians, lobbyists of all kinds, including advertisers, and the mass media. They assume they're not hearing the whole truth, and are often being simply misled. Frankly, that's my attitude, too.

A: Sure, but that applies elsewhere as well. Aren't we talking about something different here, though, at least in degree?

B: Well, perhaps we are. It's true that a sizeable majority of Germans seem to think that if something can go wrong, it probably will.

Neigung zum Pessimismus?

A: There we are, then – the doomsday syndrome.
B: Oh, no. That's over the top. This pessimistic attitude doesn't apply to the whole of life, you see. It applies primarily to the effects of globalisation on German manufacturing ...
A: What, relocation and outsourcing, you mean?
B: Indeed. And, closely related to that, it applies to the reform of the social security system.
A: Yes, but there's no way that things can possibly go on as they are, is there? I mean, you still have a very generous welfare state here, don't you? It's quite simply unaffordable, isn't it?
B: Yes, but I think ...
A: Sorry to interrupt, but isn't it still true that at the lower end of the pay scale, it makes more economic sense to live off benefits than to work?
B: No. That's a myth, frankly. It obviously takes time for the reforms introduced in 2004 – the so-called Hartz reforms – to kick in, but things are getting much tougher, I can tell you.
A: I see. Okay then. How do you explain this pessimism about the future, then?
B: Look, I think you need to take two factors into account. Firstly, the 'economic miracle' of the post-war decades enabled Germany to build a generous welfare state, including wonderful health and pensions provision. A lot of this pessimism flows from that. If you're at the top, you always fall further and land harder than people further down the pile. But that's a temporary reaction which is already beginning to wane. And that brings me to my second point.
A: And that's?
B: Well, the huge majority of Germans, young and old alike, now accept that with an ageing population and a very low birthrate, the welfare state, above all pensions, must be reformed. With the exception of a few people on the 'looney left', everybody has taken that on board.
A: What's the problem then?
B: The problem is one of social justice. This painful process of reduction must be carried by the whole of German society, not just by those least able to bear it. And until they see that happening, this 'black mood' will continue.
A: Yes, I can understand that.

2 Comparing political parties (*Politische Parteien im Vergleich*)

A: I read somewhere that you're ... uhm ... CDU, is it?

B: Right. That's the Christian Democratic Union in English.

A: Sure. Well, in this press article they were called the 'German conservatives', but isn't that a bit misleading? As far as I can see they have nothing much in common with the British conservatives at all.

B: You're right if you're comparing them to your Conservative Party, but the CDU does represent German conservatives – with a small 'c', of course. But don't forget that the German CDU is in permanent coalition with the CSU who ...

A: Oh yes. That's a Bavarian party, isn't it?

B: That's right. Anyhow the 'S' in CSU stands for 'Social', and they get a lot of votes from ordinary wage-earners who are probably SPD voters in the rest of Germany.

A: I see. So comparisons are difficult, are they?

B: Not difficult – 'impossible' would be a better word.

A: How so? Surely British and German parties have something in common, don't they?

B: Sure, but the big thing is that in British terms almost all the popular parties in the rest of the EU tend to be social democratic – again with a small 's' and 'd'. That's what makes comparisons so dangerous.

A: Ah, the 'social market economy' versus the 'free market economy', right?

B: Yes, I think that's a good way of putting it. The only Anglo-Saxon-style 'free market' party we have in Germany is the Free Democrats and they're doing well when they get around eight percent of the vote. At the moment the FDP's calling for deregulation, privatisation and tax reductions financed by cuts in social security spending and an end to subsidies. On these issues, the FDP stands well to the right of the Union.

A: Yes, that sounds really Thatcherite.

B: Indeed, it does. In fact, if I had to choose the German equivalent of Thatcherite Conservatives in the UK, I'd point to the FDP.

A: I see. So calling Angela Merkel 'Maggie Merkel' is way over the top, is it?

B: You can say that again. That's just media silliness. In fact, on social issues, Frau Merkel is to the left of Blair's New Labour party.

A: Yes, but isn't New Labour the nearest British equivalent of the CDU?

B: I think you're probably right there, but it's certainly not a one-for-one fit.
A: And the SPD?
B: Well, Blair's taken his New Labour so far to the right, that I suppose the SPD is closer to being the German equivalent of 'old labour'. That's what makes comparisons so difficult.

3 Germany's role in the extended EU (*Die Rolle Deutschlands in der erweiterten EU*)

A: It now looks as if the UK supported widening the EU mainly because this would put paid to any idea of a united Europe once and for all.
B: Yes, and they were probably right. Look what's happened to the constitution and several other measures. Nothing very much has happened since the new states joined, has it?
A: Yes, but doesn't this also mean that France and Germany will see a big reduction in their role? I mean, the Franco-German partnership was the engine of unity, wasn't it?
B: I'm sure you're right on both counts. There's no doubt that the post-war generations of French and German leaders were the driving force behind the increasing integration of the EU, if not its full union. Nobody thought that would happen in the foreseeable future.
A: Oh, so British fears of a United States of Europe were always exaggerated, were they?
B: Yes. They had nothing to do with the reality at all. The UK and other countries always had an 'opt out' of major measures such as the euro and the open frontiers anyhow.
A: But using these opt outs also tended to isolate the UK and the others, didn't it?
B: Well, if you are in a club but you don't take part in many of its activities, some other members may not think you're very committed. However, you're right. The new members on the fringe of the old EU have definitely strengthened the UK's position.
A: The British wish for a loose free trade area made up of nation states, you mean?

B: Yes. The countries of the former Soviet Bloc like Poland and the Czech Republic are still enjoying their independence far too much to cede it to Brussels. The UK knows that.

A: And where does that leave Germany – and France, of course?

B: Well, Germany and France have problems enough of their own, don't they? The further integration of the EU is very much on the back burner at the moment. However, Germany is still the biggest single contributor to the EU, which will always give it a lot of clout, frankly.

A: So France and Germany still have the final say, do they?

B: In the sense that nothing very much can happen without their support, yes.

A: So the UK may be counting its chickens before the eggs have hatched? Are you saying that once Germany and France have sorted out their domestic difficulties, they will revive their dream of a fully integrated Europe?

B: Yes and no. Obviously the idea of an integrated EU of nearly 30 states will never be a reality. We can forget that. But the idea of a more closely integrated inner core made up of the original Six plus Austria and Spain, for example, may be asleep, but it's most certainly not dead.

4 Half-day schools (*Halbtagsschulen*)

A: Is it true that in Germany half-day or morning-only schools is the general rule?

B: Well, this was once the case, but things are changing very fast now.

A: Why so? What's caused the trend away from traditional half-day schools?

B: Well, three things, really. Firstly, many people outside Germany don't realise that we used to have school on Saturday mornings as well.

A: Oh, I didn't realise that, either.

B: No? Well, we did. Unsurprisingly, this wasn't very popular among parents working a five-day week themselves. After all, it meant that somebody had to get up to see the children off to school and …

A: Sure, and nothing very much could happen before they got back again, right?

B: Right. Shopping trips and other excursions had to be delayed, which many parents found annoying. Anyhow, Saturday school is now very

rare. But this change meant that lessons once given on a Saturday had to be redistributed. The result of that was that at least some classes on some days took place in the early afternoon.
A: Yes, but did that really make much difference?
B: Well, the psychological effect was immense. The 'one o'clock barrier' had been broken, you see. Afternoon school was no longer unknown.
A: I see. But there have always been some all-day schools, haven't there?
B: Yes, indeed. That's the second important factor. Almost all the new *Gesamtschulen* or 'comprehensive high schools' set up from the early 1970s onwards were all-day schools from the very start. This was because their educational ethos was not only academic, but social as well. Obviously, you can't socialise children if they only attend school for subject lessons. You need time for extra-curricular activities and pastoral care as well.
A: Yes, that's very familiar. That's the American and British approach as well.
B: Yes, and in the old GDR (= German Democratic Republic, dt.: DDR), of course. Many secondary schools in the new states in the east were all-day as well. Anyhow, these all-day schools were a big hit with parents, particularly in families in which both parents were working. This was such an important point in favour of the comprehensives that other school forms, particularly the *Hauptschulen* or 'secondary modern schools', began to go over to the all-day system just to compete.
A: Not the grammar schools, though?
B: Oh, no. More and more grammar schools have gone over – or are now going over – to the all-day system as well. This trend is bound to increase rapidly because the policy of all the political parties is the introduction of all-day schools right across the board in both the primary and secondary sectors.
A: Ah, I get it. And I'm sure that will bring you to the third factor, right?
B: Too true. Germany is often said to be hostile to reform, but that is at best only half the truth. There is certainly a kind of inertia at the top, but huge changes are taking place on the ground. One of the most important is that more and more mothers have at least part-time jobs, often more than just one. And the same goes for fathers. At long last, politicians have recognised that schools must face the consequence of this.
A: I see. So politics is chasing reality, is it?

5 Public holidays and religious feast days (*Feiertage und religiöse Festtage*)

A: In Britain we sometimes hear about Germany's public holidays. You have more than most other countries, don't you?

B: Well – as so often in Germany – to some extent it depends on where you live. Some states have religious feast days in addition to the normal public holidays, you see. For example, Bavaria has 13 days off while Berlin has just nine.

A: What are the main German public holidays then? Are they secular like in Britain?

B: Well, New Year's Day, Labour Day in May, German Unity Day in October and Boxing Day are completely secular, but Easter Monday, Whit Monday, Ascension Day and, of course, Christmas Day are more or less religious, at least in origin.

A: What about all these other holidays, then? You know, the religious feast days?

B: In Catholic areas, or areas with big Catholic communities, they celebrate three feast days, Corpus Christi, the Assumption of the Virgin Mary and All Saints' Day. In Bavaria they also have a holiday on the sixth of January, Three Wise Men Day. Protestant areas don't celebrate these feast days, of course, but they have two of their own, Repentance Day and Reformation Day. But please don't forget that there are some differences between the states.

A: Well, lucky you! You certainly get more days off than we do.

B: Yes, but that depends on the calendar, doesn't it? In Germany, if one of these public holidays happens to fall on a Saturday or Sunday, it's just too bad. We don't get the next following Monday off instead like you do in the UK and the USA. It's just tough luck.

A: Oh, that doesn't sound so good.

6 Regional cuisine (*Regionale Küche*)

A: German cookery seems much more varied than British cookery – if there is such a thing any more.
B: I've noticed that, too. Your food's very, well, 'American', isn't it?
A: Yes. I don't know what we'd do without the Indian and Chinese restaurants.
B: Yes. They're great, aren't they? I suppose our cookery is partly a result of German regionalism. This has helped to preserve a traditional folk culture in many parts of the country, particularly in rural areas.
A: Have you got any of these regional recipes? I'd love to try some out at home.
B: Sure. Dozens of them in fact. What about *Ostfriesischer Buuskohl*, for example? I suppose you'd call it something like "Frisian white cabbage stew" in English. A funny name, I know, but it's cheap, tasty and very nourishing, especially on cold winter days.
A: It sounds great. How do you make it?
B: Well, you need a big white cabbage – about a kilo or perhaps a little less should do –, four medium-sized onions, a good pound of lean smoked bacon and about as many potatoes as you have cabbage. Oh, and you'll need some pork dripping (*Schweineschmalz*), too – two or three good dessertspoonfuls (*Esslöffel*) will be enough. They're the main ingredients.
A: Okay. I've got all that.
B: Yes, and then there are the spices and so on, of course. We use about a teaspoonful of caraway seed (*Kümmel*) – very North German, that – and then freshly-milled white pepper to taste.
A: What? No salt?
B: No. There's plenty of salt in the bacon and dripping. Don't add any more or you'll destroy the taste.
A: Okay.
B: Oh, yes, and then you'll need about half a litre of stock (*Brühe*) but you can make that from any good stock cube – Knorr or Maggi, for example.
A: Oh, yes. We can get them in the UK now. Well, how do I go about doing the cooking?
B: Well, here we go. First the cabbage. After you've removed any damaged or dirty outer leaves, cut the cabbage into quarters and cut out the stalk. Now cut the cabbage into slices about three centimetres wide, pull the

leaves apart and then wash them thoroughly under cold running water. When you've done that let the cabbage drain in a colander (*Sieb*).

A: Fine. That's how we cook cabbage as a vegetable, too.

B: That's right. Anyhow, now peel and slice the onions. After that melt the dripping in a large saucepan and cook the cabbage and the onions together over a gentle heat for about ten minutes. Stir regularly to stop burning or sticking, of course, and do make sure that you really use only a low heat, okay?

A: Okay. I'll underline that.

B: Good. After about ten minutes add the caraway, the stock and the whole piece of smoked bacon ...

A: Hold on. Does that mean that sliced bacon won't do?

B: Heavens no. That's what we call 'breakfast bacon'. You need a really thick piece, two or three centimetres, say, of unsliced bacon from the butcher's.

A: Fine. It's good that you said that.

B: Anyhow, now cover the saucepan and simmer (*ziehen lassen*) gently for about forty-five minutes or so. You can add a bit more stock if necessary, of course, but don't make the stew too thin, will you?

A: No, I'll watch that.

B: Well, we've nearly finished now. While the cabbage is cooking, peel the potatoes and cut them into roughly two centimetre cubes. Add these to the cabbage after about forty-five minutes and let the stew simmer until the potatoes are cooked through but still firm. This takes about fifteen or twenty minutes.

A: Fine.

B: Now, keep an eye on the clock because you have to take the bacon out of the pan and cut it into bite-sized cubes about five minutes before the end. When you've cut up the bacon, return it to the pan and mix in.

A: And what about the pepper?

B: Oh, yes. Add a generous amount of white pepper when you put the bacon back in. That's very North German, too, by the way.

A: And what about side-dishes?

B: Normally we eat the stew alone or with a slice of rye bread. Oh, and don't forget a nice cool lager, will you?

Weitere Rezepte

Allgäuer Käsespätzle – *cheese noodles from the Allgäu*

What you need:

350 g plain flour
approx. 1 l lukewarm water
4 eggs
3 medium-sized onions
2 dessertspoons (*Esslöffel*) butter
approx. 150 g Emmental cheese
1 teaspoon salt
pinch nutmeg
chives (*Schnittlauch*)

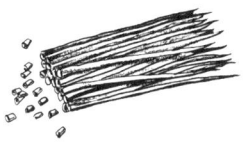

What you do: Sieve (*sieben*) flour into bowl and blend with water, eggs, salt and nutmeg to make a smooth and thickish dough. Rest for 15 minutes. Peel and chop onions and fry gently in butter until golden. Chop chives as garnish and finely grate cheese.
Spread a thin (ca. 3 mm) layer of dough on to a moistened pastry board and cut into thin strips. Push the strips carefully off the board into a large pan of gently boiling lightly salted water. Allow to simmer uncovered until the noodles float to the top. Remove noodles from pan and drain. Place noodles layer by layer in a serving bowl, sprinkling each layer with grated cheese. Garnish top layer generously with cheese, onions and chives.
This dish can be eaten alone or as an accompaniment to meat.

Berner Rösti – *Bern potato cakes*

What you need:

1.5 kg cold potatoes boiled in their skins
2 dessertspoons butter
6 dessertspoons (*Esslöffel*) cooking oil
salt to taste
parsley (*Petersilie*)

What you do: Slice the peeled potatoes. Heat the butter and oil in a heavy-based non-stick frying pan. Add salt to taste and fry, turning several times. Finally press down the potatoes firmly and fry further until underside is golden-brown. Turn on to serving dish and garnish with fresh parsley.
This dish can be eaten alone with salads or cold meats, steaks, roasts etc.

Hamburger Aalsuppe – *Hamburg eel soup*

What you need:

750 g fresh eels
100 g smoked bacon
2 onions
3 carrots
1 celeriac (*Knollensellerie*)
2 leeks
1 teaspoon each majoran, sage (*Salbei*), tarragon (*Estragon*), thyme
1 stock cube (*Brühwürfel*)
2 pears
1 cup frozen peas
1 small packet each frozen cut parsley (*Petersilie*), dill
2 dessertspoons (*Esslöffel*) plain flour

What you do: Wash eels thoroughly in cold running water and remove heads and tails. Rub eels with salt and cut into pieces about 4 cm long.
Dice smoked bacon and onions. Fry fat out of bacon and then fry onion in the fat until golden. Clean and wash remaining vegetables and add sliced carrots/leeks, diced celeriac and dried herbs to the bacon and onion. Simmer gently for about 1 minute before adding 1 litre of water. Add salt to taste and stock cube and bring to the boil. Peel, core and quarter pears. Add eel pieces and pears to mixture and simmer gently for about 25 minutes before adding peas, parsley and dill. Add pepper to taste. Thicken with flour and cook for a further 5 minutes.

Kasseler im Blätterteig –
Smoked loin of pork in puff pastry

What you need:

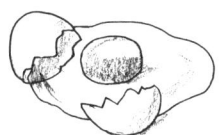

1 kg smoked boneless loin of pork
2 dessertspoons (*Esslöffel*) cooking oil
2 standard packets frozen puff pastry
1 egg

What you do: Brown bone-side of meat in hot oil for 2–3 minutes and allow to cool.

Roll both packets of thawed pastry into single sheet big enough to wrap the entire piece of meat. Put about one-third of pastry on to a baking sheet moistened with water and lay the cooled meat bone-side down on to the pastry. Moisten edges of pastry with water. Cover top, sides and ends of meat with second and larger piece of pastry, joining it to the lower piece by pressing firmly together. Make two holes in top of pastry to allow surplus steam to escape during cooking. (You can decorate the pastry with left-over strips of pastry if you want.)

Brush the pastry with beaten egg to assist browning. Place in oven at lowest level and cook at 180° C for about 45 minutes or until golden.

Serve hot with vegetables.

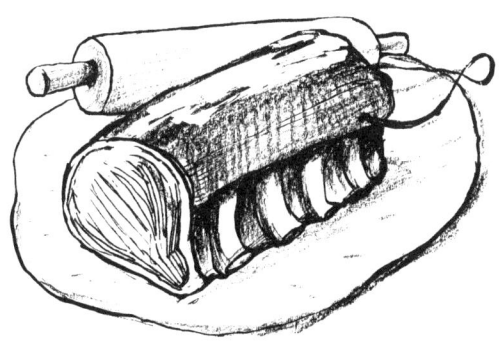

Nürnberger Gans mit Semmelfüllung –
Nuremberg goose with bread stuffing

What you need:

1 fresh or frozen goose (2.5–3 kg)
salt
salt water
4 bread rolls from day before
12 dessertspoons (*Esslöffel*) milkheart/liver from goose
40 g butter
1 smallish onion (chopped)
1 dessertspoon parsley (chopped)
salt, pepper, nutmeg (*Muskat*) to taste
4 eggs
2 dessertspoons single cream

What you do: Remove innards from goose and lay to one side for stuffing (*Füllung*). Wash goose under cold running water. Dry inside and outside thoroughly and rub all surfaces generously with salt.

Cut rolls into pieces and soften in milk. Chop heart and liver very finely and simmer (*ziehen lassen*) in butter with onion and parsley until onion is soft and transparent (here: *glasig*). Squeeze surplus milk from bread rolls and blend thoroughly with onion mix, spices, eggs and cream so as to make a firm stuffing mix. Stuff goose and close opening with thread.

Lay stuffed goose breast-side up on roasting grill with drip pan and place in middle of pre-heated oven. Roast at 180° C for about 3 hours, basting (*begießen*) frequently. After about one and a half hours turn goose over to allow underside to brown for about the last 30 minutes of total roasting time. Remove excess fat from drip pan as necessary. To get a particularly crispy skin, brush several times with well-salted water about 20 minutes before end of roasting.

Eat hot with red cabbage and croquette potatoes.

Mecklenburger Schinkenbohnen –
Bacon and bean pie from Mecklenburg

What you need:

500 g tinned sliced green beans
400 g lean bacon
750 g peeled uncooked potatoes
50 g butter
1 teaspoon savory (*Bohnenkraut*)
3 eggs
¼ l milk
l single cream
salt, white pepper, grated nutmeg (*Muskat*)
50 g grated Emmental cheese or similar
4 dessertspoons (*Esslöffel*) white breadcrumbs

What you do: Drain beans in colander (*Sieb*). Dice bacon, slice potatoes and place all ingredients in layers in well-greased ovenproof dish, sprinkling beans with savory. Add whisked eggs, milk, cream and spices. Sprinkle grated cheese and breadcrumbs evenly on top of mix, ending with a few flakes of butter to assist browning.
Bake in middle of hot oven at 175° C for about 30 minutes or until cheese has thoroughly melted and begun to brown. (Cover with baking paper to hinder burning if necessary.)
Eat with salad.

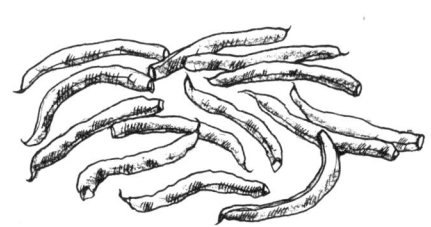

Rindsgulasch – *German beef goulash*

What you need:

1 kg stewing meat
300 g onions
2 dessertspoons (*Esslöffel*) cooking oil
1 teaspoon white pepper
1 teaspoon majoram
1 teaspoon each sweet and hot paprika
some salt
50 g goose or pork dripping (*Gänse- oder Schweineschmalz*)
¼ l red table wine (*Landwein*)
plain flour or thickening agent (*Bindemittel*)

What you do: Cut beef into roughly 2 cm cubes. Fry in hot oil, stirring occasionally to prevent sticking and burning. Add spices to meat. Dice onions and add these, the dripping and wine to meat. Simmer gently until meat is tender, stirring occasionally. Add salt to taste and thicken with flour or thickening agent if wished.

Eat with red cabbage and mashed potatoes, or just with rice.

Rheinischer Sauerbraten – *Marinated beef from the Rhineland*

What you need:

1 kg boneless roasting beef

(for the marinade)
¼ l red table wine (*Landwein*)
¼ l water
¼ l fruit-based vinegar
5 dried juniper berries (*Wacholderbeeren*)
1 bay-leaf (*Lorbeerblatt*)
1 clove (*Nelke*)
1 slice from large onion

(for roasting)
1 bunch soup vegetables (*Suppengrün*)
150 g sliced bacon
1 teaspoon freshly milled black pepper
30 g dripping (*Schmalz*)

(for sauce)
marinade
water
flour
single cream
salt, pepper to taste

What you do: Put ingredients for marinade into a saucepan and bring to the boil. Remove from heat and allow to cool. Lay meat in suitable container, cover with cooled marinade and leave in fridge for 2–3 days. If the meat is not fully covered by the marinade, turn daily.

Line bottom of roasting pan with half the slices of bacon, lay the moist meat on the bacon layer and sprinkle with black pepper. Spread flakes of dripping over top of meat and then cover with remaining bacon. Finally, add small pieces of diced and/or sliced soup vegetables and sufficient marinade to reach the underside of the meat.

Place covered roasting pan in middle of pre-heated oven and roast at about 190° C for about 1 hour or until meat is tender.

To prepare sauce, drain juices from meat and add marinade; add some water to dilute if necessary. Mix flour with cream to make thick, smooth mixture free of lumps. Thicken sauce, adding salt and freshly milled pepper to taste.

Eat with red cabbage and boiled potatoes, or German potato dumplings (obtainable from delicatessens or the delicatessen department of any big supermarket.)

Westfälischer Grünkohl mit Kasseler –
Westphalian curly kale with smoked pork

What you need:

1 kg curly kale
4 medium-sized onions
2 dessertspoons (*Esslöffel*) pork dripping (*Schweineschmalz*)
1 teaspoon sugar
salt, white pepper to taste
500 g smoked loin of pork
6 cloves (*Nelken*)
¼ l water
1 dessertspoon gravy powder (*Bratensoßenpulver*)
1 dessertspoon mild mustard

What you do: Remove leaves from stalks of kale, wash and cook gently in the lightly salted water in covered pan for about 5 minutes. Drain and cut into small pieces. Peel and dice onions and fry gently in dripping until golden. Add chopped kale, sugar, pinch (*Prise*) of salt and pepper. Press cloves into meat, put on kale and baste (*begießen*) with liquid.
Simmer (*ziehen lassen*) in covered pan for about 60 minutes and then divide the meat into pieces. Mix gravy powder into kale and then add mild mustard to taste.
Eat with fried potatoes and follow with an ice-cold aquavit.

Speisenamen

A: Have you found anything you'd like?
B: Well, I'm afraid you'll have to help me with some of these dishes. What's 'Jägerschnitzel', for example?
A: 'Jägerschnitzel'? Well, a 'Schnitzel' is …
B: Oh, I know what a schnitzel is. We use the same word in English. It's a breaded veal (*Kalbfleisch*) or pork steak. But what's a 'Jägerschnitzel'?
A: Ah, that's a fantasy name.
B: A fantasy name? What's that?
A: Sorry. I just translated the German word 'Fantasiename', I'm afraid. Anyhow, it's a made up-name, but unfortunately it doesn't say what it is.
B: I see.
A: Literally it means 'hunter's schnitzel'. It's a schnitzel covered with a thick mushroom sauce.
B: Oh, dear. I don't like mushrooms much.
A: What about a 'Zigeunerschnitzel' then? That means 'gypsy's schnitzel' – it's covered with a fairly hot sauce made of red peppers (*Paprika*) and tomato.
B: That sounds fine. I'll try that.

Alphabetisches Verzeichnis weiterer Speisen

Amerikaner	circular flat iced cake
Bauernfrühstück	scrambled eggs, fried with potatoes and chopped smoked back bacon
Berliner	doughnut without a hole
Bremer Brot	brown bread with shrimps with scrambled egg on top
Eisbein	boiled knuckle of pork
Falscher Hase	meat loaf made of minced beef and/or pork and breadcrumbs
Finkenwerder Scholle	whole fried plaice garnished with shrimps and diced smoked back bacon
Forelle Müllerin	trout fried in bread crumbs
Götterspeise	jelly
Halver Hahn	open cheese roll
Heidefrühstück	diced or minced pork in aspic

Holzfällersteak	beef steak with fried egg on top
Kaiserschmarren	pancake strips sprinkled with icing sugar and raisins
Kalte Schnauze (= *Kalter Hund*)	layer cake made of alternate layers of tea biscuits (e.g. Marie biscuits) and milk or plain chocolate
Kaltschale	cold sweet fruit soup with beer, wine or milk
Königsberger Klopse	meat balls
Leipziger Allerlei	mixed fresh vegetables in white sauce
Maultaschen	pasta envelope with meat filling for clear soups
Ratsherrentopf	earthenware pot of pork, beef, veal medallions in gravy from the meat
Russische Eier	hard-boiled eggs in mayonnaise garnished with caviar or roe ("fish eggs")
Schwalbennest	another name for *Maultaschen* (see above)
Soleier	pickled eggs
Strammer Max	open ham sandwich with two/three fried eggs on top
Wackelpeter	jelly
Wiener Schnitzel	breaded veal schnitzel without sauce
Windbeutel	round eclairs filled with cream and sometimes fruit

Deutsche Getränke

Biere

Alkoholfreies Bier	non-alcoholic beer
Alsterwasser	shandy consisting of lager and orangeade
Alt	brown ale
Bitterbier	bitter
Bockbier	strong beer (similiar to barley wine)
Krefelder	shandy consisting of brown ale and cola
Light-Bier	diet beer
Radler	shandy
Schwarzbier	light stout
Weißbier	fizzy beer from barley and wheat
Weizenbier	beer from wheat

Speisen und Getränke

Spirituosen

Korn	clear grain schnaps/spirits with 32% alcohol
Kräuterschnaps	herb schnaps/spirits
Kümmelschnaps	clear caraway schnaps/spirits
Magenbitter	bitters
Obstler	fruit schnaps/spirits (apple, cherry, pear, raspberry)
Wacholder	juniper schnaps/spirits (gin)
Doppelkorn/-wacholder	schnaps/spirits with 38% alcohol
Weinbrand	German brandy

10 Nützliche Informationen für den Englischunterricht

1 Same spelling, different pronunciation and meaning

There is an important class of word pairs in English that have identical spelling so meaning has to be expressed by changing the pronunciation (stress).

Here are the most important examples of such word pairs with the pronunciation and stress shown in phonetic script.

(1) I wound [wəʊnd] the bandage around the wound [wuːnd].
Ich wickelte die Bandage um die Wunde.

(2) We produce [prəˈdjuːs] organically grown produce [ˈprodjuːs] on our farm.
Wir produzieren ökologische Produkte auf unserem Bauernhof.

(3) The dump was so full that it had to refuse [rɪˈfjuːz] more refuse [ˈrefjuːs].
Die Mülldeponie war so voll, dass weiterer Müll abgelehnt werden musste.

(4) We must polish [ˈpɒlɪʃ] the Polish [ˈpəʊlɪʃ] furniture.
Wir müssen die polnischen Möbeln polieren.

(5) The soldier had to desert [dɪˈzɜːt] his dessert [dɪˈzɜːt] in the desert [ˈdezət].
Der Soldat musste seinen Nachtisch in der Wüste zurücklassen.

(6) I'd like to present [prɪˈzent] the bride a present [ˈpreznt].
Ich möchte der Braut ein Geschenk überreichen.

(7) AmE: When shot at, the dove [dʌv] it dove [dəʊv] into the bushes.
Als die Taube angeschossen wurde, stürzte sie sich in die Büsche.

(8) I did not object [əbˈdʒekt] to the object [ˈɒbʒɪkt].
Ich hatte nichts gegen den Gegenstand einzuwenden.

(9) The insurance of the invalid ['ɪnvəlɪd] was invalid [ɪn'vælɪd].
Die Versicherung des Kranken war ungültig.

(10) There was a row [raʊ] amongst the oarsmen about how to row [rəʊ].
Es gab zwischen den Ruderern einen Streit darüber, wie man rudert.

(11) The chair was too close [kləʊs] to the door so I couldn't close [kləʊz] it.
Der Stuhl war zu nah an der Tür, sodass ich sie nicht schließen konnte.

(12) The buck does [dʌz] funny things when the does [dəʊz] are near.
Der Hirschbock macht komische Dinge, wenn die Rehe in der Nähe sind.

(13) A milliner and a sewer ['səʊə(r)] fell down a sewer ['suːə(r)].
Eine Hutmacherin und eine Näherin fielen in einen Abwasserkanal.

(14) To help with sowing, the farmer taught his sow [saʊ] to sow [səʊ].
Um mit dem Säen zu helfen, lehrte der Bauer seine Sau das Säen.

(15) The wind [wɪnd] was too strong to wind [waɪnd] up the sail.
Der Wind war zu stark, um das Segel aufzuwickeln.

(16) After the doctor gave me a number ['nʌmbə(r)] of injections my arm got number ['nʌmə].
Nachdem der Arzt mir einige Spritzen gegeben hatte, wurde mein Arm tauber.

(17) When I saw the tear [teə(r)] in my dress I shed a tear [tɪə(r)].
Als ich den Riss in meinem Kleid sah, vergoss ich eine Träne.

(18) I had to subject [səb'dʒekt] the subject ['sʌbdʒɪkt] to a number of tests.
Ich musste den Kandidaten einer Anzahl von Prüfungen unterziehen.

2 Curious surname pronunciations

The correct pronunciation of some English surnames and place names are often a source of difficulty for both native and non-native speakers of English. Here's a list.

written	spoken
Auchinleck	Afflek
Beauchamp	Beecham
Beaulieu	Bewley [ˈbjuːlː]
Belvoir	Beaver
Blount	Blunt
Blyth	Bly
Bohun	Boon
Caius	Keys
Cholmondley	Chumley
Cockburn	Coburn [ˈkɔbɜn]
Colquhoun	Cahoon
Featherstonehaugh	Fanshaw
Home	Hume
Houghton	Horton, Howton
Knolly	Nowls [nəʊls]
Le Fanu	Leffnew [ˌləˈfnjuː]
Leigh	Lee
Magdalene	Maudlin
Mainwaring	Mannering, Manning
Marjoribanks	Marchbank
Menzies	Mingis [ˈmɪndʒɪs]
Poulett	Pawlet
Ruthven	Riven
St Clair	Sinclair
Theobald	Tibbald
Woolhardiswothy	Woolsey [ˈwuːlsi]
Worchester	Wooster [ˈwʊstə(r)]
Wymondham	Windam

3 Cockney Rhyming Slang

Traditionally, Cockneys make up a rather exclusive group of working-class Londoners of British extraction born within earshot of the bells of the church of Mary-le-Bow in the East End of London. Nowadays, however, the term has a much wider sense. It is commonly used to describe anybody of working-class British origin who was born anywhere in the East End or on the south bank of the Thames immediately opposite it.

Cockney rhyming slang replaces the intended word with a rhyming couplet, for example 'wife' with 'trouble and strife'. Although such rhyming couplets – as in the example above – can have some possible logical connection to the root word, this is not often the case. For example, rhyming slang for 'daughter' is 'bricks and mortar' and for 'money' 'bread and honey'. Hence the important thing is not a logical connection, but the rhyme itself.

As in its spoken form only the first (non-rhyming) word of the couplet is used, 'bricks' for 'daughter' and 'bread' for 'money', for example, rhyming slang is an effective secret code for those who wish to keep their conversations private. For this reason, it was often used in the presence of the police and business rivals.

A few items of rhyiming slang have gone over into more general, i. e. non-Cockney, usage and these are shown in the following list.

Cockney rhyme	meaning	expression in general usage
Adam and Eve	believe	
apples and pears	stairs	
Aristotle	bottle	
Artful Dodger	lodger	
Aunt Joanna	piano	
baked bean	queen	
baker's dozen	cousin	
bull and chalk	walk	
battlecruiser	boozer (= pub)	
boat race	face	
Bob Hope	soap	
Brahms and Liszt	pissed (= drunk)	
brass tacks	facts	
bread and honey	money	*(to) not have any/much bread*, i. e. money

bricks and mortar	daughter	
brown bread	dead	
bubble and squeak	Greek	
butcher's hook	look	*(to) give sb/have a butcher's*, i. e. look
Chalk Farm	arm	
china plate	mate (= friend)	
cock and hen	ten	
currant bun	sun	
daisy roots	boots	
dinky does [du:z]	shoes	
dog and bone	phone	
dustbin lid	kid	
frog and toad	road	
Gregory Peck	cheque	
Hank Marvin	starving	
Jimmy Riddle	piddle (= urinate)	
kick and prance	dance	
Lady Godiva	fiver (£ 5 note)	
loaf of bread	head	*(to) use one's loaf*, i. e. head
mince pies	eyes	
Mutt and Jeff	deaf	
north and south	mouth	
oily rag	fag (= cigarette)	
Peckham Rye	tie	
pen and ink	stink	
plates of meat	feet	
pork pies	lies	
Rosie Lee	tea	
round the houses	trousers	
rub-a-dub	pub	
skin and blister	sister	
sky rocket	pocket	
tea leaf	thief	
tit for tat	hat	
Todd Sloane	alone	*(to) be on one's todd*, i. e. alone
Tom and Dick	sick	
Tommy Trinder	window	
trouble and strife	wife	
Vera Lynn	gin	
whistle and flute	suit	

4 How to spell with the International Aviation Alphabet

Although we normally use the ordinary English alphabet when spelling out names on the phone, for example, this can lead to misunderstandings when you are speaking to another non-native speaker of English. Then it is best to use the International Aviation Alphabet, which has become the standard throughout the world.

The huge advantage of the International Aviation Alphabet is that it makes use only of names and international words that are used with the same pronunciation in many languages.

A	*ay*	Alpha
B	*bee*	Bravo
C	*see*	Charlie
D	*dee*	Delta
E	*ee*	Echo
F	*eff*	Foxtrot
G	*gee*	Golf
H	*aytch*	Hotel
I	*eye*	India
J	*jay*	Juliett
K	*kay*	Kilo
L	*ell*	Lima
M	*emm*	Mike
N	*enn*	November
O	*oh*	Oscar
P	*pee*	Papa
Q	*queue*	Quebec
R	*are*	Romeo
S	*ess*	Sierra
T	*tea*	Tango
U	*you*	Uniform
V	*vee*	Victor
W	*double you*	Whisky/Whiskey
X	*ex*	X-ray
Y	*why*	Yankee
Z	zed (BrE), *zee* (AmE)	Zulu

5 Acronyms to describe social groups

The first widely-used acronym of this type was 'yuppie', which became popular in the UK in the late 1970s and early 1980s. It was used to describe some of the chief beneficiaries of Margaret Thatcher's economic reforms. In those days, a yuppie was typically an ambitious young man or woman earning obscene amounts of money in commissions on financial deals in the City of London. Yuppie was quickly followed by 'dinkie' (see list below) for childless couples with two incomes.

The remaining acronyms are less than genuine, having been thought up by inventive journalists and social commentators.

BOBO	Burnt Out But Opulent
BUPPIE	Black Upwardly-mobile Professional
DINKIE	Dual Income, No Kids
DINKY	Double Income, No Kids (Yet)
DUMP	Destitute Unemployed Mature Professional
GOLDIE	Golden Oldie, Living Dangerously
GUPPIE	Green Upwardly-mobile Professional
LOMBARD	Lots Of Money But A Right Dickhead
OINK	One Income, No Kids
PIPPIE	Person Inheriting Parents' Property
SCUM	Self-Centred Urban Male
SILKY	Single Income, Loads of Kids
SINBAD	Single Income, No Boyfriend, Absolutely Desperate
SITCOM	Single Income, Two Children, Outrageous Mortgage
WOOPIE	Well-Off Older Person
YUPPIE	Young Upwardly-mobile Professional person

6 Acronyms that can be used in the chat room

BF/GF	boyfriend/girlfriend	JK	just kidding
H&K	hugs and kisses	IOW	in other words
IWALU	I will always love you.	BION	Believe it or not, …
DIKU	Do I know you?	AAMOF	as a matter of fact
HAGN	Have a good night.	BOT	back on topic
ILY	I love you.	AFAIK	As far as I know, …
LJBF	Let's just be friends.	IJWTS	I just want to say …
FOAF	friend of a friend	OTOH	on the other hand
A/S/L?	age/sex/location?	PTMM	Please tell me more.
RTBM	Read the bloody manual.	KISS	Keep it simple, stupid.
		AFK	away from keyboard
RTM	Read the manual.	NRN	no reply necessary
RYS	Read your screen.	BRB	Be right back!
FAQ	frequently asked question(s)	F2F	face to face
		BTW	by the way
IRL	in real life	NQA	no questions asked
MOTD	message of the day	POV	point of view
SLM	see last mail	L8R G8R	later 'gator
PDS	Please don't shout!	HTH	Hope that helps!
TSR	totally stupid rules	TYCLO	Turn your caps lock off.
LOL	laughing out loud	LTNT	long time no type
BWL	bursting with laughter	SWIM	See what I mean?
CRBT	crying real big tears	WAEF	When all else fails.
ROFL	rolling on floor laughing	NBD	no big deal

7 Common Latin expressions and abbreviations found in English

Expression	Abbreviation	Meaning
ab initio	an init.	from the beginning
Anno Domini	AD	in the year of our Lord
ad hoc	–	for this purpose only; spontaneously
ad infinitum	ad inf.	and so on endlessly
ad libitum	ad lib.	as much as you like
ad locum	ad loc.	indicating the place referred to
ad valorem	ad val.	according to value, not quantity
a fortiori	a fort.	with better/stronger reason
ante meridiem	am	before noon
a priori	–	from cause to effect; deductively
circa	ca. *or* c.	around
confer	cf.	compare with
cave	–	take care
caveat emptor	cav. empt.	let the buyer beware; buyer's risk
ceteris paribus	cet. par.	all else being equal
de facto	–	in fact
de jure	de jur.	according to law; by right
et alii	et al.	and other things
ex cathedra	ex cath.	'from the throne', i. e. with final authority
ex libris	ex lib.	'from the books', i. e. from the library of
ex officio	ex off.	by virtue of office, i. e. officially
ex parte	ex par.	in support of one side or party
ibidem	ibid.	in the same source
id est	i. e.	that is
in absentia	in abs.	in the absence of
in camera	–	behind closed doors, i. e. in secret
in re	–	in the matter of
in situ	in sit.	at the original location
inter alia	int. al.	among other things/people
ipso facto	–	in the point of fact itself
loco citato	loc. cit.	in the place previously cited
Magister Artium	MA	master of arts
Medicinae Doctor	MD	doctor of medicine
mea culpa	–	my fault

mirabile dictu	–	literally
modus operandi	MO	method of operating
mutatis mutandis	–	having made the necessary changes
nota bene	NB	note well
nemine contradicente	nem. con.	unanimously, nobody against
non sequitur	non seq.	it does not follow
opere citato	op. cit.	in the work already cited
per annum	pa	each year
pace	–	in spite of
pari passu	par. pas.	on the same terms
passim	–	occurring too often to cite individually
persona non grata	–	person who is out of favour
petitio elenchis	pet. elen.	arriving at an unfounded conclusion
post meridiem	pm	afternoon
post eventum	post ev.	after the event
post mortem	–	after death
per pro	pp	on behalf of
prima facie	–	at first sight
primus inter pares	–	first among equals
pro tempore	pro tem.	for the time being, temporarily
post scriptum	PS	written after
quid pro quo	–	one thing in return for another
quod vide	qv	'which see'; look earlier in same source
re	–	with regard to; in the matter of
requiscat in pace	RIP	rest in peace
sic	–	thus or literally, i. e. not a misprint
sine die	–	undated
status quo ante	status quo	the same state/situation as before
stet	–	'let it stand', i. e. do not delete
sub judice	sub. ju.	under judgement, i. e. still not decided
sub rosa	–	'under the rose', i. e. hidden, privately
ultra vires	ult. vir.	beyond one's own legal powers
vide	v.	see, look up
vide infra	v. inf.	see below
videlicet	viz	that is to say, namely
vox populi	vox pop.	the voice of the people
versus	v or v.	against

8 How to read out email and website addresses in English

.	dot
@	at
_	underscore
-	hyphen
/	(forward) slash
//	double (forward) slash
\	backslash
:	colon
http	aytch double tee pee
www	double you – double you – double you

Examples:

▶ o_duval@wanadoo.fr
✔ oh underscore duval at wanadoo dot eff are

▶ www.itv.co.uk/anglia-news
✔ double you – double you – double you dot eye tee vee dot co dot you kay (forward) slash anglia hyphen news

▶ http://www.world-records.com/formula_one
✔ aytch double tee pee colon double (forward) slash double you – double you – double you dot
world hyphen records dot com (forward) slash
for mula underscore one

9 What's the equivalent of *Arzthelferin* in English?

In Germany, there are well over 400 occupations with their own name, job description and training profile, i. e. qualifications. The problem is that in the English-speaking world many of these German occupations do not have a precise name of their own, but are included in some general term such as 'clerk' (*Schreibkraft*), 'assistant' or '... worker'.

For all that, here is an attempt at giving the English equivalents of German occupations.

Allgemeinarzt/-ärztin	general practitioner ('GP'), family doctor
Apotheker(in)	pharmacist
Arzt/Ärztin	doctor, physician
Arzthelferin (Empfang)	doctor's receptionist *sonst* practice nurse
Außendienstmitarbeiter(in) (Verkauf)	sales representative, (*Kundendienst*) service technician
Außenhandelskaufmann/-frau	export assistant/clerk
Bademeister(in)	swimming-pool attendant
Bankkaufmann/-frau	BrE: bank clerk, AmE: bank teller
Bauarbeiter(in)	building/construction worker
Beamter/Beamtin	(*in Uniform*) officer, (*Verwaltung*) official
Berufsberater(in)	vocational adviser
Berufsschullehrer(in)	vocational school teacher
Betriebswirt(in)	graduate in business management
Bootsbauer(in)	boat-builder
Chefsekretärin	executive secretary
Chirurg(in)	surgeon
Dachdecker(in)	roofer
Drogist(in)	BrE: chemist, AmE: druggist
Einzelhandelskaufmann/-frau	retail assistant/clerk
Elektriker(in)	electrician
Elektroinstallateur(in)	electrical fitter
Elektromechaniker(in)	electromechanic

Elektrotechniker(in)	electrical technician
Entbindungspflegerin	midwife
Ergotherapeut(in)	ergonomic therapist
Erzieher(in)	kindergarten teacher
Facharzt/-ärztin für ...	Privatpraxis: specialist in ..., Krankenhaus: consultant in ...
Fachkaufmann/-frau für Einkauf/Materialwirtschaft	purchasing assistant/clerk
Feuerwehrmann/-frau	fire fighter
Finanzberater(in)	financial adviser/consultant
Fliesenleger(in)	tiler, floor-layer
Florist(in)	florist
Flugbegleiter(in)	flight attendant
Förderlehrer(in)	remedial teacher
Fremdsprachenkorrespondent(in)	bilingual/multilingual assistant/clerk
Fremdsprachensekretärin	bilingual/multilingual secretary
Friseur(in) (für Frauen)	hairdresser
Friseur(in) (für Männer)	hairdresser, barber
Fußpfleger(in)	chiropodist
Gesamtschullehrer(in)	BrE: comprehensive school teacher, AmE: high school teacher
Glaser(in)	glazier
Grenzschutzbeamter(in)	border/frontier guard
Großhandelskaufmann/-frau	wholesale assistant/clerk
Grundschullehrer(in)	BrE: primary school teacher, AmE: elementary school teacher
Gymnasiallehrer(in)	grammar school teacher
Gymnastiklehrer(in)	gymnastics/physical education ('PE') instructor
Hauptschullehrer(in)	secondary modern school teacher
Hausmeister(in)	BrE: caretaker, AmE: janitor, supervisor
Immobilienkaufmann/-frau	BrE: estate agent's assistant/clerk, AmE: real estate assistant/clerk
Immobilienmakler(in)	BrE: estate agent, AmE: real estate agent
Industriekaufmann/-frau	assistant/clerk in industry

Job descriptions: English equivalents

Informatiker(in)	computer scientist
Ingenieur(in)	engineer, *mit Diplom:* graduate engineer
Innenarchitekt(in)	interior designer
Justizvollzugsbeamter/-beamtin	prison warder
Kassierer(in)	cashier
Kaufmann/-frau im Außenhandel	export assistant/clerk
Kaufmann/-frau im Einzelhandel	retail assistant/clerk
Kaufmann/-frau im Großhandel	wholesale assistant/clerk
Kellner	waiter
Kellnerin	waitress
Klempner(in)	plumber
Kosmetiker(in)	beautician
Kraftfahrzeugmechaniker(in)	automotive/motor mechanic
Krankengymnast(in)	physiotherapist
Krankenpfleger	male nurse
Krankenschwester/-pflegerin	nurse
Kriminalbeamter/-beamtin	plain-clothes (police) officer
Laborant(in)	lab/laboratory assistant
Maurer(in)	bricklayer
Modeschneider(in) (Herrenmode)	(bespoke) tailor
Modeschneider(in) (Damenmode)	fashion dressmaker
Monteur(in)	fitter
Personalfachmann/-frau	personnel/human resources assistant/clerk
Pfleger(in)	carer
Polizist(in)	police officer
Putzfrau	cleaner
Realschullehrer(in)	technical high school teacher
Rechtsanwaltsfachangestellte(r)	legal/solicitor's assistant/clerk
Rechtspfleger(in)	official with judicial powers
Redakteur(in)	editor
Redaktionsassistent(in)	editorial assistant
Regisseur(in) (Film, Theater)	director
Regisseur(in) (Funk, Fernsehen)	producer

Reiseverkehrskaufmann/-frau	travel agent's assistant/clerk
Sanitäter(in)	paramedic
Schneider(in) (Herrenmode)	tailor
Schneider(in) (Damenmode)	dressmaker
Schweißer(in)	welder
Sonderschullehrer(in)	special school teacher
Sozialarbeiter(in)	social worker
Steuerberater(in)	accountant
Tankwart(in)	BrE: filling-station/pump attendant, AmE: gas-station attendant
Tierarzt/-ärztin	vetinary surgeon ('vet')
Tierarzthelfer(in)	vet's assistant
Tischler(in)	joiner, cabinet-maker
Verkäufer(in)	sales assistant/person
Versicherungskaufmann/-frau	insurance assistant/clerk
Werbekaufmann/-frau	advertising agent's assistant/clerk
Wirtschaftsprüfer(in)	auditor
Zahnarzt/-ärztin	dentist
Zahnarzthelferin (Empfang)	dentist's receptionist *sonst* dental nurse
Zahntechniker(in)	dental technician
Zimmerer/Zimmerin	carpenter

10 Everybody knows 'Vienna' and 'Munich', but what other German place names have English equivalents?

A relatively small number of German place names are different in English. To avoid misunderstandings, it is advisable to use the English equivalent of the German name if there is one. A lot of English-speakers do not realise that the German town they know as **Brunswick**, for example, is Braunschweig.

When there is no English equivalent of the German name, English-speakers usually say the name using the English pronunciation. This can be quite confusing as it is often different from German. Please note, too, that the *umlaut* is often ignored when spelling out German place names in English.

Towns

Basel (CH)	Basle[1]
Braunschweig	Brunswick
Genf (CH)	Geneva
Hannover	Hanover[1]
Konstanz	Constance
Köln	Cologne
München	Munich
Nürnberg	Nuremberg
Wien (A)	Vienna

Please note that the English equivalents **Ratisbon** for Regensburg, **Cleeves** for Kleve and **Treves** for Trier are no longer used.

---

[1] difference only in spelling

States (Länder)

Bayern	Bavaria
Hessen	Hesse
Kärnten (A)	Carinthia
Mecklenburg-Vorpommern	Mecklenburg West Pomerania[1]
Niederösterreich (A)	Lower Austria
Nordrhein-Westfalen	North Rhine-Westphalia
Oberösterreich (A)	Upper Austria
Rheinland-Pfalz	Rhineland-Palatinate
Sachsen	Saxony
Sachsen-Anhalt	Saxony-Anhalt
Steiermark (A)	Styria
Thüringen	Thuringia
Tirol (A)	Tyrol[2]

Geographical and historical names

Alpen, die	Alps, the
Bodensee	Lake Constance
Deutsche Bucht	German Bite
Deutsche Mittelgebirge	Central German Uplands
Donau	Danube
Franken	Franconia
Friesland	Frisia
Frisische Inseln	Frisian Islands
Helgoland	Heligoland
Niederbayern	Lower Bavaria
Norddeutsche Tiefebene	North German Plain
Oberbayern	Upper Bavaria
Ostsee	Baltic Sea
Pfalz, die	Palatinate, the
Preußen	Prussia
Rhein	Rhine
Schlesien	Silesia
Schwaben	Swabia
Schwarzwald	Black Forest
Wattenmeer	tidal shallows

[1] In current usage, Mecklenburg-Vorpommern is often referred to as simply 'Mecklenburg'
[2] difference only in spelling

11 What is the correct way of saying telephone numbers in English?

In English, we say the individual numbers of telephone numbers one after the other, usually making a longer pause (-) after the area code (*Vorwahl*) and also in the middle of longer numbers.

In BrE, we usually use the letter **O** (oh) for nought (0), and in AmE **zero** (0), though zero is also becoming more common in BrE.

Here are some examples (please note the pauses):

▶ (02302) 189705

✓ BrE **oh** two three **oh** two – one eight nine – seven **oh** five
✓ AmE **zero** two three **zero** two – one eight nine – seven **zero** five

In BrE, double numbers – e. g. 22, 44 – are generally expressed as **double-two**, **double-four** and so on. In AmE, it is more usual to say these numbers one after the other, i. e. **two two**, **four four** etc.

▶ (0113) 897700

✓ BrE oh **double-one** three – eight nine – **double seven** – **double oh**
✓ AmE oh **one one** three – eight nine – **seven seven** – **zero zero**

In BrE, you can express three identical numbers – for example 777 – as either **double-seven seven** or **seven double-seven**. In AmE, the numbers are normally given one after the other, as usual, i. e. **seven seven seven**.

▶ (0191) 122999

✓ BrE oh one nine one – one double-two – **double-nine nine/nine double-nine**
✓ AmE zero one nine one – one two two – **nine nine nine**

⚠ Never use tens and units to say telephone numbers as sometimes occurs in German. If you say the number **538945**, for example, as **fifty-three eighty-nine forty-five** you will almost certainly not be understood.

12 How do you express 'Null'/'null' and 'Bitte schön' in English?

Null/null

The German *Null/null* has various equivalents in English according to the context in which it is used. Here is a review:

- In longer series of numbers such as **phone numbers** and **account numbers**, *null* is generally expressed as the letter **O** (oh) in BrE and as **zero** in AmE:
  - ▶ My account number is six – five – eight – **oh/zero** – nine – two.
  - ▶ *Meine Kontonummer ist sechs – fünf – acht – null – neun – zwei.*

- In **sports** other than tennis and a couple of other racket games, *null* is expressed as **nil**:
  - ▶ Our team won two **nil**.
  - ▶ *Unsere Mannschaft hat zwei zu null gewonnen.*

- In **tennis**, *null* is expressed as **love**:
  - ▶ A What's the score?   B Fifteen – **love**.
  - ▶ A *Wie steht's?*   B *Fünfzehn zu null.*

- In **scientific**, **mathematical** and **technical** contexts, *Null* is expressed as **nought** in BrE and **zero** in AmE:
  - ▶ There are six **noughts/zeros** in one million.
  - ▶ *Eine Million hat sechs Nullen.*

- When giving **temperatures**, *Null* is expressed as **zero** in both BrE and AmE:
  - ▶ It was five degrees below **zero** last night.
  - ▶ *Heute nacht waren es fünf Grad unter Null.*

Bitte schön

The English equivalent of the German polite phrase *bitte schön* depends upon the situation in which it is used, as follows:

- If *bitte schön* is used in the sense of *keine Ursache*, the English equivalent is **You're welcome**. In less formal situations, you will also hear **That's okay** or **That's all right**. Please note, however, that this phrase is often not used at all.

- If *bitte schön* is used in the sense of *Was möchten Sie gern?*, for example in a shop, its English equivalent is **Can I help you?**. In restaurants and pubs it is generally expressed as **What would you like?** or **What can I get you?**
- If *bitte schön* is used when giving somebody something or passing something to somebody, the English equivalent is **Here you are** or, in informal situations, **Here you go**.

13 What is the background of 'Ms', and when is it used?

An overview of forms of address

	Form	Marital status
Women	Miss [mis]	single and never married
	Mrs ['misiz]	married, divorced or widowed
	Ms [miz]	married or single (not dependent on marital status)
Men	Mr ['mistə]	married or single (not dependent on marital status)

Miss is the short form of 'Mistress', an archaic form of address for unmarried and never married women. In modern usage, Miss is seldom used unless the person concerned wishes it.

Mrs is used solely for married, divorced or widowed women. Unlike *Frau* in German, it cannot be used for unmarried women, hence the need for a neutral form of address for women (see **Ms** below).

Ms comes from the USA as a side-effect of the women's liberation movement. Many women felt the need for a neutral form of address equivalent to the male **Mr** which did not stem from their marital status. Nowadays, it is usual to address all women, married or not, with **Ms**, particularly in the world of work.

Mr is used for all men independently of their marital status. It is hence the male equivalent of Ms (see above).

⚠ It is unusual to use a form of address when introducing oneself, for example *Good afternoon. I'm Mr Fox*. On such occasions, it is better to use the first and last name as in *Good afternoon. I'm John Fox*.

14 Countries and nationalities

Notes

(1) Unless noted in the table, the noun for a citizen of a particular country is the same as the adjective and forms it plural with -s, for example 'Glen is American, and he is as patriotic as most Americans.'
(2) In the case of nationalities ending in -ese, the plural is the same as the singular, e. g. 'There is a Japanese in our street. In fact, there are a lot of Japanese in Düsseldorf.'
(3) National adjectives ending in -ch and -sh form their nouns by adding -man/-men,
-woman/-women, e. g. 'Pierre is a Frenchman'. The collective noun for the people as a whole is the same as the adjective.
(4) Very occasionally there is no English noun for a person from a particular country so the idea has to be expressed with citizen, e. g. 'a Vatican citizen'/ 'a citizen of the Vatican'.

Country	Adjective	Person if different from adjective
Afghanistan	Afghan	an Afghanistani (not Afghan)
Albania	Albanian	
Algeria	Algerian	
Angola	Angolan	
Argentina	Argentinian	(not Argentine)
Armenia	Armenian	
Australia	Australian	
Austria	Austrian	
Azerbaijan	Azerbaijani	
Bahamas	Bahamian	
Bahrain	Bahraini	
Bangladesh	Bangladesh	a Bangladeshi
Barbados	Barbadian	
Belarus	Belorussian	
Belgium	Belgian	
Belize	Belizean	
Bolivia	Bolivian	
Bosnia-Herzegovina	Bosnian	
Botswana	Botswanan	a Batswana
Brazil	Brazilian	

Countries and Nationalities in English

Britain	British	a Briton; the British
Brunei	Bruneian	
Bulgaria	Bulgarian	(not ~~Bulgar~~)
Burkina Faso	Burkinese	
Burundi	Burundian	
Cambodia	Cambodian	
Cameroon	Cameroonian	
Canada	Canadian	
Cape Verde	Cape Verdean	
Cayman Islands	Cayman Island	a Cayman Islander
Chad	Chadian	
Chile	Chilean	
China	Chinese	*plur.* Chinese
Colombia	Colombian	
Congo	Congolese	
Costa Rica	Costa Rican	
Croatia	Croatian	
Cuba	Cuban	
Cyprus	Cypriot	
Czech Republic	Czech	a Czech or a Czechoslovak
Denmark	Danish	a Dane; the Danish
Djibouti	Djiboutian	
Dominican Republic	Dominician	
Ecuador	Ecuadorian	
Egypt	Egyptian	
El Salvador	El Salvadorian	
England	English	an Englishman/-woman; the English
Equatorial Guinea	Equatorial Guinean	a Bantu, *plur.* Bantu
Estonia	Estonian	
Ethiopia	Ethiopian	
Fiji	Fijian	
Finland	Finnish	a Finn; the Finnish
France	French	a Frenchman/-woman; the French
Gabon	Gabonese	*plur.* Gabonese
The Gambia	Gambian	
Georgia	Georgian	
Germany	German	

Ghana	Ghanaian	(*not* ~~Ghanan~~)
Greece	Greek	
Grenada	Grenadian	(*not* ~~Grenadan~~)
Guatemala	Guatamalan	(*not* ~~Guatamalian~~)
Guiana	Guianan	
Guinea	Guinean	
Guyana	Guyanese	
Haiti	Haitian	
Honduras	Honduran	
Hungary	Hungarian	
Iceland	Icelandic	an Icelander; the Icelanders
India	Indian	
Indonesia	Indonesian	
Iran	Iranian	
Iraq	Iraqi	
Ireland	Irish	an Irishman/-woman; the Irish
Israel	Israeli	
Italy	Italian	
Ivory Coast	Ivorian	
Jamaica	Jamaican	
Japan	Japanese	(*not* ~~Jap~~); *plur.* Japanese
Jordan	Jordanian	
Kazakhstan	Kazakhstani	
Kenya	Kenyan	
Kirgizstan	Kirgizstani	
North Korea	North Korean	
South Korea	South Korean	
Kuwait	Kuwaiti	
Laos	Laotian	
Latvia	Latvian	
Lebanon	Lebanese	*plur.* Lebanese
Lesotho	Sesotho	a Mosotho; *plur.* Basotho
Liberia	Liberian	
Libya	Libyan	
Lithuania	Lithuanian	
Luxemburg	Luxemburg	a Luxemberger (note spelling)
Madagascar	Malagasy	a Malagasy citizen
Malawi	Malawian	

Countries and Nationalities in English

Malaysia	Malaysian	
Mali	Malian	
Malta	Maltese	*plur.* Maltese
Mauritania	Mauritanian	
Mauritius	Mauritian	
Mexico	Mexican	
Moldova	Moldovan	
Monaco	Monegasque	
Morocco	Moroccan	
Mozambique	Mozambiquean	
Myanmar	Myanmar	a Myanmar citizen
Namibia	Namibian	
Nepal	Nepalese	*plur.* Nepalese
The Netherlands	Dutch	a Dutchman/-woman; the Dutch
New Zealand	New Zealand	a New Zealander
Nicaragua	Nicaraguan	
Niger	Nigerien	(note spelling, *-ien*)
Nigeria	Nigerian	
Northern Ireland	Northern Irish	a Northern Irishman/-woman; the Northern Irish
Norway	Norwegian	
Oman	Omani	
Pakistan	Pakistani	
Panama	Panamanian	
Papua New Guinea	Papuan	
Paraguay	Paraguayan	
Peru	Peruvian	
The Philippines	Philippine	a Filipino; *plur.* Filipinos
Poland	Polish	a Pole
Portugal	Portuguese	*plur.* Portuguese
Puerto Rica	Puerto Rican	
Qatar	Qatari	
Romania	Romanian	
Russia	Russian	
Rwanda	Rwandan	
Saudi Arabia	Saudi Arabian	a Saudi or a Saudi Arabian
Scotland	Scottish	a Scot; the Scottish
Senegal	Senegalese	*plur.* Sengalese

Serbia and Montenegro	Serbian	
Seychelles	Seychellois	*plur.* Seychellois
Sierra Leone	Sierra Leonean	
Singapore	Singaporean	
Slovakia	Slovakian	
Slovenia	Slovenian	
Solomon Islands	Solomon Islands	a Solomon Islander
Somalia	Somalian	
South Africa	South African	
Spain	Spanish	a Spaniard; the Spanish
Sri Lanka	Sri Lankan	
Sudan	Sudanese	*plur.* Sudanese
Suriname	Surinames	*plur.* Surinamese
Swaziland	Swazi	
Sweden	Swedish	a Swede ; the Swedish
Switzerland	Swiss	*plur.* Swiss
Syria	Syrian	
Taiwan	Taiwanese	*plur.* Taiwanese
Tanzania	Tanzanian	
Thailand	Thai	
Togo	Togolese	*plur.* Togolese
Trinidad and Tobago	Trinidadian; Tobagan	
Tunisia	Tunisian	
Turkey	Turkish	a Turk; the Turkish
Turkmenistan	Turkmenistani	
Uganda	Ugandan	
Ukraine	Ukrainian	
Uruguay	Uruguayan	
USA	American	
Vatican City	Vatican	a Vatican citizen
Venezuela	Venezuelan	
Vietnam	Vietnamese	*plur.* Vietnamese
Wales	Welsh	a Welshman/-woman; the Welsh
West Samoa	Samoan	
Yemen	Yemeni	
Zambia	Zambian	
Zimbabwe	Zimbabwean	

15 Mathematical terms in English

$4 + 11$	four plus/and eleven
$12 - 3$	twelve minus/less three
10 ± 1	ten plus or minus one
6×5	six multiplied by/times five
$7 \div 2$	seven divided by/through two
$1/8$	an/one eighth
$5/8$	five-eighths
$7/8$	seven-eighths
$1/3$	a/one third
$2/3$	two-thirds
$1/4$	a quarter
$1/2$	a half
$3/4$	three-quarters
$=$	is equal to/equals
$\neq$	is not equal to/does not equal
$\approx$	is approximately/roughly equal to
$<$	is less than
$>$	is greater/more than
$\%$	per cent
$\permil$	per thousand
$\sqrt{}$	root/square root
$\sqrt[3]{}$	cube root
4^2	four squared
5^3	five cubed
2^4	two to the power of four/two to the fourth
p, π	pi

Übersicht: Lernjahre und Inhalte*

	Lernjahr 1/2	Lernjahr 3/4	Lernjahr 5/6	Oberstufe
Grammatik	S. 27, 31, 33, 37, 43, 45, 164–170	S. 27, 178–187	S. 194–204	
Wortschatz	S. 25–30, 32–38, 40–45, 171–174	S. 27–29, 188–191	S. 27, 205–209	S. 221–236
Syntax (word order)	S. 32, 35, 39, 41, 42, 175–177	S. 192, 193	S. 210, 211	S. 237
Phonetik	S. 25, 26, 29, 30, 31, 32, 36, 38, 41, 44	S. 29		
Prüfungsfertigkeiten				S. 212–220

*) Einzelthemen wie z. B. „Simple Past" *siehe* Register

Register

A and An (Sprachspiel) 25
Abkürzungen
   Chatten 277
   Lateinische Wendungen 278–279
   Soziale Gruppen 276
   US-Bundesstaaten 129
Adjektive
   vs. Adverb (Übung) 186–187
   Antonyme (Übungen) 207, 216
   Confusibles 140–141
   Nationalitäten 290–294
   Sprachspiele 25–26, 37
   Synonyme (Übung) 207
   in Wortfamilien (Übung) 221–222
Adverbien
   Trennungs-Regel 134
   Übungen 186–187, 211
AE *siehe* American English
Affirmative action 121
Akronyme sozialer Gruppen 276
Aktiv und Passiv (Übung) 181–182
Alkohol
   deutscher 268–269
   Whisk(e)y 113–114
   Witze 23
Allgäuer Käsespätzle (Rezept) 259
Alphabet der Luftfahrt 275
Alphabet run (Sprachspiel) 26
Alsation 97
American Creed 117
American English
   Unterschiede zu BrE 137, 156–162, 287
An and *A* (Sprachspiel) 25
Angler-Witz 12–13
Anredeformen 289
Answers galore (Sprachspiel) 27
Antonyme (Übungen) 188, 207, 216
Anweisungen
   Sprachspiele 30, 34, 44
   Wendungen für Lehrer 238–242,
   243–245, 247–249
   Witze 15
any, anybody (Übungen) 170, 174
Artikel
   A and *An* (Sprachspiel) 25
   Übungen 195, 201, 204

-ary-Endung 156
As I was going to St. Ives (Gedicht) 73
Auld Lang Syne (Gedicht) 85
Aussprache
   AmE/BrE-Unterschiede 156
   Aviation alphabet 275
   Bindestriche als Hilfe für 131
   Eigennamen 272
   Homonyme 270–271
   Null 288
   Sprachspiele 31, 32, 38, 44
   Telefon-Nummern 287
   Walisisch/Welsh 100
   Zungenbrecher 54, 74
Automatisierung (Wortschatzübung) 205
Aviation alphabet 275

Back again! (Sprachspiel) 28
Baseball 17, 29
Befehlsform *siehe* Anweisungen
Benehmen von Schülern
   Wendungen für Lehrer 244–245, 247–249
Berner Rösti (Rezept) 260
Berufsbezeichnungen 281–284
Betty Botter (Gedicht) 74
Bible Belt states (USA) 128
Biere, deutsche 268
Big Apple (Bedeutung) 117
Bild malen (Sprachspiel) 44
Bildungswesen in Schottland/England 112
Bindestrich-Regelungen 130–133
Bindewörter (Übungen) 194, 200–201
Bitte schön 288–289
Blindman's buff (Sprachspiel) 30
Blondinen 20–21, 118
Boxing Day 51
BrE *siehe* British English
Britain, Definition von 93
British English
   Unterschiede zu AmE 137, 156–162, 287
British Isles
   Definition und Karte 92–93
   Feiertage 101–107

Bücher
    Wendungen für Lehrer 238, 247
    Wortschatzübung 209
Buchstabieren
    Aviation alphabet 275
    Internet-Adressen 280
    Sprachspiele 27, 53
    siehe auch Rechtschreibung
Bühnenstücke
    Christmas pantomime 52
    Christmas Story 62–66
    Dinner for one 67–70
Bundesländer 286
Bundesstaaten (USA) 129
Bürgerkrieg (USA) 126
Burns Night 85, 113
Business (Wortschatzübung) 218–219
By heart (Sprachspiel) 36

Carol singing 49
CD-Player
    Wendungen für Lehrer 239
-*ce* /-*se*-Endungen 158
Chatten, Abkürzungen beim 277
Chinese whispers (Sprachspiel) 31
Christmas *siehe* Weihnachten
Civil War (USA) 126
Cloze text (Sprachspiel) 45
Cockney Rhyming Slang 273–274
Columbus Day 120
Comma rules *siehe* Kommasetzung
Commands *siehe* Anweisungen
Computer
    Wendungen für Lehrer 241
    Wortschatzübung 218–219
    siehe auch Internet
Concentration, concentration (Sprachspiel) 33
Conditionals *siehe* Konjunktiv
Confederate States 126
Confusibles 137–141, 226
Connectors (Übungen) 194, 200–201
Countries and people (Sprachspiel) 38

Definitionen
    British Isles 93–94
    Übung 217
Dekorationen zu Weihnachten 47

Democrats (USA) 115–116
Demokratie (UK) 107–110
Description of words (Sprachspiel) 37
Deutsche Fremdwörter (Übung) 219–220
Deutschland
    Feiertage 256
    geographische Namen 285–286
    Größenvergleich zu USA 115
    Halbtagsschulen 254–255
    Pessimismus 250–251
    politische Aspekte 252–254
    Regionalküche 257–269
Dia-Projektor
    Wendungen für Lehrer 240
Dinner for one (Bühnenstück) 67–70
Dinner zu Weihnachten 50
Diphthonge 157
Diskriminierung 84–85, 121
Dogge 97
Draw a picture (Sprachspiel) 44
DVD-Player
    Wendungen für Lehrer 239

E-Mail-Adressen, Buchstabieren von 280
-*ed* /-*ing*-Endungen (Übung) 186–187
Einfache Gegenwart *siehe* Simple present
Einfache Vergangenheit *siehe* Simple past
Endungen
    AmE/BrE-Unterschiede 137, 156, 157, 158
    Nationalitäten 290
    Trennungs-Regel 134
    Übung 186–187
    siehe auch einzelne Endungen
England
    Ortsnamen (Aussprache) 272
    Public holidays 101
    Unterschiede zu Scotland 110–113
-*er* /-*re*-Endungen 157
Essen *siehe* Nahrungsmittel

False friends 142, 224–225
Family tree (Sprachspiel) 37
Fehler
    Confusibles 137–141, 226

Fehler *(Fortsetzung)*
   False friends 142, 224–225
   Kommasetzung 135–136
   Rechtschreibung 143–144, 236
   Sprachspiel 38
   Übungen 183, 236
   Worttrennung 134
Feiertage
   British Isles 49–51, 101–107
   Deutschland 256
   USA 102–106, 119–121
   siehe auch Public holidays; *einzelne Feiertage*
Find the Mistakes! (Sprachspiel) 38
Find the words (Weihnachtsrätsel) 55, 56
Fishy (Sprachspiel) 40
Flanders Fields (Gedicht) 81–82
Flüssig sprechen (Sprachspiele) 36
Flüster-Spiel 31
for vs. *since* (Übung) 169
Frageform
   Sprachspiele 27, 29, 31–32, 34, 39, 40, 43
   Übungen 167, 168–169, 177, 202, 214
   Witze 15–17
Freiheitsstatue 118
Fremdwörter, deutsche (Übung) 219–220
Frosty the Snowman (Weihnachtslied) 58
Fruit salad (Sprachspiel) 41
Fürwörter *siehe* Pronomen
Future
   going to vs. *will* 162
   Witze 14

Gallonen 114
Games *siehe* Sprachspiele
Gap text activity (Sprachspiel) 32
Gedichte und Reime 73–91, 103–104, 273–274
Gegenwart *siehe* Present perfect; Present progressive; Simple present
Geld 77, 111–112
Genitiv *siehe* Possessiv...
Geographie
   British Isles 92–94

Geographie *(Fortsetzung)*
   Ländernamen 38, 290–294
   Ortsnamen und Regionen 272, 285, 286
   USA 115, 122, 129
Gerundium (Übungen) 203, 235
Geschenke zu Weihnachten 49
Geschichte *siehe* Historische Aspekte
Getränke (Wortschatzübung) 172
   siehe auch Alkohol
Getrenntschreibung 132–133
Gewaltenteilung in UK 110
Gleiche Bedeutung *siehe* Synonyme
going to vs. *will* 162
Great Britain, Definition von 93
Great Dane 97
Group hunt (Sprachspiel) 39
Grußkarten 47, 102–106
Guy Fawkes' Day 106–107

Halbtagsschulen in Deutschland 254–255
Half sentences (Sprachspiel) 41
Hallowe'en 106
Hamburger Aalsuppe (Rezept) 260
Hausaufgaben
   Gedicht 76
   Wendungen für Lehrer 238–239
Hausunterricht (UK) 98–99
have vs. *have got* 162
Heiligabend 47–49
Hidden words (Sprachspiel) 43
Historische Aspekte
   England 110–111
   Feiertage 102, 106–107
   USA 120, 123, 125–126
Holidays *siehe* Feiertage; Public holidays
Homework *siehe* Hausaufgaben
Homonyme
   AmE/BrE 159
   Aussprache 270–271
How many things can you think of? (Sprachspiel) 43
How to make toast (Sprachspiel) 44
Hugger Mugger (Gedicht) 76
Hunde 11, 21, 97

I, too, sing America (Gedicht) 84–85
Idiomatic expressions 144–155
If only I had plenty of money (Gedicht) 77
If-Sätze (Übungen) 200–201
-*ile*-Endung 156
Independence Day 120
Infinitiv (Übungen) 203, 235
-*ing* /-*ed*-Endungen (Übung) 186–187
-*ing*-Form/Gerundium (Übungen) 203, 235
Internationale Wörter (Übung) 218–219
Internet
  Abkürzungen beim Chatten 277
  Buchstabieren von Adressen 280
  siehe auch Computer
Interpunktion
  Kommasetzung 135–136, 237
  Private? No! (Gedicht) 77
Irish Republic 101
Irish whiskey 114
-*ise* /-*ize*-Endungen 137

Jabberwocky (Gedicht) 77–78
Jokes 10–23
  siehe auch Limericks; *einzelne Themen*

Kasseler (Rezepte) 261, 266
Kategorisieren
  Sprachspiele 33, 41
  Wortschatzübungen 172, 218–219
Kids, Witze mit 17–20
Kirchgang zu Weihnachten 49
Klassenarbeiten
  Wendungen für Lehrer 242–245
Kleidung (Wortschatzübungen) 172, 218–219
Klimazone der Sunbelt states (USA) 127
Knallbonbons zu Weihnachten 51
Kniestrümpfe zu Weihnachten 49
Knock, Knock-Witze 19–20
Kollokationen (Übung) 223
Kolonien, dreizehn (USA) 125
Kommasetzung
  Regeln 135–136
  Übung 237

Komposita
  mit Bindestrich 130, 131, 133
  Getrenntschreibung 132–133
  Trennungs-Regel 134
  Übungen 173, 223
  Zusammenschreibung 132
Konföderierte Staaten 126
Konjunktionen (Übungen) 194, 200–201
Konjunktiv
  Gedicht 77
  should vs. *would* 161
  Übungen 199–201
  Witz 14
Körperteile (Sprachspiele) 35, 42–43
Krieg
  Civil War (USA) 126
  Gedichte 81–82
Kritik und Lob
  Wendungen für Lehrer 245–247
Küche, deutsche 257–269

Ländernamen 38, 290–294
Landeskunde
  Christmas in angelsächsischen Ländern 47–52
  Sprachspiel 38
  siehe auch Deutschland; United Kingdom; USA; Geographie
Lateinische Wendungen 278–279
Lear, Edward 79, 86–87
Lesen (Sprachspiele) 28, 32
Letter to Santa (Rätsel) 54, 56
Liebesbotschaften 102–106
Lieder zu Weihnachten 49, 57–61, 85
Limericks 86–88
Linksverkehr 95–97
Listen for the sounds (Sprachspiel) 44
-*ll* /-*l*-Schreibung AmE/BrE 158
Lob und Kritik
  Wendungen für Lehrer 245–247
Lupercalia (römisches Fest) 102
-*ly*-Endung 134

Märchen zu Weihnachten 52
Martin Luther King, Jr. Day 119
Mathematische Begriffe 295
Mayflower 120
Mecklenburger Schinkenbohnen (Rezept) 263

Mehrdeutige Wörter *siehe* Homonyme
Memorial Day 120
Memory-Sprachspiele 34
Merry Christmas
  in vielen Sprachen 71–72
  We Wish You a Merry Christmas
    (Lied) 58
Miming in the middle (Sprachspiel) 32
Miss America contest 118
Miss (Anrede) 289
Mixed up words (Sprachspiel) 27
Modalverben (Übung) 198
Möglichkeitsform *siehe* Konjunktiv
Monster dictation (Sprachspiel) 35
Mr, Mrs, Ms, Miss (Anrede) 289

Nachnamen (Aussprache) 272
Nachsilben *siehe* Endungen
Nahrungsmittel
  deutsche Rezepte 257–266
  deutsche Speisen und Getränke
    267–269
  Gedicht 74
  Sprachspiel 41
  Wortschatzübung 172
Nationalitäten 38, 290–294
Nebensätze (Übung) 193
New Year 52
New York 117, 118
nobody, nothing (Übung) 174
Nonsense-Gedicht 77–78
Normannen, Invasion der 110–111
Northern Ireland 94, 101
Null (Aussprache) 288
Nummern *siehe* Zahlen
Nürnberger Gans (Rezept) 262

O Captain My Captain (Gedicht) 82–83
of-Attribut (Übung) 185
-og/-ogue-Endungen 158
On my back (Sprachspiel) 28
-or/-our-Endungen 157
Orthographie *siehe* Rechtschreibung
Ortsnamen 272, 285
Österreich, geographische Namen
  285, 286
Ostfriesischer Buuskohl (Rezept)
  257–258

Overhead-Projektor
  Wendungen für Lehrer 240
Owl and Pussy Cat (Gedicht) 79

Pairs (Sprachspiel) 40
Pantomime 31–32, 52
Parliament, British 109
Parliament, Scottish 111
Parteien
  in Deutschland und UK 252–253
  in USA 115–116
Passivsätze (Übungen) 181–182,
    199–200
Past continuous, Witze mit 13–14
People memory (Sprachspiel) 34
People's things (Sprachspiel) 33
Pessimismus 250–251
Phrasal verbs 227–229
Pinguin-Witz 10
Politik
  Deutschland 252–254
  UK 107–110, 111, 252–253
  USA 84–85, 115–116, 121
Positive discrimination 121
Possessivform (Übung) 185
Possessivpronomen
  Sprachspiele 33, 37
  Übung 178–179
Postie, Postie-Botschaften 104
Postleitzahlen (USA) 129
Präfixe mit Bindestrich 131
Präpositionen
  AmE/BrE-Unterschiede 161
  Satzvervollständigung (Übungen)
    174, 190, 204, 233–234
  for vs. *since* (Übung) 169
  Sprachspiel 43
  Verben mit (Übungen) 227–231
Present perfect
  Übung 196
  Witze 13
Present perfect progressive (Übung) 196
Present progressive (Übung) 165
Presidents' Day (US) 119
Prime minister (UK) 109
Private? No! (Gedicht) 77
Pronomen (Übungen) 170, 174, 204
  siehe auch Possessivpronomen

Proverbs 88–91
Prüfungen *siehe* Klassenarbeiten
Public holidays
  British Isles 101–102
  Deutschland 256
  USA 119–121
Publikationswesen (Wortschatzübungen) 209, 217
Puzzles *siehe* Rätsel

Queen's Speech 50
Questions *siehe* Frageform

Ransom note (Weihnachtsrätsel) 56, 57
Rassismus 84–85
Rätsel
  Gedicht 73
  St Valentine's Day 105
  Weihnachten 54–57
  -*re*/-*er*-Endungen 157
Read the sentence (Sprachspiel) 36
Rechtschreibung
  AmE/BrE-Unterschiede 137, 157–158
  Fehlersuche (Übung) 236
  häufige Fehler 143–144
  Sprachspiele 26–27, 28, 30, 32
Rechtswesen
  Affirmative action 121
  Gewaltenteilung in UK 110
  Unterschiede Scotland/England 112–113
Redensarten 88–91
Redewendungen, idiomatische 144–155
Reime *siehe* Gedichte und Reime
Relativpronomen (Übungen) 179–180
Relativsätze (Übung) 192
Religion
  Bible Belt states (USA) 128
  Kirchgang zu Weihnachten 49
Republicans (USA) 115–116
Rezepte, deutsche 257–269
Rheinischer Sauerbraten (Rezept) 264–265
Rindsgulasch (Rezept) 264
Rücken-Sprachspiele 28
Rudolf the Red-Nosed Reindeer (Weihnachtslied) 57

Satzbau *siehe* Syntax
Schäferhund 97
Schlagzeilen erweitern (Übung) 212
Schottland *siehe* Scotland
Schreibweise *siehe* Rechtschreibung
Schule
  Halbtagsschulen in Deutschland 254–255
  Unterricht in UK 98–99, 112
  Wendungen für Lehrer 238–249
  Wortschatzübung 171
Schuluniformen (UK) 99–100
Schummeln *siehe* Täuschungsversuche
Scotland
  Public holidays 102
  Unterschiede zu England 110–113
  Whisky 113–114
Scottish language 85, 110
-*se*/-*ce*-Endungen 158
Shakespeare 80–81
Shall I compare thee to a summer's day (Sonett) 80–81
should vs. *would* 161
Silbentrennung 130, 134
Simple past
  Übungen 166, 196
  Witze 12–13
Simple present
  Übung 165
  Witze 10–11
since vs. *for* (Übung) 169
Slang 273–274
Soldier, The (Gedicht) 82
some, *somebody* (Übungen) 170, 174
Sonnet 18 (Shakespeare) 80–81
Soziale Gruppen
  Akronyme 276
  Cockney Rhyming Slang 273–274
Special days 102–107, 113
Speisen *siehe* Nahrungsmittel
Spelling Banner (Weihnachtsspiel) 53
Spiele *siehe* Sprachspiele
Spirituosen, deutsche 269
Sport
  Baseball 17, 29
  Null (Aussprache) 288
  Wortschatzübung 218–219

Sprachlabor
  Wendungen für Lehrer 241–242
Sprachspiele 24–45, 53–54
Sprichwörter 88–91
St Andrew's Day 113
St Valentine's Day 102–106
Statue of Liberty 118
Straßenverkehr
  Linksverkehr 95–97
  Yellow lines 94–95
Struwwelpeter (Gedicht) 75
Substantive
  Confusibles 139
  Komposita (Übungen) 173, 223
  Singular/Plural (Übung) 204
  und Verben/Präpositionen (Übungen) 230–232
  in Wortfamilien (Übungen) 208, 221–222
Suffixe *siehe* Endungen
Sunbelt states (USA) 127
Synonyme
  AmE/BrE 159–160
  Übungen 189, 207, 215–216
Syntax
  Komma-Regeln 135–136
  Sprachspiele 27, 38, 41–42, 45
  Übungen 175–177, 187, 192–193, 210–211, 237

Tafel
  Wendungen für Lehrer 239
Täuschungsversuche
  Wendungen für Lehrer 244–245
Teatime zu Weihnachten 51
Telefon-Nummern (Aussprache) 287
Tests *siehe* Klassenarbeiten
Textverständnis (Sprachspiele) 29, 38, 44
Thanksgiving Day 120
the (Übung) 195
Theater *siehe* Bühnenstücke
Tourismus
  Regionen (USA) 124
  Wortschatzübung 206
Trennungs-Regel 130, 134
Trinken *siehe* Getränke
Twelve Days of Christmas (Lied) 59–60

Übersetzen
  deutsche Fremdwörter (Übung) 219–220
  Gerundium und Infinitiv (Übungen) 203, 235
  Komposita (Übung) 173
  Satzvervollständigung (Übungen) 225, 227, 232, 234
  Sprachspiele 34, 40
Übungen *siehe einzelne Themen*
UK *siehe* United Kingdom
Ulster 94
Unbekannte Wörter, Umgang mit 218–220
Uncle Sam (Bedeutung) 117
United Kingdom
  Definition und Karte 92, 93
  politische Aspekte 107–110, 111, 252–253
  Rechtswesen 110, 112–113
  Schulwesen 98–100, 112
  Weihnachten 47–52
  siehe auch England; Scotland; Wales; Northern Ireland
Unterricht *siehe* Schule
USA
  American Creed 117
  Bundesstaaten (Abkürzungen) 129
  Feiertage 119–121
  Größenvergleich zu Deutschland 115
  historische Aspekte 120, 123, 125–126
  Miss America contest 118
  New York 117, 118
  politische Aspekte 84–85, 115–116, 121
  Präsidenten 118, 119
  Regionen 121–128
  Uncle Sam (Bedeutung) 117
  Whiskey 114
  ZIP codes 129

Verben
  AmE/BrE-Unterschiede 137, 162
  Confusibles 137–139
  Gerundium und Infinitiv (Übungen) 203, 235
  -ise/*-ize*-Endungen 137

Verben *(Fortsetzung)*
  Modalverben (Übung) 198
  Passivsätze (Übungen) 181–182, 199–200
  mit Präpositionen (Übungen) 227–231
  Sprachspiele 31, 39
  Synonyme (Übung) 215–216
  in Wortfamilien (Übungen) 208, 221–222
  Zeitformen (Übungen) 166, 204
  siehe auch einzelne Zeiten
Vereinigte Staaten *siehe* USA
Vereinigtes Königreich *siehe* United Kingdom
Verfassung, fehlende (UK) 108–109
Vergangenheit *siehe* Past continuous; Simple past
Verhältniswörter *siehe* Präpositionen
Verkehr
  Straßenverkehr 94–97
  Wortschatzübung 172, 218–219
Verlaufsformen *siehe* Past continuous; Present progressive
Verneinung (Übungen) 164, 168–169
Verspätung von Schülern
  Wendungen für Lehrer 247
Veterans Day 120
Vollendete Gegenwart *siehe* Present perfect
Vorsilben mit Bindestrich 131

Wahlsystem (UK) 107–108
Waiter-Witze 11, 23
Wales 100, 101
want 162
We Wish You a Merry Christmas (Lied) 58
Website-Adressen, Buchstabieren von 280
Wegbeschreibung 30, 190
Weihnachten
  Christmas Day and Boxing Day 49–51
  Christmas Eve 47–49
  Christmas Story (Bühnenstück) 62–66
  Lieder 49, 57–61, 85
  Märchen 52
  Merry Christmas 58, 71–72
  Pantomime 52

Weihnachten *(Fortsetzung)*
  Rätsel 54–57
  Sprachspiele 53–54
Welsh language 100
Westfälischer Grünkohl (Rezept) 266
When you are old (Gedicht) 83
Whisk(e)y 113–114
Who am I, Santa? (Sprachspiel) 53
Wilhelm der Eroberer 110
will vs. *going to* 162
Witze 10–23
  siehe auch Limericks; einzelne Themen
Word bingo (Sprachspiel) 30
Word Find (Weihnachtsspiel) 53
Word hangman (Sprachspiele) 42–43
Words! (Sprachspiel) 41
Wortfamilien (Übungen) 208, 221–222
Wortreihenfolge *siehe* Syntax
Wortspiele
  St Valentine's Day 103
  Witze 19–20, 21
Worttrennung 130, 134
would vs. *should* 161

Yellow butter (Gedicht) 74
Yellow lines 94–95
*-yse/-yze-*Endungen 158
Yuppie 276

Zahlen
  Null 288
  Postleitzahlen (USA) 129
  Sprachspiele 35, 45
  Telefon-Nummern 287
Zeichensetzung *siehe* Interpunktion
Zeiten
  Übungen mit gemischten 184, 197–200, 204
  siehe auch einzelne Zeiten
ZIP codes 129
Zuhören (Sprachspiel) 44
Zukunft *siehe* Future
Zungenbrecher 54, 74
Zurechtweisen von Schülern
  Wendungen für Lehrer 247–249
Zusammenfassen (Übung) 213
Zusammenschreibung 132